THE ACHIEVEMENT OF JOSEF ŠKVORECKÝ

The noted scholar and critic George Steiner has called the Czech-Canadian author Josef Škvorecký 'one of the major literary figures of our time,' yet to date few books on him and his writing have appeared in English. *The Achievement of Josef Škvorecký* is the first collection of essays in any language to be devoted to his work.

Škvorecký was born in 1924, and his life spans most of the major historical events of twentieth-century Europe. An exile who left Prague after the Soviet-led Warsaw Pact invasion of 1968, he is among those distinguished writers and artists who produced much of their major work in exile. From his first book, *The Cowards* (1958), his novels have offered an indispensable fictional account of nearly a century of Czech life and history. Though Škvorecký is essentially a comic and anti-political writer, his novels engage some of the largest and most pressing political, historical, and ideological issues of the century: fascism, communism, the nature of totalitarianism, the fate of religion. Škvorecký is that rare being, a creative writer who is also a teacher, a man of letters, and an intellectual.

Sam Solecki has collected and commissioned essays from around the world that provide an overview of Škvorecký's work, place him in a larger cultural and international context, and offer readings of his fiction. Among the contributors are such well-known writers and scholars as Milan Kundera, Jan Kott, George Woodcock, André Brink, George Gibian, Igor Hájek, and Stanisław Barańczak.

SAM SOLECKI is a member of the Department of English, University of Toronto.

EDITED BY SAM SOLECKI

The Achievement
of Josef Škvorecký

UNIVERSITY OF TORONTO PRESS
Toronto Buffalo London

© University of Toronto Press Incorporated 1994
Toronto Buffalo London
Printed in Canada

ISBN 0-8020-0512-8 (cloth)
ISBN 0-8020-6947-9 (paper)

Printed on acid-free paper

Canadian Cataloguing in Publication Data

Main entry under title:

The Achievement of Josef Škvorecký

Includes bibliographical references and index.
ISBN 0-8020-0512-8 (bound) ISBN 0-8020-6947-9 (pbk.)

1. Škvorecký, Josef, 1924–   – Criticism and
interpretation. I. Solecki, Sam, 1946–

PS8537.K86Z552 1994   C891.8'63   C94-930017-9
PR9199.3.S557Z552 1994

Portrait of Josef Škvorecký © Helena Wilson, 1987

University of Toronto Press acknowledges the financial assistance to its publishing
program of the Canada Council and the Ontario Arts Council.

This book was published with the financial assistance of Multiculturalism and
Citizenship Canada.

Contents

Preface: The Writer between Two Worlds

It is particularly appropriate that the first volume of essays devoted to Josef Škvorecký's writing is international in scope, including contributions both from critics who read him in Czech and regard him as primarily a Czech writer and from those for whom he is a Czech-Canadian writer read in English. This reflects the fact that since 1968 his work, like his life, has belonged to two national and cultural traditions. On the one hand, he has received the Governor General's Award for *The Engineer of Human Souls* and has an entry in *The Oxford Companion to Canadian Literature*; on the other, his books are widely read in Czechoslovakia, he has a Czech fan club, and he figures prominently in histories of Czech literature such as Helena Kosková's *Hledání ztracené generace* (Searching for the Lost Generation, 1986) and Antonín Měšťan's *Česká literatura 1785–1985* (Czech Literature 1785–1985 [1987]).

This double career, like this volume, owes its existence to the events that occurred in Czechoslovakia in 1968, a crucial divide both in Škvorecký's life and in the history of his first homeland. At the time of the Prague Spring and the Warsaw Pact invasion of Czechoslovakia, Škvorecký was a successful Czech novelist, editor, translator, and scriptwriter with a well-known interest in American literature and American jazz. He had been an editor at *Světová literatura* (World Literature); he had worked with several of the Czech new-wave film directors; he had done well received translations of novels by William Faulkner, Henry James, and Ernest Hemingway; and the 1958 publication and banning of his novel *The Cowards* (*Zbabělci*) had been one of the more sensational Czechoslovak cultural events of the postwar era. After his arrival in North America in January 1969, he became an author in exile whose name disappeared from official Czechoslovak publications and whose books were banned. At the age of forty-four he reluctantly joined that distinguished list of European writers whose life and work are marked by the wound of exile and whose books were not readily accessible in their homelands before 1989. More unexpectedly, he also became one of those rare writers – Czesław Miłosz is another – whose writing found a place in the literatures of two countries. In the two decades following his emigration, this Czech man of letters became a professor of English literature at the University of Toronto, the co-publisher of a Czech publishing house, and a Czech-Canadian novelist.

In exile, Škvorecký was able to write novels like *The Miracle Game* and *The Engineer of Human Souls*, which he could not have published had he remained in Czechoslovakia. Not the least of the several ironies of his career is that by becoming a Canadian and thus being able to write two of the books that are among his finest works, he became a greater and ultimately more important Czech and international writer than would have been possible had he remained in Prague. The personal and national trauma that was 1968 provided him with the challenge of a great subject, to which he responded with the novels that are thematically his most profound and technically his most innovative. Whatever might have been his 'achievement' had he remained in Czechoslovakia, it would have doubtless been less impressive in originality, scope, and power than it is. This is not to underrate the work of his Czechoslovak period; *The Cowards*, *The Bass Saxophone* (*Bassaxofon*, 1963), and *Miss Silver's Past* (*Lvíče*, 1969) are among his major achievements. But exile made it possible for him to write and publish not only two of the central works in his canon but also those literary and political essays (in journals like *New Republic*, *Daedalus*, and *New York Review of Books*) that have established him among those in the West who speak with some authority about Eastern and Central European culture and politics. His literary essays usually deal with Eastern and Central European writers Škvorecký admires and wants to introduce to a Western audience; his political ones have shown him in a Cassandra-like role, bringing the bad news to the West about the pre-glasnost Soviet empire.

Looking over the past two decades of Škvorecký's career, it is fair to say that whatever critical attention and popularity he may have sacrificed by leaving Czechoslovakia in the wake of what he has called the Soviet 'ambush' have been more than compensated for by Western critics and readers. From Yorick Blumenfeld's 1968 reference to 'Josef Skovorecky's [sic] *The Cowards*' (in *Seesaw: Cultural Life in Eastern Europe*) to the reviews of *The Miracle Game*, Škvorecký and his work have gradually become as much of a presence in the English-speaking world as they were in the Czech one. He has become, like Miłosz, Milan Kundera, and Joseph Brodsky, one of those exiles with what can be called two primary audiences, one of which reads him in the original, the other in translation; and this is even truer since 1989 with the reissue of his books in Prague.

The democratization of Czechoslovakia, however, will do more than restore and enlarge Škvorecký's Czech readership. It will also have the long-term effect of allowing all of his readers to read his fiction from a new, less politically oriented perspective. Because Škvorecký's novels have from the start been concerned with political and historical issues, characters, and events, discussions of them have almost inevitably (and, up to a point, justifiably) focused on politics to the neglect of other aspects. Were he given to answering his critics – and he usually isn't – Škvorecký could justifiably complain that few of them have really given him his due as an artist. George Woodcock is right in suggesting that Škvorecký is one of those writers – like André Malraux, Ignazio Silone, and George Orwell – for whom 'style or form' is less important than 'the moral or intellectual' content. Yet, there is little doubt that an understandable concern with the latter has made most critics less attentive to his craftsmanship and artistry. Among his many critics, only the novelist André Brink and the critic František Všetička have written exclusively about his craft. Significantly, each deals with a text in which political concerns are secondary; Brink discusses 'Emöke,' and Všetička *The Bass Saxophone* (in 'How "The Bass Saxophone" Is Made,' *World Literature Today*, 54 (1980), 552–5, 555–7).

I don't want to be misunderstood, however, as suggesting that Škvorecký isn't an important political and historical novelist. In fact, as I argued in *Prague Blues: The Fiction of Josef Škvorecký*, he seems to me one of the few novelists in the century to have done something original with the political novel of ideas: in *Miss Silver's Past* he uses a mystery novel to discuss political and ideological issues; in *The Miracle Game* and *The Engineer of Human Souls* he has written about politics, ideas, and history in what are in essence comic or tragicomic novels. It is also noteworthy that the two long novels of the 1970s not only deal with a crucial recent phase of Czechoslovak history, but, on publication, seemed intended as potential interventions – the first directed at Czechoslovakia, the second at the West – in the ongoing historical process. *The Miracle Game*, for example, challenges Marxist ideology in its dialogues, subverts officially received accounts of Czechoslovak history, and, in the 1970s and 1980s, had the potential, however slight, of changing views and indirectly influencing events in Czechoslovakia. Though it was written in the West immediately after Škvorecký's emigration, its intentions clearly pointed East. It is marked by a sense of urgency that is probably unique to the sociopolitical situation of the exiled writer writing in opposition to an officially imposed amnesia in his homeland about certain events of the recent past. It is not far-fetched to see it as one of those works that subtly changed the political and cultural climate to the point that glasnost and the velvet revolution would become realities.

What I am trying to emphasize, however, is that if in reading Škvorecký's novels we need to be aware of ideology, politics, and history, we need to be equally alert to the danger of reducing their full artistic complexity to nothing more than apolitical or ideological significance. The novels may be political, but their vision is ultimately anti-political and anti-ideological; the focus is on individuals trying to evade political demands in order to live lives of freedom and common decency, to reclaim a private space within an all-pervasive politics. The fact that Škvorecký is much more explicit and dogmatic about his politics in his essays than in his fiction indicates his own awareness of the balance requisite if a novel is to engage politics and still remain responsive to the demands of art. He is fully aware, as *The Miracle Game* and *The Engineer of Human Souls* show, that one of the dangers facing the exiled novelist dealing explicitly with politics and history is that in the eagerness to score political points the play and complexity of art may be lost. Our tact in reading, then, should be as fine as Škvorecký's in writing. We need to begin with the idea that the novel responsive in whatever way to politics is both politics and art, that to ignore or overemphasize either is to misread it. And while predictions are always hazardous, I suspect that Škvorecký's future critics will probably focus more on his artistry and his place in Czech literature roughly to the same extent that his critics up to now have concentrated on the political implications of his work. Stalinism, socialist realism, the Czechoslovak purges of the early 1950s, and 1968 will become less prominent in discussions of Škvorecký's work than polyphony, his religious vision, his handling of narrative in the novels written in Canada, the influence of film montage on the structure of his later work, the relationship between swing and the rhythm of his fiction, and so on. This is not to say that the second group of topics is more important than the first, only that it, too, deserves attention, especially in discussions of fiction.

Although the publication of this volume was originally planned to coincide roughly with Škvorecký's retirement from the University of Toronto in 1990, it is not intended as a *Festschrift* in the traditional senses of that word. It seemed more important to collect and commission essays that as a group would constitute a broadly critical introduction to Škvorecký's large and impressive body of work: he has, after all, written more than forty books, and, as editor of Sixty-Eight Publishers, he has helped edit more than two hundred. It was my impression when I first thought of the volume (as it still is today) that while Škvorecký's work is popular both in Europe and North America, and although it has been warmly received by critics and writers like Stanisław Barańczak, André Brink, Anthony Burgess, Graham Greene, Jan Kott, George Steiner, and George Woodcock, it has received neither the critical recognition nor the attention that it deserves. At a time when even minor American, British, and Canadian writers of fiction have several volumes devoted to them by mid-career, it seemed curious to me that Škvorecký had received so little serious criticism. This collection, like my own *Prague Blues* (1990) or Paul Trensky's *The Fiction of Josef Škvorecký* (1991), can be seen as a celebration of his impressive achievement and as an attempt to begin serious discussion of his work and to argue a case for his importance.

Eleven of the pieces included here were commissioned for the volume. Three of the essays (by Michal Schonberg, André Brink, and Helena Kosková) are reprinted from the 1980 special Škvorecký issue of *World Literature Today*, which marked his receiving the prestigious Neustadt Prize (Czesław Miłosz and Gabriel Garcia Marquez were earlier recipients). Milan Kundera's contribution was first published as the preface to the French translation of *The Miracle Game* (*Miracle en Bohême*, 1978). Jan Kott's 'The Emigrant as Hero' and Edward Rothstein's 'New World Symphonietta' appeared as reviews in *New Republic* of *The Engineer of Human Souls* and *Dvorak in Love*, respectively; both struck me as among the best things written about Škvorecký and deserving republication.

As even a cursory glance at the table of contents reveals, the essays can be grouped in roughly two categories. The first offers an intellectual and cultural context for Škvorecký's writing and his career. This includes essays by Stanisław Barańczak, Milan Kundera, Lubomír Dorůžka, Peter Hrubý, George Gibian, and the interview with Škvorecký's wife, novelist and publisher Zdena Salivarová. The second group focuses on Škvorecký's work. Helena Kosková and Gleb Žekulin present overviews of his career; the other critics provide readings of individual novels from the very early *Konec nylonového věku* (The End of the Nylon Age, written in 1950) to *Miss Silver's Past* and *Dvorak in Love*. Considerations of space prevented me from commissioning articles on his scripts and work in film, short stories, detective fiction, dramatic works (cabaret scripts and plays), and his two volumes of poetry, *Dívka z Chicaga* (The Girl from Chicago, 1980) and *Nezoufejte* (Don't Despair, 1980).

As in all projects of this kind, there are various debts to acknowledge. Ursula Solecki helped with encouragement during the early stages; Audrey McDonagh helped with several of the manuscripts and, as always, caught mistakes and saw problems I had missed; Gleb Žekulin, Igor Hájek, and Paul Wilson helped with some Czech questions and problems; and Peter Petro commissioned four of the essays. A special thanks is due to Professor W.J. Keith, who read the final manuscript and made countless valuable suggestions.

SAM SOLECKI

Acknowledgments

André Brink, 'The Girl and the Legend: Josef Škvorecký's "Emöke,"' *World Literature Today*, 54 (1980); Marketa Goetz-Stankiewicz, 'A World Symphony in a Scherzo: *Dvorak in Love*,' *Canadian Forum*, September 1987; Helena Kosková, 'The Demolisher of False Myths,' *World Literature Today*, 54 (1980); Jan Kott, 'The Emigrant as Hero: *The Engineer of Human Souls*,' *New Republic*, 27 August 1984; Milan Kundera, 'Preface to the French Edition of *Mirákl* (*The Miracle Game*),' *Granta*, 13; Edward Rothstein, 'New World Symphonietta: *Dvorak in Love*,' *New Republic*, 1 June 1987; Michal Schonberg, 'The Case of the Mangy Pussycat: An Account of the Literary Scandal Surrounding the Publication of *The Cowards*,' *World Literature Today*, 54 (1980); Sam Solecki, '"Where Is My Home?" Some Notes on Reading Josef Škvorecký in *Amerika*,' *Canadian Literature*, 120 (Spring 1989).

A Note on the Text

Since the essays were written both before and after Czechoslovakia's 'velvet revolution,' they occasionally refer to historical facts and situations radically altered by recent history. To help the reader situate each essay, I have included with its title its date of publication or, in the case of previously unpublished material, of writing.

If a book has been published both in Czech and in English, both titles appear italicized: *Zbabělci* (*The Cowards*). If a book has appeared in Czech but not in English, the Czech title alone is italicized, while the English translation appears in Roman in a parenthesis: *Konec nylonového věku* (The End of the Nylon Age).

Throughout the text, the word *Czechoslovakia* refers to the country that existed from 1918 until 1993, while *Czech* refers to the language and the literature of the Czech people.

THE ACHIEVEMENT OF JOSEF ŠKVORECKÝ

Reflecting on Exile:
An Interview with Josef Škvorecký (1989–92)

SOLECKI As I once told you, I spent nearly the first ten years of my life living in a camp for Polish refugees in the English Midlands. And one of the most magical of English words for all of us was 'America.' Looking back I realize that for many of us the word came from the same word group as Oz or the Promised Land. Canada, on the other hand, was mentioned only if someone had relatives there or as an adjunct of the United States. Did you know much about Canada when living in Czechoslovakia?

ŠKVORECKÝ I had a vague and probably unrealistic image based on some youthful reading of James Oliver Curwood, whom I believe to be a Canadian though some say he's an American. He wrote boys' novels about Mounties and trappers and Indians and Indian girls – so my image of Canada included Mounties and deep woods and grizzly bears and a few other romantic details. Also as a boy I loved to read Ernest Thompson Seton. So I had an image of a pretty wild country and knew nothing about Canadian cities, for example. On the other hand, I knew something of the famous American cities like New York and Chicago because I had seen them or heard about them in American films. Canada was hazy and my picture of it was pretty romantic.

SOLECKI What about Western Europe?

ŠKVORECKÝ Well, that was much closer to home, next door really, so like all Czechs I knew it much better.

SOLECKI But you didn't travel extensively until after the war, did you?

ŠKVORECKÝ That wasn't until the 1950s and 60s. As you know, the political climate in Czechoslovakia improved in the early 1960s so that in 1961 or 1962 – I can't remember exactly – I was able to travel to Norway to attend a PEN club congress. After that, when *The Cowards* had been published in Denmark and Italy, I was allowed to use some of the royalties to travel in Denmark and Italy. I remember my wife and I drove to Italy. And toward the end of the sixties I attended several conferences, including a congress in Vienna that I describe in my novel *The Miracle Game*. So whatever impressions I had of the West during this period were the result of my reading, of films, and of these trips.

SOLECKI   What stands out in your memory from these trips?

ŠKVORECKÝ   The Polish writer Stanisław Barańczak mentions somewhere that he found the West simply much more colourful than Eastern Europe. I would add that it was also more joyful and cleaner. Although I should add that on my first trip I drove through Sweden, which is particularly clean and beautiful and therefore not really representative because it hadn't suffered from the war. Still, it made a deep impression on me. Similarly, when I travelled to Vienna I couldn't help noticing the abundance of everything – the fruit, for example. In Prague, you just didn't see many of the things you saw in Vienna. I had come from a world that was drab to one that was colourful. I remember driving with my wife from Italy to Czechoslovakia and having to pass through Austria, which was very bright, each of the little villages full of light. But as soon as we crossed into Czechoslovakia, everything was literally submerged in darkness. We drove through complete darkness until we reached the outskirts of Prague. It was almost symbolic. I suppose that most of my impressions of the West are probably typical.

SOLECKI   You were in the West during the invasion of August 1968, weren't you?

ŠKVORECKÝ   Yes, yes I was.

SOLECKI   Why did you decide to return to Czechoslovakia?

ŠKVORECKÝ   Partly because my wife was in her second year of study at the Prague Film Academy, to which she had been admitted after many years of being denied entrance to any institution of higher learning because her family were or had been social democrats. She simply wanted to return to finish her studies. It meant a great deal to her. So we went back. She was young and the young are always optimistic, so we decided to return. But after three months in Prague she realized that there was no future for us in Czechoslovakia, and we decided to leave for good. That was on the last day of January 1969, only a few days after Jan Palach's death by burning, really the gloomiest time since the invasion itself. Even the weather was bad. It really was a terrible time in every way. Prague was full of rumours about people who were going to be liquidated.

So we left, and an hour later we were landing in London, at Heathrow, on a sunny day, and we saw this group of English schoolgirls in their uniforms running across the hall. It made for a very sharp contrast. Again, it was almost symbolic. So that was my first impression of the West.

SOLECKI All emigration involves anxiety, but this must have been a particularly anxious period for you since you were a writer. You were forty-four and had achieved a substantial reputation as a novelist, a scriptwriter, an editor, even a cabaret writer. But this was all in Czech, a language you once described as 'that unknown, useless and difficult language of the Western Slavs.' Suddenly you were in a country where the demand for Czech writing and writers was minimal.

ŠKVORECKÝ I had no idea what I would be doing. If I had known Russian I could have hoped for a job at a university in a department of Slavic Studies. But actually I felt quite good because I knew things would have been even worse had I stayed in Prague. I also knew that if I had stayed I would have had three choices: I could recant and say that I had been wrong and that I would mend my ways; I could go back into the underground, of which I had been a member in the early fifties, but then I had been a young man and had been willing to write for the desk drawer; or I could stop writing and do something completely different. In comparison to these anything was better.

SOLECKI Did you have any contacts in Western Europe or in North America?

ŠKVORECKÝ There was George Gibian, an old friend from before the war whom I barely remembered and had not seen for years. His family was Jewish and they left in time, but he returned to Bohemia with General Patton's Third Army and then again in the sixties when he was already established as a university professor specializing in Czech and Russian. So in the sixties I saw him in Prague. When my wife and I decided to leave I wrote to him, and he contacted Kathryn Feuer, who chaired the University of Toronto's Slavic Studies Department. She invited me to Toronto for six weeks. I lectured and gave some seminars. Then Gibian arranged a visit to Cornell, and that was followed by three months at Berkeley, where my only duty was to write an essay on a Czech writer. So I wrote an essay in Czech on Vladimír Páral, and it's probably still in their archives. Then Feuer arranged another invitation to Toronto, where I had to teach one course in film for Slavic Studies and one introductory course in literature in the English department. The following year I became writer in residence, and that was followed by a permanent appointment in the English department at Erindale College.

SOLECKI So you were at Berkeley during the critical days.

ŠKVORECKÝ Oh yes. It was the height of the antiwar protests, and I remember seeing a banner announcing 'Welcome to Prague.' Ronald Reagan was the governor of California at that point, and he had sent in the National Guard. The students decided to compare the Soviet invasion of Czechoslovakia to the Guard's arrival on campus. And I must say the comparison struck me as far-fetched, remote.

My wife and I also saw the war in Vietnam very differently from the way in which the students at Berkeley saw it. For us it was a war against communism. Obviously we also had a very different view of communism from the one held by American radicals. For us the war was a war against an invading Communist nation, North Vietnam, and we were happy that the Americans and South Vietnamese were winning. And as far as I was concerned, the young people at Berkeley with their chants and burning flags didn't know much about what was really going on. Their understanding of the situation was very one-sided. Though I can sympathize with anyone who didn't want to fight, to go to war, I found the marching crowds shouting their stuttering slogans idiotic. The whole thing was really shocking.

SOLECKI In some crucial respects this anticipated some of your later reactions to North American attitudes to world politics. Like Miłosz and Kundera you tend to think of most North Americans as relatively naïve about foreign affairs or, more precisely, about those foreign affairs that were related in some way to the Soviet Union. My impression is that one of the consequences of your essentially 'conservative' stance on foreign affairs has been that many critics fail to look beyond this to attitudes and views on other issues. After two decades you must be tired of this whole topic.

ŠKVORECKÝ You're right, but it's important, very important. One of the inevitable consequences of being an emigrant or exile is that one remains tied to the old country and concerned with the fate of that country. And since in my case and in Czechoslovakia's case that fate was tied up with totalitarianism and communism, and communism had a world importance, then it's inevitable that my interest, what you call my politics, should have been primarily concerned with foreign affairs.

SOLECKI One of the results of this seems to be that you have had little interest in domestic Canadian or American politics. Similarly Kundera doesn't comment on French politics.

ŠKVORECKÝ You could say I'm interested but not as interested as I am in the other politics, which seemed to me so obviously more important or urgent. Don't forget that for my generation, at least since Hitler, politics, real politics always involved danger. You could die for saying or writing something. You could also be in danger simply because of what or who you were. From that extreme perspective, Canada and the United States and most of Western Europe don't have politics; life in these societies is free of politics. On the other hand, Czechoslovakia, until very recently, was still political in the old sense, and I'm still a Czech. So glasnost and perestroika and their effect on Czechoslovakia are more important to me than the Liberal and Progressive Conservative parties. This is probably true for most immigrants who come to Canada as adults. Those who come as children will grow up to be one hundred per cent Canadians and they will be more concerned about whether to vote for the Liberals or the Conservatives than with who is the head of the Czechoslovak government. Their politics will be mainly national politics. I came too late to be like that. It all depends on your age when you emigrate.

To get back to Berkeley, except for the war protests our impression of California and America was very positive. Berkeley and San Francisco were very beautiful, and there was very good jazz in San Francisco. Also I was very happy because my wife started writing her novel *Summer in Prague*, which gave her something to do. Since she didn't speak any English, she felt very isolated. And I guess because she was so isolated, she was able to write the novel in the three months that we were there.

SOLECKI What were you writing at the time?

ŠKVORECKÝ I was writing travel pieces for the Czech magazine *Svĕt práce*.

You see, because my exit visa was valid until the end of 1969, I was still considered a Czechoslovak citizen. Only when I refused to report to the embassy at the end of the year or to return did I really become an exile.

SOLECKI At that point you were already living in Canada. When you came here did you notice any differences between Canada and the United States?

ŠKVORECKÝ Not many, or at least not right away, but I did have the impression that the States were much older. Toronto struck me as a very new city, especially when I thought of it side by side with New York or Chicago.

SOLECKI I first saw Canada from a ship sailing up the St Lawrence, so that the first cities I saw were Quebec and Montreal. I still remember being disappointed by Ontario's towns and cities because they seemed so much less interesting than Quebec's. It was as if Quebec had a history and Ontario didn't. Only in school and even then only gradually did I start to see Ontario as 'historical' in its own way. Though I must admit it still doesn't excite my imagination in the way that Quebec's history does.

ŠKVORECKÝ You could say that I lived in history for the first forty-five years of my life so that I take castles and châteaux and medieval and baroque churches for granted. Prague is after all as full of history as any city. But to me the general conditions of life, the general intellectual conditions of life are much more important. What kind of life is possible in a city or in a country is much more important to me. Beautiful medieval churches are interesting, but they don't compensate for the fact that intellectual and cultural life is lived under conditions that from one point of view are also medieval. You know, whenever I go to Europe now, and I only go on business or to give readings, I always look forward to coming home, coming to Toronto. This is home and I feel more at ease here than I do in Germany or anywhere else in Europe. The only exception to this is England, which I like very much, perhaps because of the language or because I always remember it as very green, very beautiful. The language is very important, because Czech and English are now my main languages. Like many Czechs I used to speak German very well, but I haven't really spoken it since the war, which is almost half a century ago. I read it well but when speaking I feel rusty.

I want to return to what we were just saying about Canada and history, or the fact that Canada struck me as so much younger than the United

States. You can see this when you compare the Czech communities in the two countries. The Canadian one is really quite recent; most of the people came either before the Second World War or immediately after in 1948. Then there was the final group that came, as I did, after 1968. But the American Czechs – and I wrote about this in *Dvorak in Love*, and it is also a topic in my new novel, *Nevěsta z Texasu* (The Bride from Texas), about Czechs in the American Civil War – the American Czech community is much older. Many Czechs settled in America after the revolutions of 1848, and there was continuing immigration after that. There are now many fourth- and fifth-generation Czechs in America. Toronto has about fourteen thousand Czechs and about eight thousand of them came as a result of 1968. One of the results of this is that the Canadian Czech community has tended to be more intensely interested in what is happening in Czechoslovakia because they have come. from there much more recently. Most American Czechs, on the other hand, have little direct knowledge of the old country.

Still, I want to say that I admire the American Czechs very much because of their perseverance. Without any multicultural grants and official encouragement they remained Czechs. I was at a conference in Texas a few years ago where there were about ten mixed choirs all singing Czech songs, even though many of the singers obviously didn't understand the language. It was very impressive. There were people there in the old national costumes, which they made themselves, but the ornaments on the costumes were Bohemian and Texan. And all this was done without any kind of official governmental support or encouragement. This is also true of all the Czech brass bands in the Midwest. You can buy dozens of records of Czech music.

SOLECKI In your account there doesn't seem to be much difference between the American 'melting pot' and the Canadian 'mosaic.'

ŠKVORECKÝ I don't think there is, except that the Canadian government certainly talks about ethnic groups and multiculturalism more than the Americans do.

SOLECKI I've always thought of much of this as just political, a jockeying among parties for influence and votes with various groups. I don't really believe that any of the parties really care one way or another whether European and Caribbean cultures flourish in Canada. In fact, my own response to official multiculturalism is that it is ultimately divisive in that it creates countless small interest groups that see the country primarily if not exclusively from their own limited ethnic perspective.

ŠKVORECKÝ I wonder if one of the results of all this is that many Canadians think that European immigrants are sort of old-fashioned, simple people who do cute dances in outlandish costumes and sing in funny languages. I think that if an ethnic culture is going to survive beyond the second or third generation it will do so whether it is officially supported or not. But usually immigrants become assimilated. I think that's inevitable whether in Canada or the United States. It's ironic, by the way, that most of the folk-dances and songs that the ethnic dance groups do at officially sponsored events are no longer done in the hills of Bohemia or Poland or wherever. The teenagers there dance to rock and roll, and those dances haven't really been performed spontaneously for years.

SOLECKI I suppose you could say that if people want an image of nineteenth-century East and Central European folk-dance or folk-song, they are more likely to get it at Toronto's Caravan than in Prague or Warsaw.

ŠKVORECKÝ They would also see it in the folk groups sent abroad by the governments. My wife used to be a member of one, and like most of the other singers and dancers she was from Prague, a big city, where these songs and dances were no longer performed. Her group almost never performed in Czechoslovakia, and if they did, then it was mostly in military camps where the audience doesn't have much choice. In Czechoslovakia these dances are museum pieces.

SOLECKI Since we are speaking of Czech matters, do you think of your writing as directed at a Czech readership?

ŠKVORECKÝ Not really. I guess I don't really think about this very much. I just assume that if what you write is any good then it will always find some readers, Czech, English, French, whoever. After all, there isn't such a great difference between the readers in one country and another. If what I write is not entirely bad, then the work will find its own readers no matter in what country or in what language.

Although I should point out that some of my stories, and parts of *The Engineer of Human Souls* and *Dvorak in Love*, are probably incomprehensible for readers in Czechoslovakia because they are written in a Czech heavily influenced by North American English. Other than that, I believe that people are essentially the same everywhere and if a writer manages to write well about some aspect of life, people will read him. This is true even if the translation is awful. I remember before the war, Czechs used to read terrible translations of authors like Sinclair Lewis and Theodore Dreiser and Mark Twain. Obviously they didn't understand all the allusions to American things and they couldn't have been reading for the style – but something must have come through because everybody loved Huckleberry Finn.

SOLECKI Would it be valid to call the Central Europe of that era – perhaps even the Czechoslovakia of that 1918–1938 period – multicultural? Prague, after all, was a German, a Czech, and a Jewish city, and Czechoslovakia had many national or ethnic or linguistic minorities within it during the First Republic.

ŠKVORECKÝ The society was certainly multicultural but not in the way that Canada and America are multicultural. There was certainly a lively German culture in the country, but the Germans lived only in the Sudeten and in Prague. Similarly, the Hungarians lived in the south-east, in Slovakia, while the Ukrainians lived in the Carpathians. The various groups were fairly separate. So as a result there was a greater homogeneity in the country's culture than the term multiculturalism suggests. We didn't have the mixture that a city like Toronto has. My own home town of Náchod, for example, was a Czech town and had only about seven German families in it. That's out of a population of about fourteen thousand people. By the way, the fact that the town was almost completely Czech prevented it from being annexed after the Munich Agreement in 1938.

SOLECKI Do you ever worry about your own Czech? You left Czechoslovakia more than twenty years ago and have lived since then in an English-speaking world. The language must have changed over that period of time.

ŠKVORECKÝ Oh yes. There are always new terms, slang words, idioms, and so on. But the core of the language seems to me to have remained the same, and when I write I write in it and from it. But, you know, when I speak Czech, I have noticed that I use American or Canadian Czech, which is the Czech most North American Czechs use. I think of it as a dialect of the mother tongue. And it is more than a century old. Rosie's letters in *Dvorak in Love*, for example, which are written in that dialect, are based on a series of letters published in the 1890s in a Chicago Czech humorous weekly. They are supposedly written by a servant named Rosie. The folks back home write back that they can't understand her. She responds by telling them that they should learn English. But this situation in which the immigrant's first language is influenced by English is common to all immigrants and you can find it in every ethnic community. Henry Mencken writes about this in his appendix to *The American Language*, where he shows how European languages become corrupted by American English. My own attitude to this is fairly liberal. I see it as an interesting linguistic phenomenon with great humorous potential, which, as you know, I try to make use of in my fiction, although it is very difficult to translate into English. It needs a reader who knows both languages and can see and hear the humour that comes out of the meeting of the two.

SOLECKI Has English influenced Czech in Czechoslovakia as well?

ŠKVORECKÝ Oh yes. It's by no means a new phenomenon. The first influence came through sport and sport terminology. About eight years ago I translated Martina Navratilova's autobiography into Czech. Since I know nothing about the terms used in tennis I was a bit afraid that I would get many things wrong. But when I asked a friend who is a tennis player to help me with them, we discovered that the words are the same in both languages: topspin, lob, and tie-breaker. In recent years, especially after 1968, many English words have replaced Czech ones. Everybody now says 'job' instead of 'místo.' I saw some recent Czech films in which all the characters kept referring to their 'jobs.' All the computer language is also English, since the terms and expressions have not been translated and probably won't be: software, hardware, and things like that.

   Some of this is the result of the fact that English is a dominant international language. But another reason is that people in Central Europe and Czechoslovakia were and are very pro-American – American jazz, American movies, American literature, American democracy, American life in general. So they adopt or absorb the language, which to them symbolizes this whole civilization. Before 1989 nobody used Russian expressions and Russian syntax except the Party newspapers, which everyone knows used terrible Czech. Awful. For instance, even though 'and' in Czech is *a*, the Party orators, under the influence of Russian, frequently insisted on using the Russian form, *i*, which exists in Czech but means 'as well as' rather than 'and.'

SOLECKI Since coming to Canada you have written essays and articles in English for *Canadian Forum, New Republic*, and *New York Review of Books*, but you have never written any fiction in English. Why not?

ŠKVORECKÝ Well, fiction involves playing with language in a way that non-fiction doesn't. I use slang, various idioms, make jokes, and play with dialects. I find that difficult enough to do in the language I have spoken all my life, the one I feel at home in. I don't think I could do it in English – there I'm just a visitor who arrived late. It would certainly change my style, but I'm not sure that I could really write in it.

I enjoy writing essays and reviews in English, partly because it's a challenge, though a smaller one than trying to write fiction in an acquired language. I would even say that I *prefer* writing non-fiction in English because, though this may sound strange, I get better ideas in English and I can formulate my ideas more clearly in English. This may be because when I write in Czech I find it very easy to slip into clichés and platitudes and predictable expressions. An acquired language makes me think harder and often I somehow get better ideas. I have written only one play in my life – 'God Help Us!' – and I wrote it in English and then translated it into Czech. And I did that for a very simple reason. When I write in Czech it comes too easily, and I become too loquacious and speeches become very long, and scenes just go on and on. In English I have to write slowly and more carefully. English forces me to be more concise than I would normally be. Anyway, that play is the only *belles lettres* that I have written in English.

SOLECKI This is probably the only thing you have in common with Samuel Beckett, who gives roughly similar reasons for turning from English to French. French imposes a discipline on him.

ŠKVORECKÝ That's the right word – discipline. For various reasons, English makes me into a more disciplined writer. It presents me with obstacles, interesting obstacles, that I must overcome.

SOLECKI Milan Kundera writes his novels in Czech and his essays in French.

ŠKVORECKÝ Yes, yes. He told me that he had begun a novel in French but had to give up. Like me, he's trapped inside Czech.

SOLECKI You may be trapped within Czech, yet despite having returned several times to Czechoslovakia since 1989 you have decided to continue to live in Canada. Was it a difficult decision? And what were the main reasons behind it?

ŠKVORECKÝ It wasn't a difficult decision at all – and for several reasons that extend from selfish to sentimental, and many things in between. Let me start with some mathematics: I'm sixty-eight years old, and I have spent the past twenty-three years of my life in Canada. That is exactly one-third of my life. But it is also almost half of my adult life – if you take eighteen as the age at which we reach adulthood.

And it wasn't just any twenty-three years. Never in my life had I enjoyed the basic and most important things without which human life is not fully human: freedom, living in a democratic society not oppressed by foreign power or foreign ideology; living without fear of the all-powerful secret police, be it the Gestapo or its Czech-Communist equivalent, the StB (State Security). It was only during these twenty-three years that I was able to write and publish my books without any form of censorship, external or internal. I also found myself in a society where I never felt any discrimination, although I speak with an accent and although most of what I have written is not about Canada.

These are some of the major reasons why we have decided to stay here. You can also add the real beauty of Canada, its plains, mountains, lakes, and rivers. And there are also the creature comforts, which at my age are much more important than they were when I was eighteen or forty-five, and which present-day Czechoslovakia, although it is quickly making up for lost time, cannot yet offer.

But above everything else, this country gave me freedom. I'm sometimes asked, often sarcastically, for a satisfying, profound, scientific, maybe even Marxist definition of freedom. But like anybody who was ever forced to live in 'unfreedom' I don't really need a definition.

2

STANISŁAW BARAŃCZAK

Tongue-tied Eloquence:
Notes on Language, Exile, and Writing (1989)
(Occasioned by reading Josef Škvorecký)

Among the many hilarious, outrageous, sublime, crazy, profound, or otherwise memorable scenes that fill the pages of Josef Škvorecký's unparalleled
The Engineer of Human Souls, one brief episode seems to me particularly
pregnant with meaning. One of the novel's minor characters, Milan, a recent
Czech defector granted asylum in Canada, is throwing a housewarming
party. Except for his Canadian girlfriend, all the guests are, not
unexpectedly, Czech émigrés:

Someone is telling a joke about the Prague policeman who drowned trying to
stamp out a cigarette a passer-by had tossed in the river. There is loud laughter.
  Barbara hands Milan his glass.
  'I suppose he's telling jokes?'
  'That's right.'
  'Well,' says Barbara deliberately, 'couldn't you translate them for me?'
  'They're only word games. My English isn't good enough.'
  'Then how about making an effort? Your English is good enough for some
things.'
  But Milan ignores her ... (141)

And bad conversationalist as he may seem, he is right to do so. On a list
of things hardest to translate into another language, jokes come a close
second after rhymed poetry (whereas love entreaties, as Barbara pretends not
to realize, are among the easiest, if they require any translation at all). This
is particularly true when the jokes are Eastern European, and told anywhere
west of the Iron Curtain. Though no intellectual giant, Škvorecký's Milan
understands that instinctively and immediately.
  More sophisticated minds sometimes need a dozen years to grasp this

simple truth. I have in mind the example of a famous Eastern European wit, the poet Antoni Słonimski, who in pre-1939 Poland had been nearly idolized by the readers of his side-splitting *feuilletons* published in every issue of the most popular literary weekly. At the outbreak of war he took refuge in the West and spent the next twelve years in London, but in 1951, of all moments, he decided to go back to Poland for good. Asked many years later why he had chosen to do so, he gave a disarmingly frank answer: In England, he was unable to tell a joke. No, he had no qualms about living under capitalism, especially since Stalinism *anno* 1951 was hardly a more attractive option. No, he had nothing against the English and their ways, either: in fact, he was a declared Anglophile all his life. And no, he did not really feel lonely, or materially underprivileged, or socially degraded. What he could not stand was that whenever he tried to tell a joke to an English friend, he somehow was not funny.

For a while, he was determined to do anything in his power to succeed. He worked doggedly on his English and prepared all his jokes beforehand, endlessly chiselling their fine points and rehearsing for hours; once, before meeting some English people he particularly wished to impress, he stooped so low as to jot down a witticism on his cuff. All in vain; every joke was a flop. This would have been unbearable enough for a mere mortal. For Słonimski, who had spent twenty years building up his reputation as the wittiest man in Poland, this was sufficient reason to go back to the lion's den. There, hardships or no hardships, censorship or no censorship, he could at least sit down at his regular table in his favourite café, crack a joke, and hear his admirers laugh.

As told by Słonimski, this story of the return of the prodigal joker may well have been a joke in itself – the motives behind his decision were certainly more complex than that – but it says something about the expatriate's experience that usually escapes definition. And it says even more about the experience of the expatriated writer. After all, works of literature, like jokes, are essentially 'word games,' as Škvorecký's Milan would have it. Easy for Robert Frost to say that poetry is what is lost in translation! Squarely settled in his homeland, he wrote for an audience that shared both his experience and his language, and it was of secondary concern to him just how much of what he intended to say was lost on some distant Chinese or Chilean reader. A writer who lives in exile has to care much more about what is 'lost in translation.' His foreign readers are within earshot, since he lives among them: if they don't laugh at his translated 'word games,' it hurts.

Of course, he may choose to stay forever on the safe side, that is, to lock himself up in the comfortable cell of his native language and write exclusively for the audience formed of his compatriots, either at home, or in the diaspora, or both. (Needless to say, this solution is only relatively safer: literature that deserves its name is always a risky business, and the fact that you share a language, literary tradition, experience, and whatever else with your reader does not necessarily mean that he gives a damn.) But once the writer decides to reach beyond his native language and familiar audience, once he lets the very problem of 'translation' cross his mind (regardless of whether technically he is to be translated by someone else, to translate his works himself, or to write originally in the language of his adopted country), the balance sheet of gains and losses will always loom in his consciousness ominously and inexorably.

What makes things even more bothersome is that the whole process of balancing the necessary losses against the uncertain gains is a two-way street. Trying to adapt his work to a foreign culture, the writer living in exile has no choice but to make this work lose some of its original flavour – that seems an obvious price to pay. Less obvious is the fact that this loss has its reverse side: being, after all, an outsider in the culture he tries to conquer, the writer sooner or later realizes that some of this culture's qualities are lost on him as well. While attempting to hammer the peg of his work into the hard, resisting log of a foreign culture, he cannot help but damage both pieces of timber, that is, simplify to some extent both the work and the culture as he sees it.

Again, the telling housewarming-party episode in Škvorecký's novel illustrates this double point in a neatly symmetrical way. Barbara's failure to comprehend an Eastern European joke is paralleled by Milan's failure to appreciate an allusion to American cultural lore. Her playing with a jigsaw puzzle (to which she, left out of the Czech conversation, has resorted) is for him just 'a Canadian habit'; for her, it's an echo of a mythical Hollywood scene, one heavy with the symbolism of rejection, loneliness, and disenchanted love:

How could he know it? When *Citizen Kane* last played in Prague, Milan was not yet in this world.
'You never give me anything I really care about,' says Barbara, waiting against hope for Milan to understand. (147)

But the line is lost on Milan, as well as the message that Barbara's quotation was supposed to convey. An exiled writer similarly loses a considerable part of the intricate meaning of the culture he attempts to enter. He may try, for instance, to tell a typically absurd Eastern European story: yet in order to believe in the validity of such an undertaking at all he has to block out his awareness of the fact that his North American audience has been brought up on a tradition whose pragmatism excludes the very notion of the absurd. Thus, in trying to impose his own vision, his own set of values, his own symbolism upon the foreign culture, he unavoidably distorts it: not only by enriching it but also by ignoring some of its intrinsic laws. And the only difference between him and Milan is that he is more or less aware of his ignorance.

Natural human egotism being a factor, however, it is understandable that what strikes the exiled writer first and foremost is how much of his or her own message is 'lost in translation' or untranslatable altogether. A short poem by my contemporary and compatriot, the Polish author Ewa Lipska, expresses it better than any semantic analysis. The poem is entitled 'To Marianne Büttrich'; we are not told who Marianne Büttrich is, but it is clear that she lives on the other side of the European Great Divide, presumably in West Germany:

For a year now I've been trying
to write you a letter.
But
the locusts of my thoughts
are untranslatable.

Untranslatable are the people on duty
guarding my words and grammar.
My hours are untranslatable
into yours.

The black lilacs behind the window.
· The unbuttoned gates. The yellowed cigarette end of a day.
The dead eye in the peephole
at six a.m.

Rilke is untranslatable too.
Die Blätter fallen, fallen ...
Wir alle fallen ...

I've got so much to tell you
but

a tunnel is approaching
my delayed train.

A long whistle sounds.

I'm tired, Marianne,
I'm leaving for the Bermuda Triangle
to take a rest.

Mind you, Lipska is not an exile (though she has visited the West), and she wrote this poem from the perspective of someone living in Poland in the 1980s. Still, there is no significant difference between her and the exiled writer as far as the notion of the fundamental untranslatability of Eastern European experience is concerned. If anything, the feeling of tongue-tied helplessness is stronger in the latter case. It is exacerbated by an inevitable clash of two facts. On the one hand, any writer who moves – either voluntarily or under pressure – from behind the Elbe line to the West is convinced that he has a special mission to carry out. His task, as he sees it, is to open the Westerners' eyes to what is going on 'over there' and what threatens to engulf their free and well-to-do world as well. But on the other hand, precisely because he is now in direct touch with his new audience, he soon finds out, to his utter astonishment and horror, that the Westerners do not exactly desire to have their eyes pried open. Czesław Miłosz is a writer who should know about this: he came forward with one of the first such eye-openers when he defected in 1951 and soon afterwards published his *The Captive Mind*, to the boos of the largely pro-Stalinist Western European intellectual community. In his brief essay 'Notes on Exile,' written much later in America, he describes this sort of clash as a classic paradox: in his homeland, the writer's voice was listened to but he was not allowed to speak; in exile, he is free to say whatever he wishes but nobody cares to listen (and moreover, Miłosz adds, the writer himself may have forgotten what he had to say).

Granted, in real life the stable symmetry of this paradox sometimes wobbles. There are areas and periods of suddenly awakened or slowly growing interest in the part of the world the exiled writer came from, and his voice may come through with unexpected force. But even then his experience is hardly translatable in its entirety. Consider two skimpy lines from Lipska's poem: 'The dead eye in the peephole / at six a.m.' The Western reader's gaze will slide over this phrase as just another metaphor, perhaps a slightly macabre one: it may remind him of, say, a scene from *The*

Return of the Living Dead. For the Polish, or Czechoslovak, or Russian, or Romanian reader, the phrase's impact is much more direct and its meaning is much more specific. In the 'dead eye' he will recognize the blank stare of a secret policeman he may have seen more than once through the peephole in his own door; and 'six a.m.,' as the typical time for police raids, will refer him unequivocally to the notion of a home search and arrest. If fear is the common semantic denominator of these two readings, it is fear of two distinctly different sorts: the enjoyable and leisurely fear of a horror-movie goer versus the ugly, shabby, completely unalluring yet very genuine fear of a citizen of a police state. The former smells of popcorn; the latter reeks of cold sweat.

'Wer den Dichter will verstehen, muss ins Dichters Lande gehen' (Who wants to understand the poet must go to the poet's homeland). Old Goethe's noble adage sounded perfectly empirical in his enlightened time, but we, in our post-totalitarian epoch, should know better. Our century has known too many pilgrims who went 'to the poet's homeland' only to be given red-carpet treatment, courtesy of Intourist, and a watchful guide, courtesy of the KGB. As the well-known book by Paul Hollander has documented, under certain circumstances there is nothing more false than the so-called eyewitness account. If the eyewitness comes from a nation or system with no experience in matters of all-out deceit and especially if he is willing to be duped, it is enough to hand him a skilfully packaged reality, and *voilà* – in his account all the barbed wire miraculously disappears and citizens' happy faces shine all around. Attempts to penetrate the inscrutable East from outside usually stop at the first banquet table with a generous supply of caviar. It speaks volumes for the futility of such pilgrimages that exactly caviar was the most vivid memory Billy Graham brought home from a preaching tour of the Soviet Union. During the same tour the sharp-eyed evangelist did not notice a ten-foot-long banner with precise data about the scope of religious persecution, nearly thrust into his face by some naïve dissident.

Then would the West be, ironically, better off if it believed so-called literary fiction rather than the sort of facts that the conveniently myopic eyewitnesses provide? Perhaps things have gone so far that indeed the inhabitant of the West thirsting for firsthand knowledge of the Eastern Bloc is much less likely to obtain it by visiting one of the Bloc's countries than by reading a poem by Czesław Miłosz, a novel by Josef Škvorecký, or an essay by Joseph Brodsky?

What I am saying amounts to a praise of the cognitive potential of literature, which here, in this hemisphere swarming with deconstructionists, is a rather contemptible opinion to hold. Yet, at the risk of sounding hopelessly backward, I hereby admit that I indeed believe in literature's power to name reality – or, to put it differently, to let us hear and comprehend reality's many-voiced hubbub more subtly and fully than any other kind of account. In this sense, the testimony supplied by the literary imagination may weigh more on the witness stand than the evidence of our senses, especially when the evidence has been fabricated in order to fool us; and the imagination may be a more efficient interpretive tool than abstract reasoning, especially when we face a reality whose absurdity transcends rationalistic thinking. As witnesses go, literary fiction nearly always beats both being on the safe ground of supposedly hard facts and being in the clouds of ideological dogmas.

This also – perhaps above all – applies to the works of exiled writers. Their evidence has a special value despite the fact that their precarious balancing between two worlds, two cultures, two value systems, and two languages puts them, in more ways than one, at a special risk. For one thing, there is the aforementioned barrier of different experiences: the audience in the exiled writer's adopted country, even if not entirely indifferent, is often unable to understand not merely his interpretation of reality but simply what he speaks about. And quite naturally so, since neither the material of their own experiences nor their inherited way of viewing reality has prepared them to accept this sort of a literary world. A world in which, for instance (to draw once again on Škvorecký's *The Engineer of Human Souls*), it is perfectly possible that one day workers in a factory are called to a meeting, aligned in single file, and ordered to sign, one by one and with no exception, a petition demanding the execution of the nation's political leader whom they were told to worship only yesterday. For an American reader, this is an Orwellian fantasy; for a Czech writer, this is what in fact happened in his country and what he could have seen with his own eyes.

Yet different experiences, heterogeneous though they may be, can be forcibly brought together by the writer to reveal some common human denominator; they can be juxtaposed and compared, and their mutual differences can be defined, explained, and reflected upon. The more annoying thing about literature is that all this has to be done in this or that ethnic language, which naturally limits the defining, explaining, and reflecting to the writer's native audience. (Classical dancers are, obviously, better off in this respect: the language of their art is international. But then, I somehow cannot picture myself pirouetting in public. Toiling at my untranslatable manuscripts poses, I should think, a relatively smaller risk of making a fool of myself.)

The problem of translation rears its ugly head once again. Anyone who has ever tried to translate a literary text, his own or someone else's, knows well that the chief difficulty of this endeavour lies not in the mere tedium of rummaging dictionaries and laboriously substituting one word for another. The chief difficulty is that two different languages are never a mirror reflection of each other; their seemingly corresponding parts never exactly match. The semantic ranges of supposedly equivalent words in fact only partially overlap; or a meaning may be expressed by three different synonyms in one language and five in the other; or a word has no counterpart in the other language at all; or the emotional tinge of a word disappears in its foreign equivalent ... And we are still on the level of separate words; what about phrases, sentences, verse lines, stanzas, paragraphs? What about the nation's accumulated historical experience that reflects itself in words and expressions that have elusive connotations not to be found in any dictionary? What about complications of a literary and poetic nature that raise the elementary incompatibility of two language systems to the second and third power? There is no end to the translator's woe, and his most brilliant effort may result at best in an approximation that is more ingenious than other approximations.

But the author – particularly the author who lives in exile and harbours the ambition to conquer the minds of his foreign-tongued hosts – is not interested in approximations. He wants his one-of-a-kind message to come across in unaltered and unbent shape, just as he intended it to look and sound. In this situation, the translator is the author's adversary rather than his ally, a spoiler rather than helper, a necessary evil. Even if the translator is the author himself.

A glance at the contemporary literary scene makes one realize that the panorama of ways of dealing with this problem stretches between two extremes. One extreme solution, represented, I believe, by Milan Kundera, consists in minimizing the translator's potential interference. The author is to make his original work as translatable as possible – in fact, he makes himself write in a deliberately translatable, clear and unequivocal style, so that the translator will not be prodded into too many deviations from the intended meaning.

The other extreme, best illustrated by Kundera's opponent in other matters, Joseph Brodsky, consists in skipping translation altogether. Brodsky's literary evolution in exile – as an essayist, but also a poet – has aimed at achieving linguistic self-sufficiency, becoming capable of writing the most artistically complex works directly in the language of his adopted country, so that the translator's services would be no longer called for.

Both extreme solutions may be admired for their radical boldness, and in fact it is very rare that a writer dares adopt either of them in their pure form. The more common solutions can be located somewhere in between: these are the fairly usual cases of authors who, for instance, are capable of writing a decent essay or article in their second language, but they wisely refrain from writing poems or novels in it, and instead rely on translators (at best trying to keep their arbitrariness in check by co-operating with them). Even though the Kundera and the Brodsky solutions have their respective advantages, the risk involved in either is indeed great. In the first case, the writer constantly faces the danger of losing his unique voice, slipping into some bland, abstract, international style, sounding like translationese even before the translation as such has been undertaken. In the other, the writer is constantly engaged in a high-wire act of imposture, usurpation of a language that will never be genuinely his own; and the more breathtaking the heights of stylistic bravado he manages to reach, the more painful may be the fall. Of course, both Kundera and Brodsky are artists masterful enough to dodge these dangers. Yet even they are not shielded from criticisms of those whose opinions matter the most – the readers for whom the French or English of these authors' works is a native language.

This is also true of anybody who attempts to bypass the translation problem on a more limited scale, for instance by trying to write – like the author of these words – some relatively plain essayistic prose directly in his second language. Perfect bilingualism is not a very common ability even when it comes to you naturally (for instance, by virtue of having been raised by a nationally mixed pair of parents), much less when you try to attain it by learning. As a practical consequence, the exiled author who writes in his adopted language can do pretty well without a translator but, as a rule, he cannot do without an editor. No matter how hard he tries, and no matter how linguistically proficient he is, there will always be some wrongly used the's or a's, some misshaped syntactic patterns, some ill-fitting idioms that will expose his hopeless position as an eternal outsider. After all, even in Joseph Conrad's English some Polish turns of phrase occasionally occur. Or so I'm told by native speakers of English.

This fact, obviously, teaches you humility. The chief reason why the exiled writer tries to write in the language of his adopted country is his desire to accomplish his mission – that is, to get his message across to a broader audience. But, ironically, exactly by accomplishing his mission in this way he fails to accomplish it in another, arguably more important sense. For his mission as a writer is not merely to get his message across but also to leave his individual imprint on this message; literature's essence is not so much the message itself as the endless spectrum of 'word games' (to quote Škvorecký's Milan once more) in which the writer's uniqueness may be revealed. This is extremely hard, in fact almost impossible, to achieve if you write in a language that is not yours by birthright.

True, even though the absolutely perfect command of a language is something an outsider cannot really acquire, he can, through a lot of effort, finally attain fluency and glibness that make him sound almost like a native writer. But literature is something more than glib writing. It also includes the right – and necessity – to violate glibness, to make light of rules, to speak in a novel way without bothering to be correct. In literature, a new thought cannot emerge except from a new way of speaking: in order to say anything relevant, you must break a norm. And this is precisely what an outsider cannot afford, since if breaking is to make any sense at all, you may break only the norms that bind you, not someone else. If a native writer purposefully violates language, it's called progress; if an outsider does it, it's called malapropism.

The exiled writer is someone who has left the cage of an oppressive political system; but if he is to remain a writer at all, he must never really leave another cage – that of his native language. There, he was gagged; here, he is tongue-tied. The ultimate irony: those who are the most tongue-tied, may have most to say.

NOTE

Page numbers in parentheses throughout the essay refer to Josef Škvorecký, *The Engineer of Human Souls*, trans. Paul Wilson (Toronto: Lester & Orpen Dennys, 1984).

3

MILAN KUNDERA

Preface to the French Edition of *Mirákl*
(*The Miracle Game*) (1978)

When I arrived to spend a few days in the West in September 1968 – my eyes still seeing Russian tanks parked on Prague's streets – an otherwise quite likeable young man asked me with unconcealed hostility: 'So what is it you Czechs want exactly? Are you already weary of socialism? Would you have preferred our consumer society?'

Today the Western Left almost unanimously approves of the Prague Spring. But I'm not sure misunderstanding has been clarified entirely.

Western intellectuals, with their proverbial self-centredness, often take an interest in events not in order to know them but so as to incorporate them into their own theoretical speculations, as if they were adding another pebble to their personal mosaic. In that way Alexander Dubček may in some circumstances merge with Allende or Trotsky, in others with Lumumba or Che Guevara. The Prague Spring has been accepted, labelled – but remains unknown.

I want to stress above all else this obvious fact: the Prague Spring was not a sudden revolutionary explosion ending the dark years of Stalinism. Its way had been paved by a long and intense process of liberalization developing throughout the 1960s. It's possible it all began even earlier, perhaps as early as 1956 or even 1948 – from the birth of the Stalinist regime in Czechoslovakia, out of the critical spirit that deconstructed the regime's dogma little by little, pitting Marx against Marxism, common sense against ideological intoxication, humanist sophism against inhuman sophistry, and that, by dint of laughing at the system, brought the system to be ashamed of itself: a critical spirit supported by a crushing majority of the people, slowly and irremediably making power aware of its guilt, less and less able to believe in itself or in its legitimacy.

In Prague we used to say cynically that the ideal political regime was a decomposing dictatorship, where the machine of oppression functions more and more imperfectly, but by its mere existence maintains the nation's spirit in maximum creative tension. That's what the 1960s were, a decomposing dictatorship.[1] When I look back, I can see us permanently dissatisfied and in protest, but at the same time full of optimism. We were sure that the nation's cultural traditions (its scepticism, its sense of reality, its deeply rooted incredulity) were stronger than the Eastern political system imported from abroad, and that they would in the end overcome it. We were the optimists of scepticism: we believed in its subversive force and eventual victory.

In the summer of 1967, after the explosive Writers' Congress, the State bosses reckoned that the decomposition of the dictatorship had gone too far and tried to impose a hard-line policy. But they could not succeed. The process of decomposition had already reached a guilt-ridden central committee: it rejected the proposed hardening of the line and decided to be chaired by an unknown newcomer, Dubček. What's called the Prague Spring had begun. The critical spirit that up to then had only corroded, now exploded: Czechoslovakia rejected the style of living imported from Russia, censorship vanished, the frontiers opened, and all social organizations (trade unions and other associations) intended to transmit meekly the Party's will to the people, became independent and turned into the unexpected instruments of an unexpected democracy. Thus was born (without any guiding plan) a truly unprecedented system – an economy one hundred per cent nationalized; an agriculture run through co-operatives; a relatively egalitarian, classless society without rich or poor and without the idiocies of mercantilism, but possessing also freedom of expression, a pluralism of attitudes, and a very dynamic cultural life that powered all this movement. (This exceptional influence of culture – of literature, theatre, and the periodical press – gives the decade as a whole its own special, and irresistibly attractive, character.) I do not know how viable the system was or what prospects it had; but I do know that in the brief moment of its existence it was a joy to be alive.

Since the Western Left of today defines its goal as *socialism in freedom*, it is logical that the Prague Spring should henceforth figure in its political discourse. I note more and more often, for example, comparisons between the Prague Spring and the events of May 1968 in Paris, as if the two had been similar or moving in the same direction.

However, the truth is not so simple. I won't speak of the almost too obvious difference in scope between the two (in Prague we had eight months of an entirely original political system, and its destruction in August was a tragic turn in our nation's history), nor will I descend into 'politological' speculations, which bore me and, worse still, are repugnant to me, for I spent twenty years of my life in a country whose official doctrine was able to reduce any and every human problem to only a mere reflection of politics. (This doctrinaire passion for reducing man is the evil that anyone who comes for 'over there' has learned to hate the most.) All I want to do is to put my finger on a few reasons (without masking their hypothetical nature) that show that despite the common nonconformism and the common desire for change, there was a substantial difference in the climate of the two springs.

May 1968 was a revolt of youth. The initiative in the Prague Spring lay in the hands of adults who based their action on historical experience and disillusionment. Of course youth played an important role in the Prague Spring, but it was not a predominant role. To claim the opposite is to subscribe to a myth fabricated a posteriori in order to annex the Prague Spring to the epidemic of student revolts around the world.

May in Paris was an explosion of revolutionary lyricism. The Prague Spring was the explosion of post-revolutionary scepticism. That's why the Parisian students looked towards Prague with mistrust (or rather, with indifference), and the man in Prague could only smile at Parisian illusions that (rightly or wrongly) he thought discredited, comic, or dangerous. (There is a paradox worth meditating upon: the only successful – if ephemeral – implementation of socialism in freedom was not achieved in revolutionary enthusiasm but in sceptical lucidity.)

Paris in May was radical. What had paved the way over many years for the Prague Spring was a *popular revolt of the moderate*. Just as Ivana the Terrible, in Škvorecký's *The Miracle Game* replaces 'bad quotations from Marx with less bad ones,' so everyone in 1968 sought to blunt, soften, and lighten the weight of the existing political system. The term *thaw*, sometimes used to refer to this process, is very significant: it was a matter of making the ice melt, of softening what was hard. If I speak of moderation, it's not in any precise political sense, but in the sense of a deeply rooted human reflex. There was a national allergy to radicalism as such, and of whatever kind, for it was connected in most Czechs' subconscious minds to their worst memories.

Paris in May 1968 challenged what is called European culture and its traditional values. The Prague Spring was a passionate defence of the European cultural tradition in the widest and most broad-minded sense – as much a defence of Christianity as of modern art, both equally denied by the authorities. We all struggled for our right to this tradition, threatened by the anti-Western messianism of Russian totalitarianism.

May in Paris was a revolt of the Left. As for the Prague Spring, the traditional concepts of Right and Left are not able to account for it. (The Left/Right division still has a very real meaning in the life of Western people. On the stage of world politics, however, it no longer has much significance. Is totalitarianism left-wing or right-wing? Progressive or reactionary? These questions are meaningless. Russian totalitarianism is above all else a different culture – and therefore also a different political culture – in which the European distinction between those of the Left and those of the Right loses all sense. Was Khrushchev more Left or more Right than Stalin? The Czech citizen is confronted in 1978 neither by left-wing terror nor by right-wing terror but by a new totalitarian culture that is foreign to him. If some of us think of ourselves as more right-wing or more left-wing, it is only in the context of the West's problems that we can conceive the distinction, and not at all with reference to the problems of our country, which are already of a different order.)

All this created a spiritual atmosphere rather different from the one familiar to opponents west of the Elbe, and Josef Škvorecký represents this atmosphere better than anyone else.

Škvorecký entered literature with *The Cowards*, an exceptionally mature novel written just after the war, when he was a mere boy of twenty-four. The book stayed in a bottom drawer for many years and was not published until 1958, following the brief thaw of 1956. It unleashed an immediate and violent ideological campaign against the author. In the press and in many meetings, Škvorecký had the very worst epithets flung at him (the most famous was 'mangy kitten'), and his book was banned from sale. He had to wait until the sixties and another thaw to be republished in an edition of one hundred thousand copies and to become not only the first big best seller of the postwar literary generation in Czechoslovakia but also the very symbol of a free and anti-official literature.

But why in fact was there a scandal? *The Cowards* does not denounce Stalinism or the Gulag and does not fit what the West calls dissident writing. It tells a very simple story of a young schoolboy who plays in an amateur jazz band and tries his not always lucky hand with classmates of the opposite sex. The story is set in the last days of the war, and the young hero watches the spectacle of liberation in all its derisory unworthiness. It's exactly that aspect that was so unseemly: a non-ideological discourse dealing with sacred subjects (at a time when the Liberation was enshrined in the gilded showcases of all European museums) without the seriousness and respectfulness that is obligatory.

I have dwelt at some length on Škvorecký's first book because the author is already fully present in it, some twenty-five years before *The Miracle Game* was written in Canada: in both we find his special way of viewing history from underneath. It's a naïvely plebeian view. The humour is coarse, in the tradition of Jaroslav Hašek. There's an extraordinary gift for anecdote, and a mistrust of ideology and the myths of history. Little inclination for the preciousness of modernist prose, a simplicity verging on the provocative, in spite of a very refined literary culture. And finally – if I may say so – an anti-revolutionary spirit.

I hasten to gloss this term: Škvorecký is not a reactionary, and he would no doubt not have wished for the return of nationalized factories to their owners or for the dissolution of farm co-operatives. If I mention an anti-revolutionary spirit in connection with him, it is to say that his work represents a critique of the *spirit* of revolution, with its myths, its eschatology, and its all-or-nothing attitude. This critique does not touch on any concrete revolutionary demands or policies, but concerns the revolutionary *attitude* in general as one of the basic attitudes that man can adopt towards the world.

The Western reader can only be surprised. What can one expect from a Czech writer who emigrated after the 1968 invasion except that he should write a defence of the Prague Spring? But no, he hasn't done that in *The Miracle Game*. It's precisely because Škvorecký is a child of his country, faithful to the spirit whence issued the Prague Spring, that he writes with unwavering irony. What strikes the eye first is his critique (through anecdote more than through argument) of all those revolutionary illusions and gesticulations that tended as time went by to take the stage of the Prague Spring.

In its originating milieu, Škvorecký's view of the Prague Spring has already provoked violent polemics. In the Bohemia of the 1970s, his novel is not just banned (as are all the writer's other works), but it is also criticized by many who hold the regime in contempt, for whom – understandably enough – ironic distance is not possible when they look at themselves in the tragic and difficult circumstances in which they live. Each of us is free to enter into a polemic with this novel, but on one condition: without forgetting that Škvorecký's book is the fruit of a rich experience, in the best realist tradition.

All that is to be read here carries the stamp of truth and contains many accurate renderings of real people and events; this applies also to the main plot – a 'miracle' set up by the police, who manage thereby to convict a priest of fraud and to invent a pretext for a violent anti-religious campaign; only the real name of the village, Čihošt', has been changed to Písečnice. Ivana the Terrible, the headmistress who picked out the least bad quotations from Marx, is a real *héröine de modération*: I knew dozens of her sort. She struggles patiently, silently, against one kind of radicalism, only to fall prey in the end to an opposite kind. (Incidentally, I doubt whether any Communist writer has ever managed to create a more moving Communist than Škvorecký – a convinced non-Communist – gives us here.) The poet Vrchcoláb, the playwright Hejl, the chessmaster Bukavec are portraits of real, known, living persons. I don't know whether that's also the case for the Russian writer Arashidov, but whether or not he has a model in reality he seems more real to me than reality itself. And if you suspect Škvorecký of exaggeration, I can assure you that reality exaggerated much more than Škvorecký. Though all these portraits are marvellously malicious, the novel's hero, Smiřický (a kind of stylized self-portrait of the author), who calmly writes an official speech for Lenin's birthday without believing a single word of what he sets down, by no means represents the Truth nor does he constitute a 'positive' hero, even if he is presented in a sympathetic light. Škvorecký spares him little of the tide of irony that inundates the entire novel. This book is until further notice the only work to give an overview of the whole implausible story of the Prague Spring, while at the same time being impregnated with that sceptical resistance – in its most authentic form – that is the best card in the Czech hand.

The fire that Jan Palach lit with his own body in January 1969 to protest against the fate that had befallen his land – his desperate act, it seems to me, is as foreign to Czech history as the ghostly sight of Russian tanks – that fire brought a period of history to a close. Is what I said earlier on the spirit of the Prague Spring even very true? Can one still speak today of a revolt of the moderates? The Russian invasion was too terrible by far. Even the authorities, moreover, are not what they used to be in Bohemia. They are no longer fanatical (as in the 1950s) or guilt-ridden (as in the 1960s) but openly cynical. Can plebeian cynicism fight authority more cynical than itself? The time has come when the cynic Škvorecký no longer has a place in his own land.

NOTE

1 Despite official ideology, there was an extraordinary flowering of Czech cul-

ture in these years. The films of Miloš Forman, Jiří Menzel, and Věra Chytilová, the theatrical productions of Otakar Krejča and of the brilliant Alfred Radok, the plays of Václav Havel, the novels of Josef Škvorecký and Bohumil Hrabal, the poetry of Jan Skácel, and the philosophical works of Jan Patočka and Karel Kosík all date from the 1960s. European culture has known in our century few better or more dynamic decades than the Czech sixties, and their importance is the yardstick by which the tragedy of 21 August 1968, which killed them brutally, must be measured.

4

SAM SOLECKI

'Where Is My Home?': Some Notes on Reading Josef Škvorecký in *Amerika* (1989)

1. Translation, in one form or another, has always been an issue in the reading of Josef Škvorecký's fiction. Because of his nearly lifelong fascination with jazz, Hollywood films, and American literature, his writing has from the start been marked by the English language and the Anglo-American cultural tradition; it is tempting to see the work of his Czech period (1945–69) as pointing West, and that of his exile (1969–90) as written with one eye on the anticipated English translation. In a manner of speaking, Anglo-American culture is the tacit subtext of his novels when they are published in Czech, while Czech culture is the subtext of the translations. In both cases, we have fiction oscillating between two languages and two cultural traditions to the point that doubleness can be said to be a constitutive element in Škvorecký's vision: East/West; Czechoslovakia/America; Czech/English; socialist realism/Hemingway's realism; politics/jazz; Marxism/sceptical humanism, and so on.

2. *The Cowards*, Škvorecký's first novel, anticipates the presence in later work – *Miss Silver's Past, The Miracle Game*, and *The Engineer of Human Souls* – of intertextual material drawn primarily from sources other than contemporary Czech or even European ones. Similarly the novel's formal, stylistic, and thematic assumptions, including its choice of Škvorecký's version of Hemingway-like realism over socialist realism and its modernist mix of formal and demotic Czech (*spisovná čeština* as opposed to *obecná* or *hovorová čeština*), all point West. At a time when most Czech and Slovak novels were cautious weather-vanes turned East, Škvorecký's remarkably mature first novel – written in 1948 at the age of twenty-four though published a decade later – already indicated an opposed set of linguistic and cultural preferences, a choice not without political implications. Milan

Kundera emphasized this 'American' aspect of Škvorecký's career when he told an interviewer that 'Škvorecký is an author who was oriented towards America ... Škvorecký is one of those who were fascinated by American literature due to, I believe, jazz itself. He was a jazz musician as a young man and therefore from an early age an Americanist. He has done marvelously good translations of William Faulkner. So Škvorecký's personal originality, for a Czech, is that he is a connoisseur of American literature.'[1] In other words, if Škvorecký is now a Czech presence in Anglo-American culture, before 1968 he was perceived as an 'Americanist' in Czechoslovakia.

3. Škvorecký's semi-autobiographical hero, Danny Smiřický, is as apolitical as Huck Finn, Frederick Henry, or Holden Caulfield, and *The Cowards'* melancholy ending reflects his essential lack of interest in the momentous historical events taking place around him.

Still, a novel can be political even if its hero is uninterested in politics and if political and ideological discussions do not figure explicitly in it. The category is an elastic one and can include works as different as Alfred Döblin's *November 1917*, Arthur Koestler's *Darkness at Noon*, and George Orwell's *1984* at one end – the more explicitly political – and Twain's *The Adventures of Huckleberry Finn* and Škvorecký's *The Cowards* at the other. The last two raise questions of a political nature even while seeming not to be directly engaged in political ideas and issues or, perhaps more accurately, while leaving one with the impression that their protagonists don't consider political concerns to be especially important. Political judgments in these novels are usually generated ironically, when the reader perceives the gap between the quality of the response of the adolescent apolitical hero, on the one hand, and the implied responses of the controlling narrative voice and his own, on the other. In other words, whatever politics we perceive in such a novel belong more often to the author and the reader than to the character. (This comment doesn't apply to Škvorecký's later more explicitly political and historical novels like *The Miracle Game* and *The Engineer of Human Souls*, where the viewpoints of the first-person narrator and the author are almost identical.)

But *The Cowards* is also tacitly political in a simultaneously more obvious and more complex way by the very fact that it seems to refuse complicity with political issues in a state – neo-Stalinist Czechoslovakia – in which every aspect of social being is shaped by politics. A significant part of what, following Sartre, we could call Škvorecký's political contestation in this novel comes from his obvious refusal to offer the usual socialist-realist hero or to adhere to the formulaic, optimistic inanities of the socialist-realist plot. The very fact of writing apolitically in a culture that insists on the politicization of literature constitutes a political gesture. Even as small a detail as the title of Škvorecký's first novel sounds a resistant note different from the titles of the standard Soviet and Czech classics of the period, many of which create expectations of a happy story or optimistic ending.

4. From one point of view, *The Cowards* is a meditation on the systems of values or the philosophies governing the lives of Europeans in the twentieth century. The theme is dealt with more explicitly in the extended, often theoretical dialogues of the novels of exile, but it is already subtly adumbrated here in the novel's engagement with humanism, fascism, Catholicism, and communism. Although Danny Smiřický's frame of reference is still residually Catholic, the novel's universe or world-view is fundamentally secular and post-Christian, with no system of belief or ideology either metaphysically privileged or prioristically authoritative. Christianity, like the liberal humanism of the older generation, is shown in the novel – as it was in history – overwhelmed by fascism and communism respectively. And although Danny, like his country, century, and author, is still on occasion a sentimental Christian longing for the emotional and spiritual satisfactions faith once provided, he recognizes that, in essence, he believes neither in it nor in the equally holistic systems claiming to have supplanted it.

5. In an interview that took place in Prague in December 1966, Škvorecký told Antonín Liehm that he wrote *The Cowards* 'shortly after the February events [of 1948], filled with a kind of socialist enthusiasm (although I must admit that I was never a political thinker).'[2] Whatever may have been the intensity of that momentary enthusiasm – and the setting of the interview makes the declaration slightly suspect – it wasn't sufficiently fervid to leave its mark on *The Cowards*, in which the arrival of the Soviet army and the promise (or perhaps threat) of a Communist society leave Danny Smiřický more anxious than enthusiastic. At best, one could say that, having no real choice or voice in the matter, he is willing to suspend judgment and give the Communists the benefit of the doubt. Škvorecký's next novel, *The Republic of Whores*, takes Smiřický into the Stalinist fifties and shows both character and author radically alienated from the new social order. Written in 1954 and set in the autumn of 1952, the novel deals with the last two weeks of Smiřický's compulsory military service. The events are clearly based on Škvorecký's own term of duty between 1951 and 1953 with the elite Tank Division posted at Mladá, near Prague. Whatever hopes and illusions may have been generated by May 1945 and February 1948 – and we need only

read Kundera and Pavel Kohout to feel their intensity – they have long disappeared for Smiřický and his fellow soldiers, with the result that the novel's attitude to the society it depicts is almost completely ironic and negative.

That the novel is ultimately more concerned with Czechoslovak society than with Smiřický is indicated by the then provocative subtitle, 'Fragment z Doby Kultů' – 'A Fragment from the Period of the Cult.' Writing in a country more Stalinist than Stalin's and before Nikita Khrushchev's midnight speech to the Twentieth Party Congress in February 1956, Škvorecký must have realized that everything from his subtitle on was being written for the drawer. One of the few advantages of the drawer, however, is that one can write about anything in one's society, including the unmentionable though pervasive cult of personality. The book's focus, then, is a satiric critique of a particular period of a particular society – its distinguishing attitudes, assumptions, values, and contradictions.

6. The officers and men in the occasionally Švejkian world of *The Republic of Whores* may be equal in theory, but in practice the first group or class is predictably more equal than the second. This is particularly obvious in the scene in which the enthusiastic Lieutenant Prouza claims, as he tries to persuade the unenthusiastic men to take their exams, that 'in our people's democratic army examinations take the form of a dialogue ... We will discuss our work and our experiences and we will show how our reading helps better our preparation for combat and for politics.'[3] The lieutenant and his soldiers function in the scene rather like a traditional comedy team: he plays the straight man – Oliver Hardy, Bud Abbott – whose claims and stories are deflated by the seemingly simpler soldiers – Stan Laurel, Lou Costello – who, for the most part, are too canny either to believe their officers or to let them know that they disbelieve them. The examinations reveal the inequality between the officer and his men – an inequality based ultimately on the social power of the former and the powerlessness of the latter – and although they take the form of a dialogue, it is a dialogue of unequals in which the leading questions are designed to produce the desired answers. The examination described by Prouza at the start of the scene bears no resemblance to the examination we witness. As the discrepancy between the two grows wider and wider during this long but always lively episode, the humour and absurdity increase.

We should notice, however, that here, as in the plays of Václav Havel or in the novels of Tadeusz Konwicki, Milan Kundera, and Vassily Aksyonov, the origins or causes of absurdity are *social* rather than metaphysical. Our sense of the absurd – and of the humour implicit in it – arises when we perceive the chasm between an account of reality (a character's) and reality itself (the narrator's), and when we recognize that the essential terms of the character's account either have no referents in the latter or else are being used in a sufficiently novel way to make them incomprehensible from the point of view of common or traditional usage. In Prouza's speech, for example, we remark his use of the phrase 'our people's democratic army' and realize over the length of the scene as well as from what we have already read that this army is neither democratic nor of the people – at least not in any of the shades of meaning these words possess in Czech, English, or French. We also note that this official expression is never used by the draftees, whose vocabulary and topics of discussion belong to a world that doesn't seem to overlap that described by their officers. Prouza is also representaive of his class in his insistence on what could be termed a 'grammatical' or 'semantic' classlessness, indicated by his repeated use of the first person plural, which has no basis in the daily life of the army. Like his repeated use of *soudruh* or *soudruzi* ('comrade' and 'comrades'), his emphasis on the plural pronoun describes a non-existent set of social relationships and states of affairs, the unreality of which is implicitly indicated by his reliance on the future tense.

Prouza's relatively innocent statements are related to the more monitory exhortations of his various superiors. These, when not threatening the men with some punishment, try to encourage them to greater efficiency by evoking for them a socialist Czechoslovakia menaced by traitors at home and imperialists abroad, both dedicated to destroying this best of all possible societies. The speakers draw on a common formulaic vocabulary: duty, responsibility, honour, nobility, self-sacrifice, and hard work are emphasized; *soudruzi* is reiterated obsessively and mechanically; and every concern is related to the new 'popular democratic government and its Soviet supporters.' Most statements begin and end at a level of abstraction that never connects with quotidian social and historical particulars. Buzz-words, meaningless set phrases, and official clichés replace the language actually spoken by ordinary people. And the streams of official nonsense remain unchallenged – and therefore tacitly pass for sense – because everyone realizes that despite the claim that there are no barriers between officers and men, the speeches have the status of dogma.

Equally noticeable is the way in which the official speeches, whether dealing with cultural, social, political, or military topics, are punctuated by allusions and references to Soviet examples as well as by the occasional use of Russian.[4] The overall force of this rhetoric of power in *The Republic of*

Whores is to make the reality of army life disappear in discourses whose referents are either in Leninist-Stalinist political theory or, in what amounts almost to the same thing since Party literature is subordinate to Party ideology, in exemplary official discourses about the Soviet revolution and Soviet life. The language is still Czech, but in crucial senses its contents are foreign to the experiences of the soldiers. Putting the case more technically one could say that in the individual sign – say, the Czech word *demokracie* – the signifier or acoustic image has stayed the same but the signified – the referent or content – has been emptied and replaced by the Soviet equivalent, which, because it differs denotationally and connotationally from the Czech, changes the entire meaning of the sign.

7. The background and genesis of *Miss Silver's Past* are dealt with in Škvorecký's preface to the Picador edition. There he explains that

I began spinning the yarn of *Miss Silver's Past* as a sticking-out of the tongue at both the turncoat aesthete and the censor. *Epatez le snob marxiste, dupez le censeur staliniste!* was my credo, when I decided to tell about my *Dies Irae* experience [between 1959 and 1961 over *The Cowards*] in the form of a sort of detective story, a genre I loved, because it had helped me survive some of the worst times in my life. I decided to make it look like light literature, like an entertainment, although the subject matter was so bloody serious. To make it a melodrama, a debased genre, so that it would escape the attention of the man with the rubber stamp and make the aesthete wonder why the author of *The Cowards* and *The Bass Saxophone* was writing a crime story about such an improbable sexbomb as Miss Silver ... Was it because he wanted to please the crowds?, the former preachers of 'art for the masses' would ask contemptuously.[5]

In other words, the novel concerns not only Lenka Silver's revenge against Emil Procházka, the man responsible for her sister's death in a concentration camp, but also Josef Škvorecký's implicit settling of accounts with the Czech literary establishment that had censored and banned his books. The 'turncoat aesthetes' were those literary critics who after the 'rehabilitation' of Franz Kafka at the Liblice Conference in 1962 abandoned 'socrealism' for the more fashionable 'isms' of Robbe-Grillet, Michel Butor, and Roland Barthes. The same critics who had attacked *The Cowards* in 1959 for not being socialist-realist now attacked it for not being sufficiently modern. Škvorecký found himself dismissed condescendingly as only 'a good story-teller.' 'Deeply discouraged by adverse criticism,'[6] Škvorecký responded with his two great novellas, 'Emöke' (1963) and *The Bass Saxophone* (1967), and, most decisively, with *Miss Silver's Past* (1969). The latter, although made to 'look like light literature, like an entertainment' is nevertheless ultimately closer to 'the serious line' among Škvorecký's works than to the underrated Borůvka detective stories with which it seems to belong generically.

8. *The Republic of Whores* and *The Miracle Game* were written almost twenty years apart, years in which Škvorecký wrote screenplays, mystery novels, novellas, essays, short stories, and *Miss Silver's Past*. His interest in Danny Smiřický was confined to some stories and *The Bass Saxophone*. It is conceivable, therefore, that but for 'the fraternal help' of the Soviet invasion of August 1968 and Škvorecký's emigration, the Smiřický series would have ended with *The Republic of Whores*, *The Swell Season*, and a few stories about the war years. Instead, a national tragedy that resulted in Škvorecký's exile from Czechoslovakia served, paradoxically, to resurrect Smiřický and to stimulate Škvorecký into writing his most ambitious novel. *The Miracle Game* was begun almost immediately upon his arrival in the West in 1969, almost as if Škvorecký had not stopped looking over his shoulder from the moment the decision to leave had been made; he returned almost immediately in memory and in writing to the very place he couldn't return to in fact – with the crucial difference that, liberated by exile, he was able to write about Czechoslovakia more openly than ever before. The result is his single greatest work and a national masterpiece.[7]

Though it is obvious that *The Miracle Game* is written by the same writer as *The Cowards* and *The Republic of Whores*, it is equally evident that there is an almost qualitative difference between it and its predecessors. Responding to the private and public emotional and intellectual pressures generated by exile, Škvorecký expanded his palette and his conception of the novel in order to deal with a more complex set of historical events, giving expression, in the process, to a more profound and comprehensive vision of life. Without the fact of exile, therefore – without, that is, the pressure of the need to justify his decision to leave, as well as to settle accounts with history – it is conceivable that Škvorecký would not have become the major novelist that he is.

The continuities between this first novel written abroad and its predecessors are clear enough: comic realism and a common-sense view of language; the telltale references to Hemingway; the often invisible, sceptical, camera-like hero; the interest in jazz; the residual and problematic Catholicism; and the almost reflexive concern with how reality is described (or, more accurately, misrepresented when put to ideological uses). All of these appear in *The Miracle Game*, but with a difference: the medium of Škvorecký's message has changed. *The Miracle Game* is not only the first novel of his exile, it is also the first of his works to be obviously innovative in form. It is a generic hybrid, something immediately indicated by the unusual subtitle – 'Politická detektivka' or 'political detective story.' Its chronologically earlier narrative (set in 1949) is an occasionally autobiographical comic love story as well as a political and religious detective novel; the narrative dealing with 1968 is a *roman à clef*, a superb novel of ideas with a trenchant critique of Marxist-Leninist theory and practice, and a politico-historical novel about the fate of the generation of 1948, the same generation that is at the heart of Kundera's fiction. The vision of this sprawling novel is still basically that of a comic realist, but Škvorecký now interweaves the comic and the tragic to an extent greater than before, implying that at its most comprehensive the comic vision not only intersects with the tragic but embraces it.

9. In *The Miracle Game*, as in *The Engineer of Human Souls*, the novel's open or fragmented form should be seen as reflecting on the level of structure one of the novel's central thematic concerns: the author's profound doubts both about whether history is meaningful and about systems of thought – faiths, ideologies, philosophies – claiming to understand it. Škvorecký would agree with Iris Murdoch's comment that since 'reality is incomplete, art must not be too afraid of incompleteness.'[8] In his case, however, this is not just an aesthetic or philosophical position – it has political implications as well. The novel's fragmented form and Smiřický's commitment to 'details' – his version of Günter Grass's 'snail's viewpoint' – are both aspects of its resistance to the authoritative and often authoritarian claims of all systems of thought claiming completeness. Analogously, almost all the information gathered in Smiřický's private and casual work of detection into the religious miracle of 1949 – a church statue moved – and the political miracle of 1968 – the Prague Spring – is either absent from or contradicts official accounts of events. The optimistic homogeneity of state history, state literature, and ideology is achieved only by a calculated amnesia about anything contradicting the official point of view. The incomplete stories, rumours, newspaper clippings, and letters Danny Smiřický encounters are all fragments retrieved, so to speak, from Winston Smith's tube and, therefore, untrue as far as the state is concerned. Gathered and reassembled by Danny – and the reader following in his tracks – they constitute an alternative social and political history, an authentic, fragmented, and 'incomplete' totality challenging the factitious totality of the state.

10. At issue in both *The Miracle Game* and *The Engineer of Human Souls* is the question of the status and function of the writer – one of Škvorecký's central concerns throughout his career. In a society whose media are state controlled, the writer, when choosing to dissent, obviously has a different function – one that includes a heightened sense of moral responsibility – than he normally does in a society whose media are not state censored. To choose one example: if history books either misrepresent or are silent about certain people and events, then history can become a necessary subject of fiction and the novelist the chronicler of what Solzhenitsyn has called 'a nation's lost history.' Thus *The Miracle Game*, Škvorecký's first novel of exile, shows him more openly concerned not only with the question of the writer's role but also with the lacunae of Czechoslovak history and, inescapably, the political ideas and practice of Soviet Marxism, none of which could have been discussed openly in Czechoslovakia.

One of the results of this new concern with history and politics is the deliberate blurring of the discursive and cognitive boundaries separating autobiography, history, political discourse, and fiction. Because *The Miracle Game* includes historical figures such as Antonín Novotný, Gustav Husák, and Alexander Dubček among its characters, refers to specific historical events, and includes discussions of contemporary political ideas, it challenges our assumptions about the definition of fiction, the truth claims of fictional discourse, and the status of fictional 'facts.'

11. If some of the great East European artists of the nineteenth century – Mickiewicz, Petoffi, Dvořák – can be said to have established their national cultures, then Škvorecký, like Miłosz, Kundera, and Solzhenitsyn can be seen as preserving in exile a certain ideal of a nation and a national culture at a time when that ideal is threatened with extinction. These writers, however they may differ in their aesthetics and politics, nevertheless recognize that there is a dimension of mission in the writer's vocation. For the East and Central European exiles, this 'mission' involves a dimension of national proprietorship and salvation.

12. The complexity and ambiguity of Škvorecký's attitude toward 1968 is reflected in *The Miracle Game* in the fact that although Smiřický's position is presented as preferable because more clear-sighted than that of the idealistic students and second-time-around revolutionaries, it is not offered as normative. The attractiveness of the more 'romantic' and historically un-Czech stance of rebellion – the 'Polish' response – is clearly and strongly registered by the rhetorical force of the prose describing the student speeches

and the report of Jan Palach's suicide by burning. As well, as the novel recognizes, there is the problem that Smiřický's position also represents a surrender, however reluctant, to the corrupt status quo that he despises as much as anyone. Each stance involves a catch-22 situation: if you challenge the Soviet Union, you will lose; if you don't challenge it, you simply continue the present losing situation. The choice, as all of Škvorecký's Czech readers would instantly recognize, repeats the situations of 1938 and 1948: to fight or to surrender without resistance. One of Škvorecký's larger concerns is to show the emotional and political impasse of the contemporary Czechoslovak situation for anyone not completely co-opted by the state. Smiřický's apolitical scepticism and irony, for example, seem to offer some degree of independence and self-respect, but ultimately the position is another form – though a more honourable one – of acquiescence. It can make the status quo tolerable but it cannot help change history. In addition, there is always the dangerous possibility that the detached stance of an ironic observer will become an end in itself, an Epictetan *modus vivendi* with the world as it is – as it does in the slightly sinister, though dangerously attractive figure of Smiřický's friend, Doctor Gellen.

In the end, *The Miracle Game* seems to suggest that Smiřický's sceptical stance is safer though ultimately as futile as the reformers' revolution: neither can alter history. Much of the novel's near despair arises out of Škvorecký's clear-sighted and tough-minded awareness of the claims of both positions, as well as out of his inability to see any alternatives in 1968 beyond the usual choices – complicity, an inner anti-political emigration, a repeat of the 'romantic' Hungarian revolution of 1956, or the continuation of the 'realistic' Yalta settlement. Without access to what Max Weber calls 'the house of power' Czechoslovaks need a real miracle to change their contemporary history.

Almost two decades later, George Konrad's *Antipolitics* and Adam Michnik's *Letters from Prison* would offer pretty much the same analysis of the East and Central European dilemma. The mention of Konrad should also serve to remind us that while *The Miracle Game* may be about Czechoslovak history and the Prague Spring, its political analysis, like Škvorecký's essays, points beyond 1968 and the borders of Czechoslovakia.

13. There is little doubt that *The Engineer of Human Souls* is a sequel of sorts to *The Miracle Game*: both were written in exile and, as Škvorecký has pointed out, both share 'the multi-level structure' he developed in order to overcome the formal problem of dealing with a warehouse of materials and events separated by decades. Up to a point then, *The Miracle Game*

teaches us what to expect: there is a new amplitude in approach, a more experimental attitude to construction, a greater frankness in dealing with recent Czechoslovak history, a continuing settling of accounts with socialist realism, and a new more explicit engagement with ideas and ideologies. But a reading of *The Miracle Game* can't prepare us for a novel more reflective than anything Škvorecký had written previously; a more intellectual Danny Smiřický actively engaged in discussions of ideas; and an increased concern not just with an individual's thinking but, as in the later fiction of Saul Bellow, with ideas themselves to the point that the discussion of ideas becomes a primary focus (in *The Miracle Game*, the discussion of ideas is more closely integrated to the historic events taking place around Smiřický). Nor does it prepare us for a subject-matter more extensive and heterogeneous in scope, and a fluid first-person narration often associational in manner that shows Škvorecký has gone to school not just to Hemingway but also to Faulkner, Joyce, and Woolf, all of whom are mentioned in the novel.

Present as well is a more explicit, self-conscious, and extensive dealing with literature and aesthetic issues that seems intended as a summary of all previous discussions in Škvorecký's work – from *The Cowards* to *The Miracle Game* – about jazz, poetry, fiction, painting, and sculpture. But *The Engineer* also offers another kind of summary, which helps explain Škvorecký's use of a more elastic narrative structure. There is a possibility that the latest Smiřický novel may also be the last. If this is so, then I suspect that *The Engineer* may be Škvorecký's attempt at a summary of the series and of Smiřický's life and generation: the novel's wartime scenes recall *The Cowards*, *The Bass Saxophone*, and *The Swell Season*; the nearly three dozen letters Danny receives include many from the early 1950s, offering a new perspective on *The Republic of Whores*, *Sedmiramenný svícen* (1964 [The Menorah, untranslated]), and the chronologically earlier scenes in *The Miracle Game*; discussions of the Prague Spring and the Soviet invasion recapitulate *The Miracle Game*'s second plot; and finally, the émigré sections take Smiřický into Canada and the 1970s, the world of some of Škvorecký's later stories and of his play *Bůh do domu* (God Help Us!).

14. Looked at positively, exile or separation can be seen as conducive to the achievement of a detached and pluralistic viewpoint or of a stance tending towards an objectivity that is a privileged perspective on life. If this were all, then we could speak of exile primarily in positive terms as a situation in which the end gained, a deeper and more comprehensive experience and view of life, almost redeems the painful historical road traversed and what Edward

Said has described somewhere as 'the crippling sorrow of estrangement.' From this point of view, the exile is compensated with an originality of vision that, for the artist, may result in *The Divine Comedy, Pan Tadeusz,* or *The Engineer of Human Souls.* These are among the paradoxical 'pleasures' of exile, possible only for those who while wounded by exile have insisted on recalling the causes of the wounds, keeping the wounds open, and writing about them. Miłosz, who has described Dante as the 'patron saint of all poets in exile, who visit their towns and provinces only in remembrance,' has also speculated that 'it is possible that there is no other memory than the memory of wounds.'[9] Whatever may be the specific nature of that wound in Škvorecký's case, we find traces of it in symbolic form throughout *The Engineer.* This is most obvious, I would suggest, in those moments when memories of the Czech past, described nostalgically and with great affection, pull Smiřický away from a Canadian present he claims to prefer but to which he is less deeply attached and about which Škvorecký can never bring himself to write as evocatively and with as great an emotional intensity as he can about his homeland. Despite Smiřický's early avowal that 'the Toronto skyline is more beautiful to me than the familiar silhouette of Prague Castle' (4), the *quality* of his feelings towards Canada is closer to the description in Škvorecký's early essay 'Red Music,' where in a poignant passage he refers to 'the schizophrenia of the times' in which 'you find yourself in a land that lies over the ocean, a land – no matter how hospitable or friendly – where your heart is not, because you landed on these shores too late.'[10] Implicit in the 'too late,' of course, is a nostalgia not just for a homeland but also for a time when one was *young* in that particular homeland. This desire to return forces its way into the novel in a moving late scene in which Smiřický hears about Veronika's return to Czechoslovakia. The ending of the story of this very sympathetically presented Czech immigrant who admits to being 'obsessed with Czechoslovakia' (148) allows Škvorecký to indulge, for a moment, the unrealizable dream of going home. The dream is unrealizable, incidentally, not simply for political reasons, but because ultimately the 'home' longed for is something other than the Prague of the 1970s.

Not surprisingly, Škvorecký followed *The Engineer of Human Souls* with a novel – *Dvorak in Love (Scherzo capriccioso)* – about another Bohemian artist who also arrived 'too late' in North America but was able to return to Prague.

15. Perhaps the single most important connection between Škvorecký and Antonín Dvořák is the fact that, in middle age, each travelled to 'America.'

Škvorecký settled here in 1969; Dvořák made three crossings between September 1892 and April 1895. The America Dvořák visited was the America Škvorecký read about as a young man in Czech translations of Twain, Bierce, Harte, Howells, London, and Dreiser – it was the idealized 'literary' America (Kafka's 'Amerika') of his youthful dreams. It is even possible that had Dvořák not lived and worked in the United States, Škvorecký would not have written a novel about him. I'm not suggesting that Dvořák, without an American period, would not have been an interesting enough subject for a biographical novel, only that he would not have interested Škvorecký because one of the essential correspondences between their lives would have been missing. And without these correspondences, Škvorecký would not have been able to write a novel that is simultaneously fictionalized biography and a displaced autobiography.

The crucial difference between their journeys, however, is obvious: Dvořák travelled freely back and forth between the two countries; Škvorecký, like Solzhenitsyn and Kundera, took what seemed a one-way ticket from his native land. If one of the ways we can read *Dvorak in Love* is as a novel that is also in part an articulation of a complex of ambivalent wishes, then I would also argue that one of its profoundest desires – enacted in the historical fact of Dvořák's return to and death in Bohemia – is the author's desire to return 'home.'

Dvorak in Love allows Škvorecký to dream simultaneously about arriving 'on these shores too late' and, more important, about going home. To the question, 'Where is my home?' (the title of the Czech national anthem) the exile always points in two directions.

NOTES

When a title in the essay is followed by two dates, in almost all cases the first refers to publication in Czech, the second in English; thus *The Cowards* (*Zbabělci*, 1958, 1970). Abbreviations follow standard usage: *The Bass Saxophone* is *BS*, etc.

1 Jordan Elgrably, 'Conversations with Milan Kundera,' *Salmagundi*, no. 73 (Winter 1987), 8

2 Antonín Liehm, *The Politics of Culture*, trans. Peter Kussi (New York: Grove, 1968), 170

3 Josef Škvorecký, *Tankový prapor* (Toronto: Sixty-Eight Publishers, 1971), 86. The translation is my own.

4 The Soviet references, made almost without exception by the officers, include

Lenin, Stalin, Kalinin, the Komsomols, the 1917 revolution, as well as such less significant names as Oleg Kochevoi and Pavel Morozov.

5 *Miss Silver's Past*, trans. Peter Kussi (London: Picador, 1980), xvi. Substantial portions of the Czech text are missing in this version. The French translation reproduces Škvorecký's text in full.

6 'I Was Born in Náchod,' in *Talkin' Moscow Blues*, ed. Sam Solecki (Toronto: Lester & Orpen Dennys, 1988), 56–7

7 On the subject of the positive or beneficial aspects of exile see the following sentence from Adam Michnik's essay 'Shadow of Forgotten Ancestors' (1973): '[Pilsudski] had been an exile himself for some time, and he knew that for a conquered nation emigration is a priceless treasure, an eye and an ear on the world, a mouth that can speak freely and breathe fresh air, absorbing it into the nation's body' (*Letters from Prison and Other Essays*, trans. Maya Latynski [Berkeley: University of California Press, 1987], 204).

8 Iris Murdoch, 'Against Dryness,' in *The Novel Today*, ed. Malcolm Bradbury (London: Fontana/Collins, 1977), 31

9 Czesław Miłosz, *Nobel Lecture* (New York: Farrar, Straus & Giroux, 1981)

10 *The Bass Saxophone* (Toronto: Lester & Orpen Dennys, 1980), 29

5

HELENA KOSKOVÁ

The Demolisher of False Myths (1980)

Between 1948 and 1980 the very existence of Czech literature was severely threatened: the first instance came during the fifties, when the doctrine of socialist realism changed official literature into a mere tool of political propaganda; the second came during the seventies. Milan Kundera character- ized the situation in an interview that appeared in *Le Monde* on 19 January 1979: 'I weigh my words carefully: neither in length nor in intensity nor in systematization has the massacre of Czech culture which has been taking place since the year 1968 had a parallel in the country's entire history since the Thirty Years' War.' Despite this, Czech literature experienced a remark- able revival during the brief liberalization period of the sixties, the signifi- cance of which is comparable to the famous avant-garde of the twenties and thirties. Even the forcible repression exerted by the power apparatus could not stop this development. In 1980, the best part of contemporary Czech literature is no longer in the hands of the official Czech publishers and appears in underground editions or in exile.

For anyone living in the free world it is difficult to grasp the significant role literature plays in Czechoslovakia, a country where the consciousness of cultural autonomy predated the political formation of an independent state and where, in 1968, writers and journalists played a more important role than politicians. Literature is frequently a substitute for non-existent political expression; it becomes a collective experience of freedom in non-freedom, a symbol of the indestructibility of the human spirit, which outlasts a hopeless political reality. Under such circumstances literature has to cope with many obvious as well as hidden obstacles. Apart from the official pressure there exists also the influence of the underground, which has its own myths and fashions. The measure of political persecution could, for example, become the criterion for artistic qualities. Such a situation is entirely understandable in a context where in fact all literary life takes place illegally or abroad in emigration.

It is against this background that we must assess Josef Škvorecký's admirable creative power and strength of character, which have made it possible for him to avoid all external influences and to continue writing without regard for fashionable, artistic, or political trends. In this way he became, despite himself rather than as a result of a program, a demolisher of false myths. In *The Cowards*, written in 1948, he draws an anti-heroic picture of the May Revolution in Prague in which he deals not only with the 'liberating Red Army' but also, above all, with the Czech lower-middle class. When the novel was published in 1958, the author was criticized for his 'lack of taste' because of his intensely realistic style. In fact, the then theoretician of underground avant-garde literature, J. Chalupecký, returned the manuscript to the author with the remark that this was not literature at all.

In 1954 Škvorecký wrote his next novel, which, if published, would have earned him a lengthy prison sentence at the time. *The Republic of Whores* is a satire on the army and indirectly on the entire Stalinist system. During the second half of the sixties, in the detective novel *Miss Silver's Past* (1969) he describes the circumstances in Prague editorial offices so truthfully that not only the Stalinists appear in an ambiguous light but also many of those who later became the representatives of and spokesmen for the Dubček regime. When it was published in Czech in 1972 *The Miracle Game* caused a scandal in certain circles of the Prague underground because Škvorecký had the audacity to deflate the living myths of the Prague Spring. It is symptomatic of the time that discussion about the work centred upon the question of whether an author had the right to write negatively (albeit, as many admitted, truthfully) about the idols of the year 1968, whether by doing so he indirectly served the occupational regime. Five years later, *The Engineer of Human Souls* deals with the numerous prejudices of the various generations of Czech emigrants, so that many are likely to reproach the author again with a lack of reverence for any ideals. One would have to replace the word *ideal* with *ideology* in order to be able to agree with this kind of attitude. In this sense James Jones's epigraph to *The Miracle Game* could serve as a motto for all of Škvorecký's writings: '... it's so easy to kill real people in the name of some damned ideology or other; once the killer can abstract them in his own mind into being symbols, then he needn't feel guilty for killing them since they're no longer real human beings.'[1]

The perennial and often seemingly hopeless struggle of mankind – threatened by false dogmas, prejudices, illusions, and myths – for survival in a dehumanized world is the basic theme and unifying principle of

Škvorecký's whole work as well as of his philosophy of life. He belongs to the generation that was moulded by the experience of the German occupation as well as by the totalitarian regime of communism. These experiences are the source of his profound mistrust of ideologies and the way they are misused in sociopolitical and philosophical areas. In practice, ideology changes into an instrument of power that reduces the individual to a mere part of the machinery of society, a part that is deprived of any personal responsibility and that, moreover, is easily replaced. The result is that a collective is formed whose members, as is well-known, are best identified by their hatred for all who are outside this collective. Against this form of dehumanization, in which the value of human life is measured against superior collective forces and man is regarded as only a means or an obstacle to their attainment, Škvorecký develops a pattern of ethics that centres on the dignity of the individual human life, based on the Christian credo of not harming one's neighbour. Against the forcibly imposed collective the author pits the individual with his basic needs and motivations for action. He breaks up the rigid structure of systematized society and its petrified hierarchical value system by revealing the hypocrisy of an ideology that in practice becomes a list of mechanically repeated phrases. Škvorecký's humour is at its best when he stresses the paradoxical discrepancy between people's real motivations for actions and their various ideological poses. Lofty words and noble aims are revealed as opportunistic manoeuvres to achieve personal ambitions; yet, on the other hand, fine human qualities are frequently hidden behind unassuming behaviour or real modesty. The truth is always concealed in the absurd mixture of the lofty and the base, for the world is infinitely complex.

It is in Škvorecký's personal experiences that we must seek the roots of his philosophy of life. Ideology, degenerated into political demagoguery, pretends to be an axiomatic system that includes everything there is to know about life. Škvorecký, however, constantly stresses the relativism of each form of truth. Not claiming the right to see and penetrate the consciousness of all his characters, he often stresses the one-sidedness of his view by using a first-person narrator. Danny Smiřický is not a judge or a critic or an expounder of generally valid principles; he is an observer, and he is deflated and treated with irony just as all his surroundings are. Danny is the centre of a consciousness that the author constantly tells us is limited by its own individual conditions. Many critical misunderstandings have arisen from critics' mistaken comparisons between the narrator and the author.

Although he keeps returning to his own experiences, reality is for Škvorecký increasingly merely a point of departure: beginning in the reality as perceived through the senses, he strives to penetrate beyond the surface and to ask questions about the true, basic causes for human actions and the sense of life, to decipher the signs that emerge in human behaviour. The truth about life that the author is seeking to convey is not to be found in the individual realistic episodes but rather in the implications between the lines. Literature is for him 'an expression which in a way deceives in regard to the surface in order to be able to say, by the same means, the truth about the essence.'² Again and again Škvorecký asks questions and avoids unequivocal answers. The multilevel nature of his work increases and deepens from *The Cowards* to *The Engineer of Human Souls* – parallel to his own deepening experience of life.

In his initial creative period – which, in addition to *The Cowards, Konec nylonového věku* (The End of the Nylon Age), and a number of stories, includes *The Republic of Whores* – he is an onlooker, an outsider or witness who tells about his own experiences. The narrator in *The Cowards* shares with the author the instinctive sensitivity of a young man and an intimate knowledge of the environment, which helps him distinguish the falseness of various social roles that come to one's help if one lacks the courage to preserve the simple basic principles of human decency. The great historical moment of the end of World War II and the Czech nation's revolution against the Germans undergoes a change when regarded from Škvorecký's point of view. It becomes a kaleidoscope of individual human fates in which the discrepancy between the official image of great historical moments and their real nature is sustained throughout. The revolution at Kostelec simultaneously becomes a miniature rendition of the 'Great National War' in which we have become accustomed to counting the victims by the millions. In the Kostelec variation historical events no longer appear as anonymous generalizations, and therefore we experience each sacrificed human life as a personal tragedy.

Škvorecký's style in *The Cowards* is closest to realism, which he absorbed above all from American prose, particularly from Hemingway. The brief, terse sentences lack any lyrical quality and give the story a powerful epic momentum. Through their telegraphic brevity they simultaneously awaken the reader's imagination and urge him or her to read between the lines, to follow, as it were, the subtext of the novel. The whole composition is, in fact, based on abbreviated perspectives. For the return to his youth the author has chosen a period of only eight days, which form the culmination and centre of gravity of the novel. Into these eight days Škvorecký has managed to concentrate an entire chronicle of a small Czech town, including a representative sampling of all layers of society and political currents. At the same time he has succeeded in sketching the characters and their individual fates in so lively a manner that frequently real people have recognized themselves in these literary figures.

One of the typical features of Škvorecký's prose, already apparent in his earliest writings, is his absolute ear for the spoken language. One of his works, the prose collection *Babylónský příběh* (A Babylonian Story, 1967), is based largely on dialogue. Henry Kucera used a computer to analyse one chapter of *The Cowards* and compared it with the actual language of people recorded in the particular region of Eastern Bohemia in which the novel is set. He found that the two idioms are indistinguishable. Dialogue plays a very important part in *The Cowards* by implying what has not been directly expressed, yet is characteristic of people and situations. It stresses the dynamic tension between what is said and what is felt, between fiction and reality; it shows the inability of language to express a complex set of circumstances.

Language, however, can also become a cliché, a set of political phrases, which deliberately manipulate reality. Škvorecký has the rare ability to seek out and unmask the empty phrase that is used without contact with what is really happening. Thus he exposes the potential comic ingredient that comes to the surface whenever there is an unintended discrepancy between the ideological, institutionalized quality of the set phrase and reality. What emerges is the schismatic difference between people's real lives and the comedy in which they must take part. Škvorecký expresses this tension primarily through language. The principle never to confuse what is lived with what is said is displayed particularly skilfully in *The Republic of Whores*.

First Lieutenant Ruzicka, who until then had been persistently silent, rose. He had decided to help the clueless greenhorn out of this increasingly knotty situation.

'Wait, Macha,' he said, turning to the second lieutenant, 'the comrade private here has the right idea, he just has to be helped to put it a trifle more precisely. Macha, what do we say about the First Republic?'

Face to face with his immediate superior, the political commentator lost his talkativeness.

'It was a bourgeois democracy,' he said briefly.

– 'And what else do we say?'

– 'Capitalistic.'

– 'And who served in the army?'

– 'The people.'

– 'And who were the officers?'

– 'Capitalists.'
– 'Whereas today?'
The private finally saw the light.
'Today we say,' he said quickly, 'that the officers are sons of the working class.'
– 'And what do we say in our country that the people do?'
– 'Rule.'[3]

In a military context the political phrase frequently becomes a fixed form of communication between officers and men. What emerges, with the help of the illiteracy of the officers, is an odd kind of Czech whose syntax betrays that the ideological component is due to a literary translation from the Russian. ' "I fail to observe," said the lieutenant who under the spell of military instructional sessions tried to speak literary Czech in official communications, "in which way the discipline was unfulfilled by me" ' (175). As is evident in the above quotation, Škvorecký's humour is based on resourceful work with the language itself. This is exceedingly important, because during the Stalinist period it was the political phrase that was the chief tool for alienating man from himself. Jiří Voskovec once wrote that Švejk was 'a modern St George, the hero of the saga about the triumph of one head over the many-headed monster of authority, of the system, the triumph of reason masked as simple-mindedness in its struggle against absurdity, which in turn masquerades as wisdom and dignity – the sense of nonsense against the nonsense of sense.'[4]

In Škvorecký's work the single person in his struggle against the absurdity of the army and a totalitarian regime disguises himself by a certain basic primitivism. The appropriateness of this disguise becomes apparent when one remembers that *The Republic of Whores* was written in 1954, when the official, so-called socialist-realist literature produced schematic events to order schematized stories whose heroes had in their veins political phrases instead of blood. Danny Smiřický and his Rabelaisian friends provoke the Party and the government just as Gargantua and Pantagruel provoked the Holy Church. They announce a resurgence of human qualities, which were to re-emerge during the sixties. Together with the liberalization of political life, the early sixties brought a sudden resurgence of Czech prose, primarily due to writers like Škvorecký and Bohumil Hrabal, whose work finally reached a broader spectrum of readers and inspired both the avant-garde growing in small theatres and the new wave in Czech film. Škvorecký became an active member of this avant-garde and collaborated with nearly all the significant directors.[5]

The atmosphere of the sixties had a strong influence on Škvorecký's work.

His vision of reality deepened; the epic core of events became the background for more profound philosophic reflections. The sociopolitical aspects of man's alienation in a totalitarian society were viewed increasingly as merely part of the problematic nature of human life in general. A sense of existential anxiety, regret about lost, frittered-away years of living, hatred of indifference, the awareness of the simultaneity of many time levels in a human being, questions about past events, about guilt and punishment – all these are woven into the texture of a contemporary consciousness. In addition to this philosophical dimension, the work reflects at the same time a deeply felt personal experience. Milan Kundera has tried more or less successfully to explain to his French students and to critics in Czechoslovakia that Franz Kafka's work was regarded as a virtually realistic description of what was happening – he was expressing what people were experiencing day after day. It is in a similar vein that we must regard the existential aspects of Škvorecký's work of the sixties.

The year 1963 was not only the year of Škvorecký's 'rehabilitation' as a writer but also the year when the victims of past political reprisals were rehabilitated. In both cases the guilty parties decided upon the measure of 'grace' to be allotted to their victims. For this reason Škvorecký's prose collection *Sedmiramenný svícen* (The Menorah, 1964) was topical in several ways. In his own case as well as in all Czech literature of the time a Jewish theme was not merely a polemic against the anti-Semitism of Stalin; the Jews were also symbols of all those victims about whom it was forbidden to write. One of the volume's selections, 'Příběh o kukačce' ('A Story about a Cuckoo'), with its questions about the nature of guilt and punishment and about the possibilities and justification of personal revenge, anticipates the novel *Miss Silver's Past*. ' "There are certain crimes which the law cannot touch, and which therefore, to some extent, justify private revenge," ' is the latter's epigraph (the quotation is from Sherlock Holmes in 'The Adventure of Charles Augustus Milverton').[6] The victim in this 'detective novel' is in fact a murderer who kills because of his indifference to the fate of others. He has on his conscience not only his Jewish fiancée but also a whole gallery of destroyed talents and lost values in Czech literature.

Revenge can perhaps be justified, but it is always useless. Spoiled existences, destruction of talents, the loss of innumerable years of life cannot be compensated for. Škvorecký lived through this himself, and his awareness of having lost fifteen of the most productive years of his life awakened in him a strong sense of the impossibility of recapturing past possibilities, of the need to submit to the relentless passing of time. The personal, emotional basis for his possibly subconscious existentialism is his sympathy for all other victims, combined with a deep hatred for human indifference.

The suggestive poetic note about the loss of possibilities is struck most strongly in 'Emöke' (1963), a love story in which the rare human emotion of love is betrayed and lost for good. The contact between two individuals is explored at its deepest level and related to the very meaning of life itself. The symbols of love, beauty, friendship, and absolute values do not reside in the title figure of Emöke but in the poetic expression of two people's yearning to rise through the magic of love above the superficiality of life and to give it a deeper significance. Both feel the possibility of achieving this, yet miss each other at the crossroads of their lives. As their relationship reaches its zenith and approaches its fulfilment, it is destroyed by outer circumstances. The figure of the teacher represents 'vandalism,' that same vandalism that Milan Kundera defined during the Czech Writers Conference of 1967 as the prime enemy of Czech culture. The teacher also embodies typical forms of aggression informed by baseness, stupidity, and lack of character, which are inevitably combined with self-righteousness and the conviction that anything that goes beyond can justifiably be destroyed. 'Emöke' can certainly be interpreted in different ways because of its numerous layers of meaning. For the Czech reader of 1963 there was, however, little doubt about which particular form of stupidity it was attacking.

The Bass Saxophone, like 'Emöke,' abounds in free associations, and although it, too, deals with personal memories, it moves on the borderline between reality and fantasy. In addition to being a declaration of love to jazz and to the beauty of art, it expresses the author's view of life as a whole, touching frequently and subtly on existential questions.

– and suddenly I saw myself among those spectres, how terrible it all was; a sharp, pointed, cruel instant of realization: how I had been led into this stuffy, inhuman failure of a world, a soft baby woven of a dream; how the dream kept breaking through, but not a grandiose dream at all, a pathological dream of helplessness and incapacity, marked by illness, girls' derisive, pointed laughter, lack of talent, lonely afternoons at the movies, nightmares, night fears; how it will all end someday, how it will all collapse; a baby touched from its first pastel perambulator by death, by the fear of eyes, of ears, of contact, the foolishness of those who do not understand, a lonely bad job of a baby – I played, and the immense bass saxophone bent over me; like the frame of a sombre painting. I suddenly felt, knew, that I always had and always would belong to Lothar Kinze, that I had made that entire migration of failure with him and would always be on the move with him, to the bitter end ...

But it was no dream: for that desperate scream of youth is still inside me, the challenge of the bass saxophone. I forget it in the rush of the day, in the rush of life, and I only repeat I love you, I love you, mechanically, because the tears and the callous disinterest of the world have given me this countenance, this thick skin; but there is a memento – an intimate, truthful moment God knows where, God knows when, and because of it I shall always be on the move with Lothar Kinze's orchestra, a sad musician on the mournful routes of Europe's periphery, surrounded by storm clouds; and the sombre bass saxophone player, the adrian rollini, will time and again remind me of dream, truth, incomprehensibility: the memento of the bass saxophone.[7]

'Emöke' and *The Bass Saxophone* are the peaks of Škvorecký's work of the sixties. In addition to their artistic and poetic qualities they share an aura of the author's awareness of the real values of life, reachable only as 'an intimate memento of moments of truth' within the rough reality of day-to-day living, which is indifferent to these values. In 'Emöke' the narrator's return to these values is represented by a long train journey; in *The Bass Saxophone* the dream itself and its fulfilment are mingled with a reality that seems to have emerged from the paintings of Hieronymus Bosch. The musical qualities of Lothar Kinze's little band show that any real contact with the truth is nothing but a relative, fleeting, personal feeling that occurs despite the Kafkaesque reality of life and is marked by our own imperfection.

During the sixties a new view of the past became topical, prompted by a sense that the past continued into the present like an open wound. Like a flash of lightning, this awareness broke through the texture of daily life and illuminated all its layers of time. Decades of lost years, hundreds of compromises that had to be made within oneself as well as in relation to one's surroundings, numerous heroes who showed themselves to be cowards and vice versa, currents of words that rarely touched the truth – everything appeared condensed into a single fraction of the present. This sudden awareness of the omnipresence of the past, which was typical for many members of Škvorecký's generation, forms the basis for the extremely complex composition of *The Miracle Game*. A period of nearly twenty years, a whole mosaic of figures and events slowly jells into a whole, and the reader cannot escape the increasingly intense feeling that the world has gone mad. How else could a former prisoner from Jáchymov pick up golf balls for Dr. Hrzan, who rides his Party activities to the position of full professor at a university in the United States? How else could he simultaneously listen to the cautious stories of M. Kohn, who after thirty years finally has the courage to visit his old home country on 20 August 1968?

The author himself writes in *Samožerbuch* that he moulded the novel by ordering small episodes on two basic historical levels. One is the detective reconstruction of 'the miracle' that had been staged some time ago by the state police as part of an anti-clerical campaign; the second traces the fortunes of Danny Smiřický from the fifties to the end of 1969. The detective aspect also has a deeper meaning, however. The author expressly leaves the conclusion open; the miracle is at the same time a symbol of what human life is really about. 'Meanwhile I thought about life which was to come. About that cheap detective novel, the main character of which is called Truth. But the detective never manages to catch it. From time to time the possibility of a solution seems to flash, but it is inevitably farfetched and unlikely. It may look attractive, but it occurs only in literature' (283).

In the course of his life Danny meets with symbols and forms of truths more profound than his own personal desperate realizations. Those symbols, however, are a part of our confusing and absurd world and are experienced and interpreted by the narrator on his own level, limited necessarily by his own character and talents. In Škvorecký's work humanity is conceived as a puzzling mixture of higher and lower forms that cannot be separated. Life is a Schopenhauerian tragedy that in its single traits is farcical. In this sense *The Miracle Game* is an extended analogue of *The Bass Saxophone*. Ideals, dreams, and mementoes of the truth are presented on a stage where apocalyptic absurdity is mingled with a cheap farce.

In *The Miracle Game* Škvorecký develops his new style, which consists of the best aspects of his former works, enriched by his experience of working with films. In the merging of realistic detail, structured around vivid dialogue, spoken in characteristic linguistic patterns, we recognize Škvorecký's unique ear for the spoken language, his graphic precision of detail, and his ability to delve below the surface of false masks and poses. The cinematographic technique of editing and distributing realistic detail gradually pieces together an absurd whole. Between the Danny of *The Cowards* and the Danny of *The Miracle Game* there are twenty years of living. He has long since lost the ability and the right of an observer, endowed with the sixth sense of youth, to unmask the false roles of the adult world. The observer has entered the world of active collaborators in these absurd endeavours. Through his eyes and his experiences we re-experience the atmosphere of the fifties, the preparations for the outburst of the Prague Spring, and finally the complete deflation of those who took part in it. Those twenty years and the many human tragedies about which Škvorecký writes have one common denominator: an ideology misused by a totalitarian regime. For that reason, instead of dwelling on various aspects of ideology, Škvorecký concentrates on the concrete details that destroyed so many lives.

The Engineer of Human Souls continues along the lines of *The Miracle Game*, developing and perfecting its technique. This novel is among the best works the author has yet written. This time the broad canvas, a chronicle of the society in which Danny lives, consists of two main parts: Danny's experiences as an emigrant after the events of August 1968, and those as a professor of literature at the University of Toronto, where his 'thoughts are running away from the duty for which he is paid to the opulent memories by which he lives.' These memories lead him back to his homeland, to Kostelec during the last years of the war, to the time of total mobilization and his own part in the revolutionary activities, inspired by a boyish romanticism and a desire to impress the girls.

In addition to these two main themes, the panorama of memories – often in the form of letters – broadens to include the fortunes of Danny's friends at home and on other continents. There is also a whole gallery of various human types, above all those who represent the waves of Czech migration. Many of these emigrants have kept, together with their ideals, the prejudices that they imported decades – or months – ago from their homeland, prejudices that prevent understanding and tolerance toward other emigrants as well as toward the populace of their new country. It is made clear that this understanding is very difficult to attain despite a maximum of goodwill on both sides. It seems that people may speak the same language but the words may have different meanings, different associations. Škvorecký uses this fact for such delightfully comic episodes as the clash between the publisher Ms Santner and Mr Senka, or elsewhere the increased difficulty of communication between Professor Smiřický and his students: 'Here too the difference is a matter of life experience. Wendy's comes mostly from television whereas mine from the European *teatrum mundi* ... It occurs to me that at the root of everything there are associations. Associations in time, in image, in theory, in one's heart, all-powerful and omnipresent.'[8]

In this way the same fact and the same thought can sound entirely different, if the natural generation gap is intensified by differences in sociogeographic background. At the same time, however, despite these differences, many things prove that certain things are shared by all young people, perhaps by people in general. But it is difficult to make contact, to find a common language, and it is almost impossible to pass on one's life experience, even if heavily paid for. The charm of the book is precisely in that sense of the huge distance – and simultaneously the close proximity –

between the Czech town Kostelec during of the years of the German Protectorate and the Toronto of the seventies.

As to form, Škvorecký here uses for the first time the method he began testing in *The Miracle Game*. In the consciousness of the narrator free associations evoke certain real episodes from his youth, which emerge and wedge their way into his experience of the present. As in the best sections of the earlier novel, the reader of *The Engineer of Human Souls* discerns a chronological structure to the narrator's mind. This allows the reader to follow the narrator's psychological development, which in turn accounts for his reactions to his surroundings and his beliefs about life in general. The complexity of the composition is functional in the deepest sense. It expresses a situation typical of the author's generation: the constant changes in the rules of society, ideologies, prejudices, and referential frameworks affect and harass the individual, interfere with his life as well as the lives of those near to him and constantly cast doubt on his identity: 'The bow of time is bent to breaking. Is this still me? It is. There is room for so much in one single life' (331).

Škvorecký's ability to tell stories, his profound knowledge of people, his absolute ear for language, and his tendency to use dialogue often create the impression that the single episodes are photographic and acoustically precise renderings of reality, most frequently in its daily banalities. Ultimately, however, they are an artistic abbreviation in which the text is only an outer sign of the profound subtext, which poses questions about the sense of man's existence in the tragicomedy of the contemporary world.

Škvorecký consistently takes the part of the concrete individual against any abstractions that simplify reality and against all ideologies that become the tools of power structures. In our television world we have become accustomed to counting the dead by hundreds and thousands, and the inability to kill or at least theoretically to sanction violence is considered by many to be a punishable non-commitment. Marxist philosophy programmatically places the life of the collective above the life of the individual. All these are abstractions as long as they do not touch the human being personally. It is easy to accept death and the destruction of others in the name of ideology; it is much more difficult to kill with one's own hand one single person, and most difficult of all is to die oneself. It is not easy consciously to harm another person, nor is it easy to resist movements or other motivations that offer a ready surrogate for the earnest search for the sense of life. Therefore the author is suspicious of any theory and infinitely tolerant regarding human qualities. He knows that man is much less explicable and much more complex than dogmatic simplifiers ask us to believe. He also knows that his own notion of the truth is only one of thousands.

NOTES

The essay has been translated from the Czech by Marketa Goetz-Stankiewicz. Translations from *Samožerbuch, Mirákl, Tankový prapor,* and *Příběh inženýra lidských duší* are by Helena Kosková.

1 Josef Škvorecký, *Mirákl* (Toronto: Sixty-Eight Publishers, 1972). All quotations are from this edition and page references are incorporated into the body of the essay.

2 Josef Škvorecký, *Samožerbuch,* (Toronto: Sixty-Eight Publishers, 1971), 115–16.

3 Josef Škvorecký, *Tankový prapor* (Sixty-Eight Publishers, 1971), 81–2. Quotations are from this edition and page references are incorporated into the essay.

4 Jiří Voskovec, introduction to *Tankový prapor,* 8

5 See Josef Škvorecký, *All the Bright Young Men and Women: A Personal View of the Czech Cinema,* trans. Michal Schonberg (Toronto: Peter Martin, 1972)

6 Josef Škvorecký, *Miss Silver's Past,* trans. Peter Kussi (New York: Grove, 1974), xix

7 Josef Škvorecký, 'The Bass Saxophone,' in *The Bass Saxophone: Two Novellas,* trans. Káča Poláčková-Henley (Toronto: Lester & Orpen Dennys, 1979), 178, 185–6

8 Josef Škvorecký, *Příběh inženýra lidských duší* (Toronto: Sixty-Eight Publishers, 1977), 93, 151

GLEB ŽEKULIN

Life into Art: From Josef Škvorecký to Daniel Smiřický (1989)

Speaking of the emerging Northern School of Czech writers, František Stárek, editor of the underground journal *Vokno*, characterized it as a 'school ... which has moved away from traditional novelistic forms and towards quasi-diaries or documentary literature, which actually isn't entirely factual but deals with concrete experience.'[1] It might seem strange that the above definition of late 1980s Czech underground literature appears to fit the fiction of Josef Škvorecký, the self-confessed believer in inspiration and in 'a special kind of lying, called imagination.'[2] But those of Škvorecký's books that are literature and not entertainment (the distinction is his own) and whose main protagonist is the autobiographical Danny Smiřický, can be seen by the reader – as they are by their author himself – as 'quasi-diaries' and as 'documentary literature, which actually isn't entirely factual but deals with concrete experience.'

Škvorecký has provided us with a great deal of information about his life and art in the form of autobiographical essays and interviews. To read *Samožerbuch* and *Talkin' Moscow Blues* one would think that one knew all there is to know about his art and the genesis of his books. And yet, perhaps because he tells, in the inimitably smooth and charmingly entertaining manner that is the trademark of all his writings, the story of his creative life, he remains elusive as a person and partly as an artist. Is he one of the most important Czech writers of the second half of the twentieth century who, together with Kundera, Hrabal, and one or two others, has elevated the little-known literature of a little-known Central European country to the level where it has become a familiar part of world literature, or is he just a good entertainer whose well-crafted books win literary prizes from time to time but are destined to have a short life?

The impact of the publication of *The Cowards* in 1958 on Czech literature and its development has been compared to that of Aleksandr Solzhenitsyn's *One Day in the Life of Ivan Denisovich* in the Soviet Union; according to Solzhenitsyn's publisher Aleksandr Tvardovsky, after the appearance of *One Day* it became impossible to write in the old manner.[3] The works of these two contemporaries, Solzhenitsyn and Škvorecký, bear, on the surface, little resemblance: the main themes, the individual motifs, the milieu in which the action takes place, and the society represented in their writings are different. There are, however, one or two features that reveal certain parallels and affinities more profound than just 'the mutilation of the literary language' of which both writers have been widely accused. Most strikingly, both the pre-*Gulag* Solzhenitsyn and Škvorecký seem to be able to transpose into their fiction only that which they have lived through and/or personally observed. Solzhenitsyn is less overt about it: only 'Matryona's Homestead' has a first-person narrator; in the other works narrated by an omniscient narrator, the protagonist, be it Nemov, Nerzhin, Kostoglotov, or to a lesser degree Alex, is quite unmistakably Solzhenitzyn's thinly disguised *alter ego*. Škvorecký, however, seems to reduce the distance between himself and his personal protagonist, Danny Smiřický, to the point that readers at times have been known to be unable to distinguish between the author and the character (*S*, 255, 260; *TMB*, 41). On occasion he has even used a form of his character's name – Daniel S. Miritz – as his pseudonym (*TMB*, 181). Both Solzhenitsyn – as he himself writes in the afterword to the first YMCA-Press edition of *The First Circle* – and Škvorecký – as Sam Solecki convincingly demonstrates in *Prague Blues* – use their art to mediate between real events and readers in order to deal with history. Both have recognized that in the modern world there are two ideologies, Christianity and the Revolution, each of which claims to know what history is and how to deal with it in the only correct way. Solzhenitsyn and Škvorecký oscillate, as it were, between the two prevalent ideologies, hence their at times ambivalent, even ambiguous, attitude to both Christianity and the Revolution. Their art, however, permits them to consider the problems of history from the point of view not of ideologies but of everyday life (John LeCarré, in *The Little Town in Germany*, calls it 'little history' as opposed to 'great history'), and in this way to convey to their readers the touch, smell, and taste of events, and thus to show the truth about the life that is, as the cliché goes, more truthful than the truth itself (*S*, 299).

Except for his works of fiction about the Stalin period, Solzhenitsyn, however, tends to be a dogmatist swayed by ideologies: as an adolescent inspired by Marxism he planned a work on the Russian revolution, to be titled *I Love Revolution*; in his mid-fifties he began writing the monumental history of the same revolution, the still unfinished *The Red Wheel*, which is inspired by his Christian, specifically Russian Orthodox, understanding of history. Not so Škvorecký. Probably due to his Central European bourgeois upbringing – he is quite content to possess 'the impressive values of the bourgeois lifestyle'[4] – and certainly under the influence of certain greatly admired American writers, he chooses art as the *tertium datum* when dealing with history. Art permits him to stand at a distance from the events, to see the pros and cons, to doubt and to question, and in the end, by assembling the fragments of the 'small history,' to achieve an authentic powerful image of the social, political, and cultural history of the period.

There is one more feature that relates these two seemingly so different writers: the belief in the humanizing effect of art. In his Nobel Prize speech, Solzhenitsyn quotes Dostoevsky's dictum 'Beauty will save the World,'[5] and goes on to say: 'What is it? ... Perhaps it is the old triad of Truth, Goodness and Beauty ... If the tops of these three trees have to be joined together, as the interpreters insist they do, but the too visible, too straight shoots of Truth and Goodness get crushed or cut off and are not allowed to push through, then, perhaps, the unpredictable, the unexpected shoots of Beauty will find their way up to the top and thus will do the job of all three.'[6] He then proceeds to claim that writers can 'conquer the lie! ... In this way literature becomes the live memory of the nation; in this way she keeps alive and preserves the lost history – in a manner which is not exposed to perversions and lies.' While Solzhenitsyn acknowledges the insolubility of the Platonic triad, he follows the Russian tradition and considers the ethical component as primary because it is the only one that is the result of man's own free action. For Škvorecký, who grew up in the democratic, pluralistic, parliamentary republic of the 'philosopher-president' T.G. Masaryk and who was brought up in the Western cultural conventions where the division of a being into autonomous spheres is traditional, such 'old-fashioned' understanding of the Platonic triad would be foreign. And yet, the close connection between Truth and Goodness permeates all his works. Perhaps it is at least partly due to the profound influence of Catholicism, which, though not openly acknowledged, underlies all his attitudes and ideas. 'The writer's job is to tell the truth,' he quotes Hemingway, and continues: 'That is as simple as a commandment, and it is a commandment that is difficult to evade' (*TMB*, 78). Škvorecký would agree with the sentiment expressed by Anatole de Meyrargues, the protagonist of Eric Deschodt's novel *Le Royaume d'Arles*: 'Le seul moyen de ne pas s'ennuyer, c'est de servir quelque chose de grand.'[7] It is to overcome this *ennui* that is the *malaise de siècle*, that Škvorecký writes: 'Why do I write? ... For the fun of it. For amusement'

(*S*, 344). This amusement, however, has a serious purpose: 'Man, if he does not die young, will mature, will acquire the ability to analyse himself and the world ... he will become, or rather, he should become master of his conscience. That is his obligation if he is a college educated person and a humanist. This also imposes upon him certain obligations' (*NB*, 278–9). Furthermore, 'All art is a manifestation of a more or less critical attitude towards society. Artists usually have a strong moral consciousness' (*TMB*, 77). Of course, the writer's main obligation is to write not necessarily in order 'to solve the problems of the world but to tell a story about it, even though this, too, is, naturally, a *sui generis* solution' (*NB*, 216), and to convince the reader about the truthfulness of what is being written by means of 'this unique suggestivity ... which will force us to accept this world with all its small and big imperfections' (*NB*, 170). This is as far as Škvorecký will go in defining Beauty. We see here the basic difference between Solzhenitsyn's vocabulary and Škvorecký's. The former, with his traditionally Russian tendency to maximize and his predilection for abstractions, refers throughout his Nobel speech to the capitalized Beauty, Truth, and Goodness. The latter prefers less grandiose words and phrases, such as 'to write well,' 'to convince,' and 'obligation.' But both, when speaking about their art and their role as writers – and Škvorecký, compared to the very reticent Solzhenitsyn, speaks out on this subject often and in considerable detail – take their work and their obligations equally seriously, as seriously as all good writers do who lived through the profound political, social, and cultural changes over the past fifty years in Central and Eastern Europe.

Škvorecký has told the story of his twenty-five years as a writer in postwar Czechoslovakia in some detail and with a great deal of wit, both in his essays and in his fiction. The striking aspect of this literary biography is that one finds little or no mention of Czech writers, predecessors or contemporaries, who might have had an influence on him. He mentions Jaroslav Hašek, the creator of Švejk, in connection with *The Republic of Whores*, but only in order to say that he had not read *The Good Soldier Švejk* prior to writing it and therefore could not have been influenced by him. His acknowledged teachers are the American writers, among them first and foremost Hemingway, followed closely by Faulkner, whom, he says, 'within the limits of my capacities, I tried to emulate' (*TMB*, 58). This is not to say, however, that Škvorecký's writings are totally outside the sphere of Czech literary tradition: as a product of the Czech school system and a voracious reader since childhood, he knows very well his native literature and, as a writer, continues *volens nolens* the work of predecessors such as Jan Neruda, Karel Čapek, and yes, Hašek, writers who, each in his own time, introduced new ways of seeing, assessing, and representing the life around them.

One of Škvorecký's major innovations was the notion – learned from Hemingway (*NB*, 200; *S*, 290) – that the writer's interest should be almost exclusively centred on the analysis of subjective feelings. In Hemingway's words, 'A writer's job is to tell the truth about his own feelings at the moment they exist,' and that truth is, of course, to be defined only as the truth about those feelings. It is out of the matrix of such assumptions that Škvorecký's fictional *alter ego*, Danny Smiřický, was born. Danny is his most original, most important, and most successful invention. Time and time again, in his numerous *confessions d'un écrivain*, Škvorecký claims that 'basically, I only endeavoured to tell what I have lived through' (*S*, 117). He has done this by *recreating* himself and what he has 'lived through' in Smiřický. Danny is the same age as his creator – twenty-one in 1945 in *The Cowards*: even their birthday, 27 September, is the same. His surname Smiřický is that of a Bohemian noble family with whom the Škvoreckýs had a close connection in the seventeenth century.[8] The topography of Kostelec where Danny lives is that of Náchod where Škvorecký lived. Danny's adventures repeat, on the whole, the author's adventures as they took place or as he, wished them to have taken place. In short, starting with *The Cowards*, through such collections as *Sedmiramenný svícen* (The Menorah), *The Swell Season* (both have a pre-*Cowards* Danny as their protagonist), and *Hořkej svět* (The Bitter World), through *The Republic of Whores*, 'Emöke', *The Bass Saxophone*, and *The Miracle Game*, to *The Engineer of Human Souls*, Danny Smiřický is 'Pepa' Škvorecký as seen, understood, and 'lived' by the writer Josef Škvorecký.

But since Škvorecký knows his craft, he realizes that a work of fiction is never a simple copy of real life but art, and that art always distorts life, gives it an artificiality, a form of its own, and creates an independent world not so much by the veracity and accuracy of representation as by the creator's craftsmanship and convictions. What holds this fictitious world together is a 'strange kind of lying called imagination,' (*S*, 109) which comprises selection, invention, disremembering, and structuring. He also knows that a writer does not and cannot write just about himself. 'Some writers may *think* their only subject is themselves: if they are any good they are in fact telling the history of their times and of their people in the form of a self-portrait. For the self-portrait has an open landscape in the background, with little human figures toiling and frolicking in it, the way the Dutch masters used to paint' (*TMB*, 61). In Škvorecký's novels, however, these 'little human figures' do not remain in the background, with the foreground occupied solely by Danny. The contrary is true. They are seen and judged by Danny; they cannot be, therefore, other than 'flat' characters whose inner life, feelings, and attitudes are revealed only if they are prepared to share them with Danny. Yet, ultimately, they are the ones who complete and add colour and life to the image of the world provided by Danny. Thus, paradoxically, Danny – the protagonist, the hero, the *corpus* and the *spiritus agens* of the novels – becomes more difficult to define as he moves from one novel to the other, while the touch of the real creator of the image becomes more prominent.

The creation of the Danny character is almost inconceivable and inseparable from the first-person narrative mode; in fact, the whole Smiřický sequence, with the exception of *The Republic of Whores*, is written in the first person singular. But in that work Danny remains 'the centre of consciousness' practically all through the novel. This allows Škvorecký to exploit the advantages this form of narration presents, especially the manipulation of time. If in *The Cowards* the use of this device is limited to short and relatively rare flashbacks and insertions of 'time-less' tangential stories that show Škvorecký's special talent at storytelling, in *The Miracle Game* and *The Engineer* the manipulation of time, whether action, narration, or real time, becomes the main feature of these multiplot novels. Another feature of first-person narration exploited in the novels is the possibility for the narrator to avoid the analysis of his own feelings and attitudes and to limit himself to mere statements about them. This does not mean, however, that Danny is slowly removed to the fringe of the stage on which the human comedy is played out under the direction of Škvorecký the author. He always remains our eyes and ears.

Speaking of his own works, Škvorecký maintains that he wrote them in order to satisfy the need to relive his own past. Of the *The Cowards* he says: 'What I had in mind was recreating events in my past life so that they would, as if magically, return to me' (*TMB*, 44). And he does so, letting his *alter ego* Danny Smiřický relive the eight final days of the war in the life of Náchod/Kostelec. He wrote the novel in the autumn of 1948, with the events described in it, as well as with his then dreams and urges, thoughts and attitudes, still fresh in his memory. How true and how autobiographical was this Danny?

In May 1945 Škvorecký was twenty-one years old; he had finished his secondary education in 1943 and had worked for two years as a forced labourer in a German-run war factory. He could not have been as 'immature' and naïve as his Danny appears in the novel. Danny in *The Cowards* is actually indistinguishable from the Danny of *The Swell Season*, which covers the war years, that is, roughly Škvorecký's and Danny's middle and late teens. But *The Swell Season*, written after its author settled in Canada, is a piece of nostalgic recollection of 'the good times,' good because of the innocence and the resulting natural ebullience and selfish optimism of youth. This does not mean that the horrors and hardships of the war are left out: the shocking ending, in which Danny's fellow-musician Lexa is told while playing a beautiful clarinet solo that his father has been shot by the Nazis, is a good example of how much the war-years' reality intrudes into the life of these young people. But the focus remains on the 'normalcy' of everyday life for ordinary adolescents.

Danny's naïveté can be also defined as lack of dogmatism. It is this openness, this absence of engagement, that shows the confusion, the uncertainty, the cruelty, and the tragedy of the very last days of the war – 'Náchod was the scene of probably the last fighting at the end of the war in Europe' (*TMB*, 31) – and allows Škvorecký to show as objectively and fairly as possible the way the events really took place. As a result, *The Cowards* acquired for Czechs the characteristics of a documentary, of history in the making. The 'historical' value of the novel is reinforced by Škvorecký's manipulation of his protagonist. He makes Danny, the ostensibly unengaged participant in events of grave consequences, tumble unwittingly into every happening that marked the progression of fateful incidents foreshadowing the future upheavals in the life of every inhabitant of this provincial town, as well as, by extension, of the whole nation. The embellishments, the inventions, the little lies that accompany the telling of Danny's story are the stuff from which art is made, the flesh a writer puts on the bones that are the facts: 'The basis for *The Cowards* was formed by about five pages of a diary ... simply a description of the main events that happened around Danny each of the eight days described in the book. And then I just began to number, embroider and plaster with details these five terse pages' (*S*, 117). The war's events are not quite comprehensible to, and loom threateningly before, Danny as originally they had for Škvorecký. The only escape was into the life, the freedom, the 'fraternity' (*TMB*, 71) of jazz. 'You cannot lie if you play jazz,' Sidney Bechet says somewhere: 'You cannot despair of life if you love jazz,' could be added by Škvorecký and Danny with him. Another means of escape that tempted both of them was a change of place and, with it, of life. 'To Prague!' – the wistful, longing cry with which *The Cowards* ends – recalls Chekhov's sisters' 'To Moscow, to Moscow!' Škvorecký, accompanied by Danny, was more lucky than they were: he got to Prague.

The next twenty-five years, from 1945 to 1969, Škvorecký spent in

Prague. This sojourn was interrupted only by a year-long spell as teacher of social sciences – the Kostelec episodes in *The Miracle Game* – and two and a half years' military service in the army – *The Republic of Whores*. These were also years of literary apprenticeship; of gaining entrance into the literary – first underground, later official – circles; of work as editor and translator; and finally, in the mid-sixties, of recognition as a 'successful and exceedingly popular writer' (*TMB*, 51).

The Republic of Whores is, as mentioned before, the only novel in the Smiřický series of books written in the third person. The intention of the novel was to capture the experience of army life: hence, another autobiographical work. The result was the creation of probably the funniest, most ribald, most Rabelaisian work of Czech literature in the twentieth century. The underlying seriousness lies in the revelation of the discrepancy between reality and ideological concepts. The resulting absurdity extends, through Danny's contacts with civilians, to life as a whole under the Stalinist régime in Czechoslovakia. Again, as in *The Cowards*, the autobiographical facts are altered, twisted, embellished, added to, mixed, and restructured, to become the essential truth as perceived by Danny. However, the older and much more sophisticated Danny, now a university graduate with a doctorate in philosophy, appears to stand, due to the distance created by the third-person narrative, at the side, looking at the action on the stage with the cynicism that makes him a predecessor of Karel Leden, the protagonist of *Miss Silver's Past*, a novel not in the Smiřický cycle. In *The Republic of Whores*, the distance between the creator and his *alter ego* is also increased by the author's distinctly heard voice. If Danny is the 'centre of consciousness' in this novel, as Škvorecký claims (*S*, 286), then this centre is quite different and less appealing than the one in the other Smiřický novels: perhaps the dehumanizing experience of military life has affected not only the character in the novel but its author as well – which would, of course, only confirm the author's claim that his work is 'plain realism' (*S*, 44).

The Danny of *The Bass Saxophone* is the first hint of the development this character will undergo in the 1970s with *The Miracle Game* and *The Engineer*. Though still the Danny of Kostelec and still confused by his emotions and puzzled by problems of life as he encounters them, he begins to think, to seek the answers both by observing the life around him and by looking inside himself: he begins to develop his own scale of values and to doubt the values acquired in the family, in the schools, and in the provincial Kostelec. The dilemma Danny faces in this case is whether to reject any kind of contact with the Germans or to ignore this absolute *Verbot* based on nationalistic feelings elevated to the level of a principle; whether to give in to the temptation to try out the bass saxophone, an instrument previously only heard about, or to give up the only chance he will probably ever have to do so. The bass saxophone belongs to a German travelling band arrived in Kostelec to perform before the exclusively German audience that did not tolerate any other music but the oom-pa-pa kind prescribed by the Nazi watchdogs of pure Aryan mores. The temptation wins. Danny, disguised, plays the bass saxophone on a few pieces with the band, aware that in the eyes of his Czech compatriots, and to a certain extent in his own eyes, he can and even should be considered a traitor and a collaborator with the enemy. But as the music slides somehow, unaccountably, into a beautiful jazz piece, it dawns on him that these German musicians are as ordinary and normal, and even, possibly, kind human beings as he is, and he realizes that ready-made answers are not necessarily correct and acceptable to him. *The Bass Saxophone* is an exquisite piece of writing, which shows that Škvorecký has matured as a writer and that he has learned perhaps the most difficult lesson a writer has to learn, namely, how to tell a story about a specific, simple, and seemingly trivial occurrence and at the same time make an important comment on life (*TMB*, 57).

In *The Miracle Game*, the first Smiřický novel written after Škvorecký settled in Canada, he 'tried to create a world out of the mess of my life in our messy century' (*TMB*, 61). The plot is developed on two time planes: the most difficult years of Stalinist terror in the early 1950s and the years of liberalization that led to the Prague Spring of 1968 and ultimately to the occupation of Czechoslovakia by the Soviet army.

When a small wooden statue of St Joseph moves apparently of its own accord during the service in a small chapel on the outskirts of Kostelec, the faithful believe that a miracle has happened. The police, under the instructions of the local Party functionaries, accuse the priest of rigging the statue, arrest him, and torture him to death. During the later, more liberal years, the Catholics who venerate the priest as a martyr try to prove that the police rigged the statue *post factum* in order to discredit the priest and the Church, and accuse them of murder. Danny was present but asleep in the chapel when the 'miracle' took place and is, in the later years, involved in helping to find the truth about the incident.[9] The Kostelec part of the novel is based on the real event, as well as on the familiar autobiographical material that, again, is adjusted, mixed, bent and twisted, richly embroidered, and partly invented. Danny is in his mid-twenties, still not a fully developed individual. As a teacher of social science, he is expected to represent the orthodox Party teaching, though as a non–Party member, he is allowed in his private life slight deviations from the behaviour demanded from a member of the Party.

Privately, he knows that what he teaches is utter rubbish, totally rejected by the overwhelming majority of his students and of the population at large; but he knows that they, as well as he, are more or less willing actors in an absurdist play. His attitude towards the miracle that he did not see is not dissimilar to his attitude towards Communist propaganda: he does not believe in the unreal but is not willing to take part in dissuading the believers. In the episodes that take place in the liberal sixties, Danny, who was shocked by the murder of the priest by secret policemen, becomes involved in the attempt to prove the guilt of the murderers. In the end, he solves the mystery of the 'miracle' by proving that neither the murdered priest nor the murdering police were involved in rigging the statue but that a third person played a tragic joke on both. However, he does not make public his solution of the mystery.

In this novel with a very complex structure Škvorecký deals with or presents two Dannys simultaneously – the young one who is still in the process of growing up emotionally, intellectually, and especially morally, and the middle-aged one who has established for himself his own scale of values but is not willing to declare it in public. The explanation of how and why this change in the protagonist's character actually occurred has been left out of the narrative. The ambiguous character of the older Danny, who both debunks the Communist ideologists and demystifies the Dubček reforms and the Prague Spring, angered both the Right and the Left. Particularly bitter were the so-called reform Communists (whose unabashed dogmatism is exposed by Danny), who retaliated by presenting the author as someone who betrayed the very spirit of liberalization that they attempted to appropriate. The Right attacked him for selling out to the Moscow-appointed Communist old guard. What neither side wanted to see was that in *The Miracle Game* Škvorecký has made his two Dannys face the same problem his protagonist had faced in *The Cowards* and in *The Bass Saxophone*, namely, how to make a choice. He once again allowed Danny to see that to make a choice was, in fact, impossible. With each succeeding novel he made the situation to be resolved more complex and the choice before his protagonist more difficult – in fact, due to the mess in which the whole world finds itself, impossible to make. The attacks on Škvorecký only show how artistically successful he has been in *The Miracle Game*. The distance between the author and his *alter ego* had been reduced to such an extent that not only the readers but the critics as well have tended to confuse the two.[10]

Two lengthy quotations from Škvorecký's autobiographical essay 'I Was Born in Náchod' will introduce the discussion of its successor *The Engineer of Human Souls*, the last novel to date in the Smiřický series. 'Since passing the halfway point of my life, it has been here, on this continent of Poe, Twain, and Faulkner, that I set out to recapitulate my life in fiction.' And: 'To be a ripe epic novelist ... you have to retain the freshness of emotions well into your declining years when you have accumulated a wealth of experience: the hundreds of real-life stories of which you were a part, the hundreds of characters – sweet and funny, sad and obnoxious – who crossed your way, the decades of historical upheavals, political somersaults, the wisdom and stupidities of your age' (*TMB*, 59).

Reaching back in this recapitulation of his life to *The Cowards*, Škvorecký, it could be argued, rewrites this novel in *The Engineer*. On the continent of the American writers who have 'produced their magnificent responses to the rawness, freshness of life' (*TMB*, 58), and inspired, perhaps, by the directness, naturalness, and 'innocence' of his present-day young North American students, Škvorecký seems to have relived more clearly, fully, and honestly the sweetly sad war years, the 'messy' postwar decades, and the even messier post-1968 years. In this novel he shares with his new compatriots the hundreds of real-life stories and the extraordinary experiences accumulated over the years. He creates the kindly, understanding, patient, and tolerant 'American' Danny, the college professor of American literature who uses the works of Poe, Hawthorne, Twain, Crane, et al. to impart to his students the wisdom of understanding and accepting life as it is, and the truth about mankind that only art is capable of giving.

And yet, Danny is not quite comfortable in his new intellectual and social surroundings. His colleagues, though knowledgeable and well-read in their narrow fields of specialization, strike him as lacking a personal experience of real life and as deprived of wider vision. They appear to be, to borrow Dostoevsky's phrase, humans made of printed paper: he is surprised by the ease with which they adopt ideas that are à la mode and follow the latest scholarly fads. He cannot find among them a single friend with whom he would want to share everyday pleasures and pains or exchange thoughts and discuss feelings as young Danny used to do in Kostelec with Benno, Haryk, and Lexa. He does not know, nor does he seek to know, many Canadians outside of his college. The few he encounters are concerned mainly with organizing their lives to be as pleasantly uneventful and routinely comfortable as possible, and intellectually undemanding. But at the same time he cannot but be moved by their innocence, their kindness, their tolerance, and their insistence on fair play. He is more critical of his former compatriots, with whom he maintains some social intercourse, consisting mainly of attending parties and going to restaurants. He finds them intellectually unexciting, uninterested in politics (specifically in the tragic fate of their former homeland), exceedingly materialistic, selfish, and intolerant. Only on occasion does he find among them a young post-1968 refugee – Veronika – who had experienced one short period of happy, exciting, and exhilarating life during the Prague Spring and who, haunted by nostalgic memories and unable to find fulfilment in the unvarying course of predictably orderly life in Canada, decides to return to Czechoslovakia. Remembering his Kostelec years, he sympathizes with her, because he understands her futile longing for the past that will never come back, though he disapproves of her decision, which will bring her even more unhappiness.

The Danny of this latest metamorphosis has, then, acquired new features. He does not actively involve himself in the life around him, rather he stands aside, observes, and – for the first time since we have met him – passes judgment, without, however, imposing his views on others or preaching to them. Though not a loner, he has built around himself an enclosure that he is loath to leave or to let anyone into. Even his sexual prowess, with which the author has so richly endowed his *alter ego* in previous novels, seems to be subdued, and his amorous pursuits, whether imaginary or real, are less persistent and very much less enthusiastic.

Thus, in *The Engineer* we have once again two Dannys – the young Danny of Kostelec, who seems to be far removed from the reminiscing author, and today's Danny, the author's contemporary, who is in fact nearly indistinguishable from him. For the most part, we do not see or understand this latter Danny as a separate, a created character, but rather as a slightly touched-up self-portrait.

It would appear that Škvorecký has closed the circle. He starts with the young Danny Smiřický of *The Cowards*, who is doubtless the author's *alter ego*. He closes with the older Danny of *The Engineer*, where the *alter ego* becomes more and more confused with its creator, Josef Škvorecký. Sam Solecki is right when he argues in *Prague Blues* that *The Engineer* may be the last Smiřický novel. Danny Smiřický was born, as his author claims, to recall his, the author's past. As a participant in Škvorecký's Czechoslovak past, Danny turned out to be a trustworthy, observant, and intelligent witness who provided 'a more or less continuous picture of the last four decades of Czechoslovakia's history' (*TMB*, 63). In Canada, all that is left for Danny is to transmit gently and tactfully to his new audience his vast knowledge of life. Having done this in *The Engineer*, he has accomplished the task for which he was created. From now on, Josef Škvorecký, the Canadian novelist of Czech origin, will find inspiration for his current writings in his North American homeland.

NOTES

1 Interview in the independent Polish quarterly *Obecność*, translated in *Uncaptive Minds*, 1: no. 2

2 *Samožerbuch* (Toronto: Sixty-Eight Publishers, 1977), 109, 330; *Talkin' Moscow Blues*, ed. Sam Solecki (Toronto: Lester & Orpen Dennys, 1988), 74. References to these books are included in the body of the essay and indicated by the abbreviations *S* and *TMB*. (All translations from the Czech and Russian are mine.)

3 Škvorecký acknowledges (*S*, 108) the fact that *The Cowards* 'delivered, in the 1950s, a mortal wound to socialist realism.'

4 Antonín Brousek – Josef Škvorecký, *Na brigádě* (Toronto: Sixty-Eight Publishers, 1979), 282 (abbreviated in the rest of the essay as *NB*). See also *TMB*, 32.

5 Aleksandr Solzhenitsyn, *Nobelevskaia lektsia po literature 1970 goda* (Paris: YMCA-Press, 1972), 2–3

6 Ibid, 9

7 Paris: Lattès, 1988

8 In *Samožerbuch*, 301–7, Škvorecký explains Danny Smiřický's genesis by providing some genealogical information about his own ancestry, embellished, as is his wont, by more or less relevant but as always beautifully told anecdotes. He omits to mention an ancestor of his who played an important role in the still earlier history of Bohemia: Olbram of Škvorec (Wolfram von Skworek in its Germanized form) was a nephew of Jan of Jenštejn, the influential and politically very active archbishop of Prague in the reign of Wenceslas IV; he succeeded his uncle in 1396 and occupied the Prague see until 1402. Škvorecký, while explaining how he chose the surname Smiřický for his protagonist, does not explain the choice of Daniel for the latter's first name. Is the Old Hebrew meaning, *my judge is God*, a tongue-in-cheek hint at how the author feels about the reaction to his writings of critics and readers?

9 The title – *Mirákl* in Czech – is ambiguous: it is a Czech colloquial form of a foreign word – *zázrak* would be the correct Czech form – that contains elements of irony, doubt, and a little contempt. The title, thus, seems to imply that it is not a true miracle the author is talking about, that perhaps there are no miracles, as there are no definite, definitive, absolute truths, whether Catholic or Communist, when we deal with life.

10 See letters from the readers in *Samožerbuch*, passim.

7

LUBOMÍR DORŮŽKA

Remembering 'The Song of the Forgotten Years' (1989)

At the beginning of the seventies I was attending a jazz festival in the Italian town of Bergamo. Among the stars was Gerry Mulligan, one of those Greats whom all jazzmen in our country regarded with awe. After the concert there was a party at a small Italian restaurant, high above the town, right – as it seemed – under the sky full of glistening stars. Somehow I got to the same table as Gerry and we began to talk. It was easy, since in contrast to some other Greats I had the opportunity to meet, he was a kind and wise man of wide interests, knowledgeable about many things and anxious to learn more about anything touched on in our conversation.

After some two or three hours of talk and I don't know how many carafes of Italian red wine, he thought it no longer impolite to ask about my accent: I told him I came from Czechoslovakia. His reaction was immediate and I could hardly believe its intensity: 'Why – this can't be true! Half a year ago I hardly knew that such a place existed. But then I got hold of a novel about young Czechs playing jazz at the end of the war. I just couldn't believe it: suddenly here were young people who talked and acted the same way I did at their age. They felt exactly the same not only about music and jazz, but also about their parents, their plans, girls, the world – well, about everything. Since that time I've been just burning to meet someone from that country. Do you happen to know the author of that novel? If you do, give him my very best regards and wishes.'

I looked at my wristwatch: it was three o'clock in the morning on Saint Joseph's day, and all Josefs in Czechoslovakia were in their dreams preparing themselves for this feast, which in our country is celebrated with much more effort than individual birthdays.

The author who was the subject of our talk was totally unaware of what was happening at Bergamo.

The connection between jazz and life is as complicated as the connection between life and fiction. When a novel acquires the reputation that some 'real' characters are depicted in it, the readers who know the scene set out on their private sleuthing trips: Who is this – and when did this story told here really happen? But such relations are always much more complicated and sometimes they reverse the one-way connection between life and its literary reflection. The author creates his characters as an amalgam of many persons and things he has seen in his life, and the simple equation 'This one is that one' seldom works in such a simple way. But if he really can imbue himself with the spirit, the atmosphere, the pulse of his own time, he may live to see the one-way connection between fiction and life reversed. Sometimes, long after his works have been published, he may learn there were real people behaving in the way he described and meeting the fates he wrote about without his knowing them at all.

After *Miss Silver's Past* was published in 1969, I realized I had known a man who might have been a model for one of the book's most important characters – a man of letters who changed his political views as the winds blew, behaved with a lot of irresponsibility in his private life, made it to the top echelon of his professional association, where he slept during most committee meetings in a drunken stupor, and finally was found drowned, fallen from a fishing boat, at the very place where the author had his character meet his fate in his novel. As a matter of fact, Škvorecký did not know this man at all, neither did he hear of what happened to him. Life sometimes can play such jokes on us. Is this mere chance or proof that a book permeated with the spirit of 'real' life will automatically call to the minds of the readers 'real' characters and situations that they have encountered but of which the author himself was quite unaware?

Let me illustrate this with a 'true' story from the history of Czech jazz.

Among the author's works dear to the hearts of Czech jazz fans is a short story with the title 'The Song of the Forgotten Years.'[1] It tells of a girl singer – a canary, as they were called in those blessed years of adolescent swing – who pays a high price for an obvious lack of caution. She happened to swing a famous military march at a time when this was hardly advisable in Czechoslovakia and was 'sentenced to silence.' (There were a lot of such sentences, never pronounced in any courtroom and never made public in any way, but all the same working very reliably in practice.) Silent during the years that would have been her best ones, she returned to the scene 'after the storms of anger have passed,' as the seventeenth century's Czech émigré Jan Amos Comenius put it, only to find the dance floors ruled by a different kind of music with a different set of tastes and fashions followed by a different generation of dancers and listeners, for whom, to put it mildly, she was just a pathetic old-timer.

Readers who believe every novel or story from contemporary life to be a crossword puzzle they have to solve by inserting the 'right' names into the blank spaces that the author obviously tried to camouflage by fictional names, immediately got to work and offered their guesses. Because of some details in the girl's description, some of them identified the heroine as the late swing and early bop vocalist Vlasta Průchova, wife of one of the pioneers of Czech swing, Dr Jan Hammer, and mother of the keyboard player Jan Hammer, Jr, later of *Mahavishnu* and *Miami Vice* fame. In her singing and voice there were many echoes of the story, but hers was not the typical 'crime and punishment' fate – that, again, was an amalgam of things that happened to hundreds of other unknown jazzmen of those times, of emotions and memories that every one of those adolescent swing cats in our country felt as part of his personal heritage.

But, according to a quotation from a widely publicized work of postwar Czech literature, 'there were no nameless heroes.' Each of them had his own face, name, hopes, and dreams. And the fate of the singer from 'The Song of Forgotten Years' had a very 'real' parallel in what happened to a real singer whom everybody knew in her years of fame, but whose fall from stardom passed somehow unnoticed at a time when most people had too many other things to care about.

Her name was Inka Zemánková, and she was the queen of Czech swing. It was she who first succeeded in bending the accents of the Czech language in such a way that syncopation and off-beat phrasing sounded as if they had been invented just for her; it was she who could just naturally play with glissandos and blues inflections at a time when only a very few instrumentalists in Prague could do something similar. There was a glamour about her, but there was also some mystery. In his memoirs, *Já nic, já muzikant* ('I'm Nothing, I'm a Musician'), Jiří Traxler, a prominent swing songwriter and pianist (now resident in Canada) writes: 'Now I come to think of it, she was a strange girl, this Inka Zemánková. Somewhat mysterious. For instance her age was a subject of guess work, and since she did not show her birth certificate to anybody, everyone was entitled to his own theory. For me, the most interesting thing was that from one day to the next she could look five or even more years younger or older. Her family background was also unknown to anybody and as for that, she might have been hatched from an egg. I always had the impression that she was living under great tension and I suspected her private life to be very chaotic.'

Well, it took four decades to learn a bit more about those mysteries. As for her family, Inka was a modest Czech counterpart of Billie Holiday: her mother was the youngest child of a large, poor, mining family and her father – the heir of a very well-to-do village miller, who was disinherited by his father for marrying such poor trash – died by the time she was two. Her mother being luckless in her choice of partners, the child lived with changing stepfathers but without any fatherly love. Eventually mother and daughter moved to the Slovak capital, Bratislava, and the girl trained there in the ballet corps of the Slovak National Theatre. The mother died suddenly, and Inka (at an unspecified age, but probably in her teens – here the mystery remains) came to Prague to stay with a recently divorced friend of her mother to help her take care of her little house. She even accepted the name of the friend's family, Zemánková.

It must have been 1937 or 1938, when the swing generation of Škvorecký (aged fourteen or fifteen), charmed by Fred Astaire – Ginger Rogers film musicals and slightly acquainted with Louis Armstrong, Benny Goodman, and Bob Crosby's Bobcats, was still without local heroes. These arrived in 1939 or 1940: the Karel Vlach Band with American swing charts as well as with original Czech tunes penned by Jiří Traxler or the 'hot accordion player' Kamil Běhounek. And the singer was Inka, flying over those molasses-flavoured honeycombs of the saxophones and chattering with the biting responses of the brass, declaring in her lyrics the burning confession of that generation: 'Today Jazz Is My Life, My Desire, My Dream.' After one of her country-wide hits she was called 'The Girl Born to Swing,' and in the opinion of her worshippers she had it all – glamour, glory, and goods.

Four decades later we see that this was too optimistic. At the time of her greatest successes, Inka was living on a bed-and-breakfast basis as a tenant of a kind old lady – the career of a jazz singer being obviously not acceptable to her mother's lonely friend. She was entitled to a cup of coffee, two rolls, a piece of butter and some jam, and often this had to last all day. In the afternoon, when coming to sing at a five o'clock tea on the popular terraces of the Sharpshooters Island, she looked with envy at the cake-loaded plates of her listeners. Karel Vlach's band, though idolized by the entire generation, was still an amateur group at that time. He used to phone her: 'Oh, baby, don't you forget to come tonight. I can't pay you any fee, but it's important – the radio's going to put a wire into the hall!'

Fame was one thing, but bread and security another. In 1941, to get rid of the 'great tension and chaotic conditions' mentioned by Traxler, Inka accepted a one-year contract from a popular coffee-and-cabaret hall. The contract was extended in 1942, and – near the end of the war – she was sent with other singers on tours of working camps and factories in Germany to which Czech workers (many of them former students or young people of the swing generation) had been previously transported as slave labour. Immediately after the war, there were the three years of what Škvorecký calls 'the age of nylon' with big bands playing swing all over the country. Inka was singing with the Ladislav Habart Band in a huge hall in the middle of Wenceslas Square, still shooting out her swing numbers, while in the basement of the same house, in Prague's first jazz club, the Pygmalion, the young Vlasta Průchova, with Jan Hammer, Sr, was beginning to explore the regions of boppish scat. But that period was brief and came to an abrupt end. Soon, the powers that be dismissed swing and jazz as decadent, bourgeois music that had no place in the new model of socialist culture. Syncopated rhythms were banned from the scores, and the singers were supposed to stand stiffly in front of the microphones, without a single movement that could be interpreted as an attempt at that tasteless hip-shaking, finger-snapping jazzy behaviour. HAU, the Musicians and Artists Agency, was the only organization entitled to sign contracts for engagements and gigs, and thus had absolute control over all musicians and singers. At its head stood a sworn and professed enemy of jazz, acting at the same time as the Official Music Critic and monopolizing the important task of directing Czech popular music towards greener, but above all safer, much tamer pastures.

In Prague's Lucerna Hall, once the scene of history-making concerts, dances, and battles of Czech wartime and postwar swing bands, HAU decided to stage a magnificent All Singers Show. Participation was compulsory for anybody who wanted to continue in his or her professional career, and right in front of the singers, seated behind a long table, was a jury, following with hawks' eyes every illegitimate movement or voice inflection. The singers were supposed to appear in alphabetical order, as if called for a strict examination. Each had to offer three titles, but, of course, no American or jazzy tunes, please, or more precisely, if you *wanted* to please.

Inka, safely placed by her initials as the last item on the menu, was waiting nervously in the wings. She realized that by the time her turn came, the people would be tired and she might not even get a hand – what a terrifying idea for any singer! Well, at last her turn did come. She opened her set with Harold Arlen's 'Accent-tchu-ate the Positive,' an American tune, but a snappy, swinging, and very optimistic one. The song was attributed, however, to a clever Czech lyricist, a well-known practice used whenever any real name was considered undesirable. The audience warmed up to this: no danger of them falling asleep yet. Then came the safe choice, a song by Jaroslav Ježek, the granddaddy of Czech jazz from the thirties. Ježek was an exceptionally gifted composer. Born half-blind and with a kidney condition, he was so full of vitality that he made it through the Prague conservatory and the Maestro School and then became the house composer and bandmaster of the Liberated Theatre. The theatre presented works by avant-garde artists, used a lot of jazz, and offered outspoken anti-fascist satire when Mr Hitler came to power. When the theatre was dissolved in 1939, Ježek, together with the comedians Jiří Voskovec and Jan Werich, who co-directed the theatre, had to flee to the United States, where he died soon after his arrival. Because he had been an anti-fascist and fate had given him no opportunity to reveal his postwar politics, he became a hero of Czech culture, and his songs from the thirties, witty, inventive, and catchy early swing hits, became deeply rooted in the Czech national tradition. Inka's second tune was Ježek's lovely ballad, 'The Dawn Comes and Lovers Have to Part.' Themes like that were never subject to dispute; the audience swallowed it as did the jury.

But Inka had to close her set with a fast number that would raise the listeners from their seats. And here there was a problem. She chose another Ježek tune, 'David and Goliath,' the eternal story of a small and weak hero fighting a giant. Ježek, Voskovec, and Werich used it as a parable for their fight against Hitler. It was again a swinging, catchy tune, and you just can't sing such tunes standing stiffly in front of the mike. When Inka came to the line 'David turns around and swings his sling,' she just had to act this out, and the audience went with her. And suddenly it was all back to what the current aesthetics of stage shows abhorred: Inka couldn't help falling into the hip-swinging, finger-snapping routine; swing was here, and the audience could not refrain from hand clapping and – what an unbelievably horrible thing to do! – even whistling their approval. Inka added another chorus as an encore and her success was tremendous. But the results were grave. Her friends, some opera singers from the National Theatre, came to see her after the show and told her, 'You were great, Inka – but we doubt it you're going to sing in public anymore.'

They were right. Next morning she was summoned to the HAU. She was met by the director, who was wearing a blue shirt, the uniform of the Union of Czechoslovak Youth. He did not bother to let her sit down and told her straightaway: 'Comrade Zemánková, The Girl Born to Swing shan't appear any more on our scene. All that finger-snapping, hip-swinging formula, that's something basically inimical to socialist culture. The HAU will not sign any contract issued in your name.'

So Inka had to withdraw from public performances. She married a man who was appointed the director of a State Tractor Service Station. She actually learned to drive a tractor and sang driving it on the huge fields of an agricultural co-operative – the very image of what new 'pop songs' of the fifties were telling people to believe. She studied classical singing techniques at the same time, and from time to time she parked her tractor at the church of the nearby village and sang Gounod's 'Ave Maria' from the choir. And she kept in touch with whatever was happening on the pop scene. She made a small comeback when a prominent band's vocalist got ill a few days before an important concert and the bandleader could not think of anybody else to replace her. He fixed the strings with the Agency, and they agreed to make an exception for once. But at the concert there were some people from the Polish State agency; they heard Inka, liked her, and offered her a two-week job at a fair in Poznan. Two weeks extended to two years, Inka's passport expired in the meantime, but the Poles still paid the commission due to the Czech agency (which changed its name and director, but not its basic policy). The Poles also recorded Inka for their Radio International Exchange Service and offered her recordings to the BBC, the Swiss, and the East Berlin radio, so that Inka's recordings got to Prague – where, officially, she was declared 'unacceptable' for radio transmission – via East Berlin. The Czech agency was suddenly no longer reluctant to sign her contracts for jobs abroad, from which it took a fat commission, although it hardly did anything to help her at home. When recording for Radio Zurich, she was told by the producer: 'You know, Mrs Zemánková, what especially appeals to me is that Slavonic character of yours.' She could hardly fail to remember the former HAU director, who by that time probably lived close to Zurich: after 1968 even some of those who in the fifties acted as self-appointed guides for new socialist culture decided it might be better to have a look at some alternative.

So Inka survived somehow. Even in the 1980s, from time to time she appeared on Czech TV when there was some anniversary of any of her contemporaries (not her own, however; her birthdate remains a mystery). Her recordings from the 1939–42 period were even reissued on an LP. But those years in which she might have been a real star were desperately and hopelessly lost. It was like the promise of a young love that never reached its consummation – like Scott Fitzgerald's hero confessing in the closing paragraph of 'Winter Dreams': 'Long ago ... long ago, there was something in me, but now that thing is gone ... That thing will come back no more.'

Škvorecký knew Inka – she was the idol of his adolescence – but it is doubtful how much he knew of her real fate. He even did an interview with her in the sixties, but Inka, sometimes too emotional and reluctant to talk, and sometimes just bursting with memories and reminiscences, tended to change her stories with each interview. Anyway, whatever he may have learned from her – and perhaps he even wrote the story before having spoken to her; the chronology isn't clear – he wrote 'The Song of the Forgotten Years' not as the story of one particular singer but as the story of the times. It is the privilege of great authors to condense the feelings, emotions, aspirations, hopes, and disappointments of thousands of people so that the result speaks not only to the people who actually lived under those circumstances, but also to people growing up in quite a different set of conditions who, to their own surprise, suddenly find in all those dreams something akin, something universal that they share. In 'The Song of the Forgotten Years,' the times are caught in a much more convincing and effective way than they would be in a 'true story' – however precisely and painstakingly it might have been told.

But Škvorecký's stories are not only the stories of the times – they are also the stories of jazz. The honorary titles like 'The Girl Born to Swing,' the lines like 'Jazz Today Is My Life, My Desire, My Dream,' may sound like a set of commonplace platitudes to cold, critical ears. But to those bitten by the jazz bug, they are part of an experience that is valid and everlasting whatever the times may have done to it. Škvorecký's jazz stories will always remain something personal for them, no matter if they were born in a small border town of Bohemia, in the country's capital, Prague, or in Marion, Ohio, where Gerry Mulligan first saw an old Greyhound bus with the inscription Red Nichols and the Five Pennies. Musicians have played out that experience in their solos and singers have sung it, but not many writers have managed to capture it in writing, so that its message is as strong and powerful as the music itself.

Škvorecký, no matter whether in a novel (*The Cowards*), novella (*The Bass Saxophone*), or in a number of short stories, has succeeded perhaps better than anyone else. If you've got a thing under your skin, it must get out, whatever medium you choose. Those 'wildly sweet, soaring, swinging saxophones, the lazy and unknown voice of an unknown vocalist' will always speak of 'the love of youth which stays firmly anchored in one's soul.' Doubtless this was inspired by events and persons from real life; doubtless some members of the Dixieland band from *The Cowards* are still living in different parts of the world; but what's the use of looking for them? There is no need to search for the 'true' and 'real' heroes behind those stories: what's real and true about them is the basis, the intensity of feeling, emotion, belief, and confession. If that is true, 'real' characters and actions lose the ties binding them to this common world and inch a step closer to some limitless, universal space – perhaps, as Mahalia Jackson sang, somewhere 'to the upper room.' I believe Škvorecký's works are, among other things, unique upper-room jazz writings.

NOTE

1 'The Song of the Forgotten Years' ('Píseň zapomenutých let') first appeared in the magazine *Repertoar malé scény*, 4: no. 5 (1966), 2–6. It was published the following year in the short story collection *Babylónsky příběh a jiné povídky* (Praha: Svobodné slovo, 1967), 7–21. A translation appeared in *The New Writing in Czechoslovakia*, ed. George Theiner (Harmondsworth: Penguin, 1969), 70–80.

8

MICHAL SCHONBERG

The Case of the Mangy Pussycat: An Account of the Literary Scandal Surrounding the Publication of *The Cowards* (1980)

Early in 1958 rumours began circulating in Prague literary circles about the imminent publication of a novel by Josef Škvorecký, titled *The Cowards*. Škvorecký was known in the publishing industry and among the liberal members of the intellectual community as the fine young editor at the prestigious National Publishing House of Belles Lettres, Music and Art, an author of several introductions to translations from Anglo-American literature, an anglophile since his student days and a great jazz lover. Only a very few among his friends knew that he was also the author of many short stories and of two novels which due to their contents had remained for several years in manuscript only. There had been one attempt by the publishing house Československý spisovatel (Czechoslovak Writer) to publish the short novel 'The End of the Nylon Age,' but the censor refused to allow it on the grounds that it was erotic.

Rumours about publication were nothing unusual in a city with a literary life as active as that of Prague, but this time the situation was somewhat different: those who had read *The Cowards* in manuscript realized that the book's contents were highly controversial, as it dealt most unconventionally with the touchy subject of the last days of the German occupation of Czechoslovakia and the comic-opera attempts by the burghers of the small Czech town of Kostelec (based on Škvorecký's home town, Náchod) to bring about a revolution and hasten their liberation. Formally the book was just as controversial, as it was written in the 'I'-form and all the events were seen through the eyes of a teen-ager, Danny Smiřický, whose principal interests in life seemed to be jazz and girls. The language of the characters consisted of an unusual mixture of the zootsuiters' street talk and refined literate Czech. Furthermore, the book contained no positive characters in the sense of the limited code of socialist realism. There had not been a book like that published in Czechoslovakia since Jaroslav Hašek's *The Good Soldier Švejk* in the first quarter of the twentieth century.

There were other factors that made the rumoured publication a special event: for one, the book was written when the author was twenty-four years old, and some very knowledgeable people identified it as one of the best things written in Czech in recent times (Zdeněk Urbánek in a letter to Škvorecký); secondly, the book was not announced in the official publication plan of Československý spisovatel for 1958. Instead a blanket note was made concerning 'new, hitherto unknown authors.'[1] This was a precaution taken by the publishers, who were not certain whether the book would be approved by the Main Office of Press Supervision (HSTD). The book was submitted to the censor in manuscript, which was an unusual procedure allowed with works of controversial character; otherwise page proofs were submitted.

Writing in his 1977 volume of reminiscences and letters entitled *Samožerbuch*, Škvorecký relates that he was very surprised when approached by the director of Československý spisovatel, Ladislav Fikar, with the proposal concerning the publication of *The Cowards*, and even more surprised to hear that, save for eight minor corrections, the censor had approved the book for publication as it stood.[2] The book appeared in time for the Christmas market in a relatively modest run of 10,000 copies. Still insecure about the book's controversial contents, the publishers provided an interpretive description on the flap of the dust jacket in which the book was identified as a searing satire of petit-bourgeois cowardice and aimlessness. The book was out, the initial responses were encouraging, and Prague seemed to have a brand-new literary star.

Before I proceed any further, a brief review of the political situation in Czechoslovakia might serve a useful purpose. After the Communist takeover in 1948, seven years of hard-line Stalinist rule ensued, with all the political and police terror that the world had seen on a larger scale in the USSR. Then came the Twentieth Party Congress in 1956, and the shocking disclosures of wholesale murder, jailing, and all other forms of oppression seemed to move the politicians as well as the artists toward a fundamental re-examination of the values and the political system in which they were living. The process of moral and political regeneration was abruptly interrupted after the unrest in Poland and especially after the abortive Hungarian Revolution in the fall of 1956. The Soviet invasion of Hungary signalled the return of the hard-liners to the forefront of political activity and the launching of an intensive anti-revisionist campaign both within the Party apparatus and in all walks of public life. The disclosures of the Twentieth Congress had an effect on the form and intensity of the measures taken against the so-called revisionists, but the ideological war was as intense as it had been earlier under Stalin. Therefore, after a very brief respite, the old bugaboos of American imperialism and Yugoslav revisionism were revived, and the search for and identification of internal enemies began.

In the literary community this meant doing away with the effects of the cathartic Second Congress of Czechoslovak Writers (April 1956); the first concerted step was taken at the plenary meeting of the Writers Union in June of 1957, where some of the activists of the Second Congress recanted and performed self-criticism. The process was intensified after the Twenty-First Party Congress of the USSR and the subsequent Eleventh Congress of the Czechoslovak Communist Party. In short order all the separate groups in the arts held ideological conferences with the purpose of purging their ranks of liberals and of those who had deviated from the hard-line tenets of socialist realism in their particular discipline. Thus *The Cowards* appeared at the moment when the conservative wing of the Writers Union was in the midst of final preparations for its ideological housecleaning, and the publication of the book took on the definite look of a deliberate setup.

It is of course impossible to determine at what point *The Cowards* was selected as the conduit for the conservative attack, but whether it was done as early as the spring of 1958 when the manuscript was being censored, or sometime in the fall of that year, the fact remains that a particular tactical move by the editors of the oppositionist literary magazine *Květen* (May) contributed to the decision to choose *The Cowards* for special treatment. The group of young authors and critics who had managed to gain control of *Květen* and who pursued a policy of polemical confrontation with the conservative groups had managed to obtain page proofs of *The Cowards* and, together with three other new novels, had them pre-reviewed in *Květen*. Possibly in order to strengthen their position or, conversely, in search of still another confrontation, they solicited the reviews from the Slovak novelist Vladimír Mináč, who was well connected within both the Party and the Writers Union and who in 1958 was a peculiar maverick hard-liner. Whether deliberately or unwittingly, *Květen* gambled in choosing Mináč, and insofar as *The Cowards* and Škvorecký were concerned, the move backfired. In fact, as will be demonstrated, the affair was the kiss of death to the magazine as well.

Not surprisingly, Mináč did not like *The Cowards*. A professed socialist realist, though not of the Lukács school, he considered the work of the young Czech writers to be chaotic, and additionally, he did not like their penchant for Anglo-American literature: 'There is a chaos in them, and not only chaos that indicates searching, but also chaos that comes from a lack of knowledge. ... A clearer picture of the attempts of some of our young writers is afforded by their loves and inclinations. The names mentioned here are usually those of Hemingway, Faulkner and Dos Passos, but also those of Joyce, Proust and Kafka. I do not know to what extent the inclination toward these names represents only an empty faddish gesture and to what extent it is based on real knowledge and experience.'[3] Needless to say, the first three authors belonged among Škvorecký's favourites, and he had written and translated extensively from their work.

In Mináč's review there is a clear preference for the books of the other three Czech authors discussed (Ptáčník, Otčenášek, and Lustig), with Ptáčník's *Město na hranici* (The Town on the Frontier) receiving special praise as 'a strong novel with weak points.'[4] Still positive about Otčenášek's 'Romeo, Juliet, and Darkness,' Mináč felt that it 'could have been more focused,' while Lustig (*Diamonds of the Night*) he considered to be 'an exceptional talent who ... should become independent ... and stop emulating his American literary models.' By comparison, the review of *The Cowards* was wholly negative. It seems that Mináč considered the novel an exercise in literary brinkmanship.

The Cowards moves on the border between literature and pamphlet, between revolt against convention and anarchy, between good and bad taste, and on the border of chasteness ... The book presents a one-sided view, a surface psychology, a psychology of gesture ... It is one-sided and therefore distorting. Only in some places is it really strong; for the most part it is only 'machismo.' It is Danny's gesture and the author's gesture that is used to throw dirt, too much dirt, so much dirt in fact that it finally becomes incredible and we don't believe it ... And, my god, I am really not prudish or oversensitive about these things, but why is there so much lewdness here? Obscenity loses its charm when the boundaries of chastity are obliterated, and in this case they were.

Apparently there is a basic mistake in the narrative principle. The use of the 'I'-form did not allow the author the distance from his character, his illumination from another side, the judgment of the character ... So the blasphemy that in many cases is justified turns into a mean and sometimes even cynical sneer.

No doubt it is an interesting look and many things are seen freshly and revealingly, without myths, legends, or illusions. But it is a view that is interesting at all cost, at the cost of truth and true dimensions.

While Mináč's article has very little, if any, critical validity and was subsequently refuted point by point in *Květen* by Josef Vohryzek,[5] it is very important within the context of the campaign against Škvorecký, for it served the authors of subsequent reviews and essays as a theoretical model from which they freely drew and modified their ideas. It is also quite likely that the article was used by the appropriate officers of the ideological section of the Party in drawing up the directives according to which the campaign against Škvorecký was then co-ordinated.

Vohryzek's polemical reply to Mináč illustrates the tremendous gap that existed at the time between the liberal democratic movement in Czech literature and the conservatives. It points out the fundamental misunderstanding of Škvorecký's method and purpose in writing the book and maintains that Škvorecký's work is not only authentic and original but also ideologically quite sound. While the polemic in *Květen* was under way, two more positive reviews appeared: first Svatoslav Svoboda wrote in the daily *Mladá fronta* (Youth Front) about the changing nature of the contemporary literary hero. Svoboda begins with an examination of books by Lustig and Otčenášek, then turns to *The Cowards* and relates Danny Smiřický to the more schematically positive characters of the other authors: 'For various reasons Škvorecký's *The Cowards* might appear alien in this conjugation. And indeed Danny's view of the people ... is marked by the faintness of the Occupation; it requires very little to make Danny satisfied ... And yet even this hero who finds himself at the very edge of a terrifying caricature, of a cynical sneer – and who has much in common with our own hooligans – suddenly finds an altogether different note. Maybe only for a short while. Who knows? But it relates him to the other heroes.'[6] Then Jiří Lederer wrote a short laudatory piece in the Prague tabloid *Večerní Praha* (Evening Prague).

You read the novel with bated breath. Not because you are afraid for the embarrassing little characters, silly and swollen with gluttonous selfishness, but simply because – it is well written. The novel surprises, provokes the reader, elicits arguments – actually calls for them. If for no other reason than because nobody has ever written about the May revolution like that. Nobody has presented such a deliberately incomplete picture of the revolutionary days, so terribly deformed through focusing. But precisely this deliberateness renders *The Cowards* into a unique literary testimony about the disintegration of the world that through the adult characters vainly plays at patriots, at fighters. Vainly, because not even the children – Danny and his whole group – can see its future; they have ahead of them only 'some new and equally senseless life' ... [By] revealing a considerable layer of dirt and cynicism, Škvorecký proves that his novel contains a powerful positive charge. He does not glorify the dirt; he simply says: This is how we lived and nothing can be done about it – and there is no point in writing about it with kid gloves. The novel's undercurrent leads the reader to a clear conclusion that life cannot go on like that, that the revolution is on its way with a scalpel.[7]

The notice had most unfortunate consequences for Lederer, who became one of the first victims of the anti-Škvorecký campaign. He lost his job at the newspaper and could not work in the field for more than a year. There was one other positive review in the Socialist Party organ *Svobodné slovo* (Free Word) by Vl. Brabec. The only remarkable thing about it was that it appeared after the review by Jiří Hájek in *Literární noviny* (Literary Newspaper) and indicated that the author and editors of the paper had either little political savvy or a great deal of courage.[8]

The first really important review of the book in so far as the general readership was concerned appeared on 23 December in the important weekly *Literární noviny*. It was written by one of the paper's senior writers and is a classic example of what Václav Havel calls dialectical metaphysics. It was, as the great dramatist would say, 'on the one hand good, but on the other hand also bad,'[9] and demonstrated above all else the consternation on the part of the old guard – that is, the majority of that group that did not belong to the decision-making inner circle with direct contacts to the Politiburo – over the very act of the book's publication. Obviously not having been instructed on how he should react, Hájek tried to write in a manner that would maintain the official critical line of the day, while at the same time allowing for a potentially positive interpretation of the review, should future developments move in that direction. Thus the first and last paragraphs of the piece are encouraging, while the middle part of the article contains the critic's reservations.

There is something quite appealing about Josef Škvorecký's first novel *The Cowards* – unlike others that we so often read. It is certainly not an overanxious book calculated for unequivocal consent and success. It is polemical and provocative from beginning to end. Under its excessively ostentatious and flashy literary stylization, gleaned from contemporary American prose and including many unpleasant details, I nevertheless find intentions more serious than a mere youthful attempt to cause a literary scandal, break a few windows, and find fame with certain provincial proclaimers of internationalism. This compels us to speak about it with the seriousness with which it is written. All the more so, as it is written with talent and cleverness.[10]

The final paragraph is equally positive and seems to be meant as an apology for the negative comments in the body of the article: 'Why am I telling the author all these unpleasant things ...? Because I feel in him a penetrating talent, despite all that is problematic and artistically derivative in his first novel. It is a talent capable of sharp psychological analysis, capable of fighting its way out of the excessive enchantment with its beloved literary mentors to some future original, rough, and uncompromisingly truthful look at reality, at the life that we are living.' And in an apparent contradiction of his own first paragraph, he concludes: 'It would be a shame if a person of his potential were to remain content with causing small literary tempests in teapots.'

In the critical part of his article Hájek reproaches the author for being too close to his character and thus being unable to pass proper judgment on his actions and philosophies. He also touches upon the far-reaching problem of truth in literature: he rejects the validity of the author's subjective view of reality and advocates the socialist-realist view of reality as it should have been. In the conflict between the real and purposeful, the raw and the processed, Hájek takes naturally the side of the latter, shielded by the ideological and educational utility of literature. In attacking the shortcomings of The Cowards Hájek fires the opening shot in the critical cannonade of invective. In comparison to what was to come, his was decidedly a small-bore weapon, but it did set the tone of the campaign. His reference to Danny Smiřický as 'a not yet full-fledged petit bourgeois clucking pullet, or rather rooster' initiated the theme of the denial of the characters' humanity and the repeated use of epithets from the lower orders of fauna and flora. He also introduced the term nihilism to describe Danny's depression over the sorry state of his own life and of public affairs at the end of the German occupation.

Most interesting, however, is Hájek's recognition of the novel's potentially harmful effect, which was, in view of the book's date of composition (1948–9), quite unintentional. Hájek accuses Škvorecký of failing to identify and analyse the root causes of the principal characters' aimlessness and failure to find meaning, but these causes are quite obvious to any reader (including Hájek) with an elementary knowledge of the effects of any form of prolonged terror on the human psyche. When Hájek writes that 'comparable feelings concerning life are elicited in one segment of today's youth,' he is unwittingly but quite correctly drawing a parallel between the effects of the terror during the German occupation on the outlook of that younger generation during the Protectorate, and the effects of ten years of Communist totalitarianism. It was not Škvorecký who drew the parallel; it was Hájek. Finally, Hájek accuses Škvorecký of a 'lack of measure and taste' and of using slang in a manner that renders the dialogue into 'a naturalistic photocopy of hooliganism in which especially expressions related to known physiological functions and appropriate bodily organs are emphasized with a demonstrative (but unfortunately cheap) pompousness.' And borrowing unabashedly from Mináč, he concludes: 'Here Škvorecký strongly confuses strength with machismo, and truthfulness with exhibitionistic tendencies.'

In a typically paradoxical exercise of wishful thinking the liberal Prague intellectuals preferred to see the positive side of Hájek's review, reasoning that neither Hájek nor the Literární noviny could have been expected to reverse policy completely and like the book unequivocally. Even Škvorecký expected the sort of criticism that Hájek sounded in his review.[11] He recollects meeting Kamil Lhoták, the designer of the book's graphics, who greeted him cheerfully, waving a copy of Literární noviny with Hájek's review and announcing: 'It's in the bag. We won!'[12] The jubilation continued into the new year, when Literární noviny published the results of an opinion poll in which prominent Czech authors were asked to name the contemporary Czech book that had affected them most profoundly. Of the thirty-one replies, there were four that mentioned The Cowards. The novelist František Rachlík thought it was one of the best books of the year. Karel Ptáčník actually gave a reason for thinking so: '[The Cowards] deals with the present in an unartificial, uncostumed, uncompromising, courageous, unschematic, and revealing way.'[13] And the highly regarded young poet Jan Skácel even wrote a miniature review of the book: 'I was captivated by ... The Cowards. It may be that his heroes do not have the brawny souls and powerful brains to be able to carry all the inner monologues ... and the author's dependence on models may well be great, but the book is not cowardly. Škvorecký knows life; he doesn't copy it from books or the daily press. His interesting view of the May revolution from below is well cast, and his crooked mirror reflects accurately. I am not saying that I liked everything about the book, but I don't think that the author wanted me to.'[14] Most interesting, however, was the reply by the almost seventy-year-old Distinguished Artist Karel Nový. After indicating the book he liked best, Neff's Císařské fialky (Imperial Violets), he went on to speak about two other books that he did not like quite so much. First he mentioned Ptáčník's 'Town on the Frontier,' 'a compilation of important material for the purpose of writing a great novel'; then he added the following: 'As far as Josef Škvorecký's The Cowards is concerned, the talented author reminds me of a kitten that is quite clever and worldly-wise, but that is also dangerously infected with mange. If it is to be kept alive, then one must do what the editorial board of Československý spisovatel failed to do: take it immediately to a veterinarian!'[15]

For a week nothing happened, but the 'veterinarians' were getting their instruments ready. On 11 January 1959 the trade unionist daily *Práce* (Labour) carried an article by Václav Běhounek entitled 'A Slap in the Face of the Living and the Dead,' and it suddenly became clear that *The Cowards* had been awarded the dubious distinction of selection as the *casus belli* in yet another Party purge within the literary community. The choice of *Práce* over the official Party paper *Rudé právo* (Red Rights) is noteworthy: although there was no difference in the orientation of the papers, priority was given to the unionist paper, which implied that it was not the Party alone that was dissatisfied but that the voice of the working class as a whole was being heard.

The initial part of the article was uninteresting; Běhounek simply repeated the attacks made earlier by Mináč, Hájek, and Nový concerning vulgar language, excretive organs, 'verbal athletics,' and exhibitionism. He then accelerated the attack and added some pathos and melodrama: '[Škvorecký] chooses as heroes of his novels zootsuiters who, during the horrible darkness of the Protectorate when Death lay in wait at every step for everybody, played jazz, wallowed in jazz, and made love to broads.'[16] To drive the point home, he accused Škvorecký of 'glorifying the lifestyle of his principal character,' and as proof he offered completely distorted descriptions supposedly taken from the novel. Here he was on fairly safe ground, since the novel had been withdrawn from the shops and libraries, and its author was in no position to sue him. To Běhounek, Danny Smiřický was 'a show-off, a cynic, a nihilist. [*The Cowards*] reads like a latter-day Sanin [the eponymous hero of Russian author Mikhail Artsybashev's 1907 novel], like Céline's *Voyage au bout de la nuit*.' Later in the article Běhounek also throws in Smerdyakov (from *The Brothers Karamazov*) for good measure. It is hard to imagine what the readers of *Práce* made of the references, since most of them very likely had never heard of Céline or Artsybashev, whose books were simply not available in Czechoslovakia.

Feeling compelled to refute the earlier praise of the book's formal aspects, Běhounek wrote: 'And what does Škvorecký's literary know-how mean? The Czech philosopher Klíma during the period of liberalistic capitalism promoted an aphorism that art in his day meant the presenting of a turd in pretty form – which sounds as if it were made to measure for Škvorecký's *The Cowards*.' The aphorism rhymes in Czech, but the sensitive Běhounek made a comical slip: 'Alas, I am not convinced that Škvorecký wanted to judge Danny. Rather he is laughing with Danny at the senselessness and confusion of the life and of the order for which we are striving.' In closing, Běhounek called *The Cowards* 'dirt that must be swept from our threshold.'

Běhounek's article was followed up in *Rudé právo* on 14 January by one from another prominent hard-liner, Josef Rybák. Titled 'Wormy Fruit,' the article concentrated on further discrediting the positive opinions about the book, which was compared to another of Céline's works, *Mort à credit*. The latter, according to Rybák, is a book so despicable that *Voyage au bout de la nuit* 'was by comparison harmless reading for girl scouts.'[17] Like his 'literary father Céline,' Škvorecký 'lacks taste and shame,' and like Danny, he suffers from 'jadedness, cynicism, and intellectualism.' Further on, Rybák writes: 'You see how the author delights in the moral morass, how he enjoys himself in his characters as one of them.' Later in the article the critic deliberately misquotes the text in order to show that Škvorecký insults the Soviet soldiers who were liberating Kostelec. In fact, Škvorecký is not referring to them at all but rather to the Czech Johnny-come-latelies who had both actually and symbolically joined the soldiers in their triumphant entry into the liberated town. The only originality that Rybák concedes to the 'cynical photographer' Škvorecký lies in his ability to 'show his own low moral character better than anyone before him.' On 18 January 1959 it was the turn of the Army daily *Obrana lidu* (Defence of the People). František Kejík calls *The Cowards* 'the methodological handbook from which the remnants of the Golden Youth draw their means of expression rather than, as was believed formerly, getting them from the ... penny dreadfuls, the illicitly distributed pornography, and the even more illicitly circulating trashy American literature.'[18] In Kejík's descriptions *The Cowards* gives the impression of being a dirty book: 'And as he views the women's world exclusively through visions of a gaping dressing gown or a raised skirt, so he regularly ends his zooter's twenty-four hours in bed, where he indulges, if we believe the author, in erotic thoughts only.' The writer also deduces that Danny is probably not good at playing his saxophone, 'because a good saxophonist is usually a good musician, and musicians are usually good people.' After Kejík's conclusion 'the book is no milestone but rather a wandering stone,' the weekly publications took over from the dailies.

First Jan Nový (the son of Karel Nový) wrote a long piece entitled 'The Zooters' Zoology' for the Party weekly *Tvorba* (Creation), in which he added nothing substantive but did use a few new epithets such as 'seething hotbed,' 'moral mould' and 'warped individuals' in his description of 'epicurean living according to the law of *carpe diem.*'[19] Otherwise he borrowed Mináč's 'one-sidedness ... that falsifies the truth of life,' repeated Rybák's and Běhounek's anathematic 'nihilism and cynicism of Sanin and Céline,' and blatantly plagiarized Mináč's view of the book as 'a pamphlet of reality.' He also accused Škvorecký of 'using weapons from the verbal arsenal of Goebbels' and of desecrating 'things that to everyone are almost sacred through the use of coarse, insulting words and a repulsive tone.' An unintentional light note is added to the article when Nový, in trying to borrow Rybák's 'moral morass' (*marast* in Czech), uses the word *marasmus* instead. On second thought, it may not have been a malapropism at all, for Nový concluded sadly that 'the book written ten years ago has now become a stimulant for snobs whose taste buds have become dulled and need a spicy "enticement."'

One of the symptoms of marasmus may also be the 'odour of decay of the Golden Youth and the breath exuded by the concoction of American contemporary literature,' as noted in the introduction to the revised views of Jiří Hájek toward *The Cowards*, which appeared on 17 January 1959 in *Literární noviny*.[20] There are two interesting points concerning this piece. First, it was supposed to have been delivered as a speech on 8 January at the Tenth Plenary Conference of the Central committee of the Czechoslovak Writers Union, a fairly large forum that included, among others, Ladislav Fikar. Yet, until the attack in *Práce* three days later, Škvorecký was unaware of the magnitude of the storm that was gathering around him. The second point of interest is that Hájek had not yet received clear instructions, as he still labelled Škvorecký 'the talented young author.' He must have none the less been aware of something, because in a radical departure from his earlier opinion, he now called the book, 'an oftentimes revolting and tasteless as well as extremely naïve bookish alchemy written according to poorly digested literary models calculated solely for effect.' He went on to say that he saw *The Cowards* as 'a symptom of the atmosphere that has an effect on parts of literature ... and that also has considerable influence on the creation of artistic criteria and opinions concerning what is and is not art, what is really modern and contemporary, what is useful forever, and what is good only for immediate social consumption.'

Next the voice of the military was heard once again in Ivo Štuka's 'I Disagree with *The Cowards*!,'[21] in which he tries to present a condemnation of the novel on behalf of the insulted younger generation. After the customary borrowing from his predecessors, Štuka concludes hysterically: 'Škvorecký in *The Cowards* naturalistically distorted the picture of the May events and of our youth. This is why I disagree with the opinion on the dust jacket that the book is a satire of the middle class. Rather, I maintain that it is the credo of the petite bourgeoisie. And I protest against it!' If the article in *Československý voják* (The Czechoslovak Soldier) was meant to show the anger of the young people in uniform (Štuka pointed out that he was five years younger than Danny Smiřický), then Jan Kloboučník's 'Why Do We Have *The Cowards*?' in *Mladý svět* (The World of Youth) was presumably supposed to express the dissent of the other part of the nation's youth.[22] Kloboučník answers the title question by declaring *The Cowards* to be an intolerable 'artistic-political program ... that must be rejected'; and just in case young people should become interested in all that wickedness, he declares the book boring because it is full of 'verbal trickery, lacks character development,' and generally contains nothing but 'horror from emptiness, horror from hopelessness, horror of life.'

On 29 January Škvorecký achieved another distinction when he became the subject of a 'satirical' poem by Karel Bradáč. Called 'In the Café,' it was published in *Dikobraz* (Porcupine), a national satirical magazine.[23] Since *Dikobraz* invariably dealt only with matters that were no longer current, it may have been assumed that the affair of *The Cowards* was finally over; but that was not the case. After an embarrassing and sad attempt at a review in the literary-critical journal *Host do domu* (A Guest to the House) by its managing editor Bohumír Macák, in which the basic incompatibility between critical integrity and Party discipline was clearly demonstrated and in which the author's shame could be read between the lines, came the final heavy rounds of the campaign. The venue now moved to the monthly journals and to the lecterns at public gatherings, from which the highest officials of the Party and the Writers Union condemned the book and its author.

First came an unsigned long article in the Party theoretical organ *Život strany* (Party Life), 'To Instill Culture and the Arts with Party Spirit,'[24] a call to arms in the fight against revisionism. After *Květen* was attacked as 'the tribune of a few over-intellectualized "theoreticians" who are poisoning the healthy flow of ... socialist literature,' Škvorecký was singled out as one 'who has assumed an ideological position completely alien to the Party.' The essay then continued: 'One of the most shameless examples [of revisionistic tendencies] is Škvorecký's "novel" *The Cowards*, which brutally insults our national and democratic revolution and disparages the liberating role of the Soviet Army.' Without again mentioning Škvorecký by name, the article then calls for vigilance, 'because here in the sphere of ideology and culture the revisionists and international imperialists concentrate their diversion ... It is not by accident that the enemies, who range in touching unity from Yugoslav revisionists to the émigrés of Radio Free Europe, encourage our artists to create works independent of Party politics and the interests of the people. They call on the artists to promote ideas in their works that would by implication lead to the weakening of the moral and political unity of the people, to the strengthening of bourgeois individualism, and to civic passivity.' These words, which now sound absurd, had an ominous ring about them at the time – although, as Škvorecký writes, 'they were published in a journal that nobody read.'[25] In 1959 people were still being jailed for lesser transgressions of the Communist Party line.

On 1 and 2 March 1959 the Congress of the Writers Union took place in Prague. The major ideological and programmatic statement was made by Ladislav Štoll, Deputy Chairman of the Czechoslovak Academy of Sciences and Rector of the Institute of Social Sciences, which was attached to the Central Committee of the Communist Party and was responsible for ideological direction. Štoll was the leader of the ultra-conservative group in the Writers Union and the direct link between the inner circle of the Party's Central Committee and the writing community. Štoll's book-length speech 'Literatura a kulturní revoluce' (Literature and the Cultural Revolution) concentrated on 'doing away with the tradition of the spirit of the Second Writers' Conference.'[26] In the concluding portion ('New Perspectives') he criticized some of the writers who, according to him, had misinterpreted the message of the Twentieth Congress and declared that 'literary history would not be able to take a conciliatory attitude toward such works as Milan Kundera's "Monologues," ... the latest work of our very talented young prose writer Karel Ptáčník, or the book ... by the remarkable Slovak author Alfonz Bednár [*Hodiny a minuty* or "Hours and Minutes"].' But while his criticism of those authors was brief and mild, he reserved a different treatment for Škvorecký.

And finally I wish to mention a book that does not belong to the category of the work of the artists I have just mentioned. It is a book by Škvorecký, which I would prefer not to deal with at all, because its whole spirit is profoundly alien to our beautiful democratic and humanistic literature. It is an artistically dishonest thing, untrue and cynical. This was not caused by the theme, or by the choice of hero, or by the 'I'-form of its narrative, but rather by the author's ideological stand, his ideological source, which nurtures also his imitative provincialism of expression. The great historical event that our literature depicted in a number of excellent works with the most truthful and beautiful pathos served him as nothing more than a gaudily painted backdrop for the description of the amorous campaign of a zootsuiter. The whole composition of the novel is based on that campaign. The provocative piling up of expressive vulgarities together with the erotic exhibitionism of the story proves that we are not dealing with any artistic originality, but with a cheap, slanderous sensation, with something like a Czechoslovak best seller.[27]

Štoll's speech was the last important specific and direct attack against *The Cowards*. Other speakers at the congress paid their political tithes by attacking Škvorecký – the author Josef Toman, the professor František Buriánek – but their remarks were nothing more than echoes of Štoll's summation. At the important ideological gathering in June 1959, the 'Conference of the Cultural Revolution,' Škvorecký was already left alone.

The consequences of the campaign against *The Cowards* were far-reaching. The Party used it to purge the publishing house Československý spisovatel of all its liberal-minded editors and dismissed among others Kamil Bednář, Jan Grossman, Josef Hiršal, and Vítězslav Kocourek, besides forcing the director, Ladislav Fikar, to resign. Josef Lederer was fired from *Večerní Praha*, and the whole editorial board of *Květen* was scattered when the journal was closed down. It is one of the paradoxes of the system that the editors and columnists are usually meted out more severe punishment than is the author, because Škvorecký in comparison did not suffer as severely as could have been expected. He lost his job as associate editor of *Světová literatura* (World Literature) but was immediately hired by the parent company of that journal, the National Publishing House of Belles Lettres, Music, and Art. This was facilitated by the fact that Jan Řezáč, a well-connected Communist of liberal leanings and a former surrealist, directed both establishments. When the Party found out about Řezáč's move, pressure was put upon him to punish Škvorecký further, but this was solved by lowering his salary. At the end of the year Řezáč made up the salary cut by giving Škvorecký a bonus.

Other punitive measures included subjecting Škvorecký to self-criticism before his colleagues. To that end he was summoned before the Central Committee of the Writers Union. Škvorecký describes the session in *Samožerbuch*: there were the obligatory speeches by Rybák, Buriánek, and others; there was the glaring Běhounek, who grudgingly admitted that had he known Škvorecký personally he would not have been so hard on him; and finally there was the revered Communist author Marie Majerová, who silently chaired the session and who finally declared, 'The comrade is young; he doesn't know the working class. If you like, Comrade, come with me to my coal mine.' Škvorecký gladly went with Majerová to the mine named in her honour to meet the working class. As it turned out, he never did meet the miners, only a few bureaucrats and schoolchildren. He also never got to make his self-criticism. But the chairman of the Writers Union was able to report to the plenum at the Writers Congress that the author and the book had been analysed and criticized.[28]

Škvorecký's publishing activity was of course severely restricted. For the moment there was obviously no question of bringing out any original work, but there was also a major decrease in the number of translations and book introductions that he was allowed to author. Whereas in 1957 he had published six major pieces and in 1958 nine (including *The Cowards*), in 1959 only two introductions appeared under his signature, and in 1960 he was down to a single item, a publisher's note to Sinclair Lewis's *Main Street*. The first original work to appear after *The Cowards* was a short story, 'My Dad the Show-Off and I,' which appeared, with a delightfully Czech touch of the absurd, in *Plamen* (Flame), the new literary journal that was established to replace *Květen*, and that was managed by no other than Jiří Hájek. Škvorecký's story is followed in the issue by a piece from his erstwhile educator cum saviour Marie Majerová.[29] Škvorecký did not completely recover from the effects of the campaign against *The Cowards* until his full rehabilitation in 1964.[30]

The critics, on the other hand, fared much better: Karel Nový was named a National Artist, a title that accorded the highest artistic distinction along with significant tangible benefits. Jiří Hájek was named director of *Plamen*, while Jan Pilař, who attacked Škvorecký at a session of authors in Prague,[31] was given Fikar's position at Československý spisovatel. Josef Rybák became the managing editor of *Literární noviny*, Ivo Štuka was allowed to move after six years at *Československý voják* to *Plamen*, and another of Škvorecký's detractors, Ivan Skála, became First Secretary of the Writers' Union and eventually a member of the Central Committee of the Communist Party.

Finally, there is a question of why Škvorecký was singled out to serve as the catalyst in the showdown between the conservatives and the liberal reformers in Czechoslovakia. Apparently there were others who were being considered at the time.[32] Most prominent among them was Karel Ptáčník and his 'Town on the Frontier,' but he had received the National Prize for his debut novel *Ročník jedenadvacet* (The Class of '21) in 1954 and was a Party member with a strong class profile. Škvorecký, on the other hand, was the perfect victim. As a novelist he was a newcomer, he was not a Party member, and he came from a middle-class background, much like his hero Danny. Also, he had a doctorate in philosophy and could be tagged with the pejorative label of 'intellectual.' His background in American literature, his recent participation in the literary polemic on modernism in contemporary literature,[33] his interest in jazz, his active participation in and association with members of the Czech literary underground and with the group around *Květen*, as well as his Catholicism in an atheistic state made his selection obviously quite easy. That the consequences of the attack on Škvorecký were not more serious is indicative of the fact that, despite the temporary setback of the liberal movement in Czechoslovakia, the conservative faction was not able to regain complete control of the cultural apparatus, nor for that matter of the Party. Moreover, by now there was no popular support for the moves against him; on the contrary, *The Cowards*, which circulated illegally, became the most widely read book of the Czech literary underground, and its author one of the folk heroes of the literary youth of Czechoslovakia.

NOTES

1 'Návrh edičního plánu nakladatelství Československý spisovatel na rok 1958,' *Literární noviny*, 6:34 (1957), 11

2 *Samožerbuch*, ed. Zdena Salivarová and Josef Škvorecký (Toronto: Sixty-Eight Publishers, 1977), 124

3 Vladimir Mináč, 'O modernosti, svetovosti, a iných veciach,' *O literature* (Slovenský spisovatel, 1972), 38. The article is dated 1958.

4 Vladimir Mináč, 'Proud proti proudu,' *Květen*, 3:12 (1958), 666. Subsequent comments by Mináč on Otčenášek, Lustig, and Škvorecký are taken from this article, 666–8. Mináč mentions Steinbeck's *Of Mice and Men* as a particular model used by Lustig.

5 Josef Vohryzek, 'Próza dnes,' *Květen*, 3:14–15 (1958), 780–5, 842–6

6 Svatoslav Svoboda, 'Cesta za hrdinou současné prózy,' *Mladá fronta*, 12 December 1958, 5

7 Jiří Lederer, 'Zbabělci Josefa Škvoreckého,' *Večerní Praha*, 20 December 1958, 3

8 Vl. Vrabec, 'Trojí slibný úspěch naší románové tvorby,' *Svobodné slovo*, 30 December 1958, 3

9 Václav Havel, 'On Dialectical Metaphysics,' trans. Michal Schonberg, *Modern Drama*, 23:1 (1980), 6–12

10 Jiří Hájek, 'Zatím jen svědectví,' *Literární noviny*, 7:51–2 (23 December 1958), 4. All immediately subsequent remarks by Hájek are taken from this review.

11 *Samožerbuch*, 124

12 Michal Schonberg, interview with Josef Škvorecký, 1 June 1980

13 Karel Ptáčník, 'Novoroční anketa,' *Literární noviny*, 8:1 (January 1959), 5

14 Jan Skácel, ibid

15 Karel Nový, ibid

16 Václav Běhounek, 'Políček živým i mrtvým,' *Práce*, 11 January 1959, 4. All subsequent comments by Běhounek are taken from this article.

17 Josef Rybák, 'Červivé ovoce,' *Rudé právo*, 14 January 1959, 4. All subsequent comments by Rybák are taken from this article.

18 Františak Kejík, 'Bludný kámen,' *Obrana lidu*, 18 January 1959, 7

19 Jan Nový, 'Živočichopis pásků,' *Tvorba*, 24:3 (1959), 62–3. All subsequent comments by Nový are taken from this article.

20 See the introduction to Jiří Hájek's article 'Novoroční úvahy o nové české próze,' *Literární noviny*, 8:3 (17 January 1959), 1–3. All subsequent comments by Hájek are taken from this essay.

21 Ivo Štuka, 'Nesouhlasím se Zbabělci!,' *Československý voják*, 8:3 (1959), 24

22 Jan Kloboučník, 'Proč jsou tu "Zbabělci"?,' *Mladý svět*, 2 February 1959, n.p.

23 Karel Bradáč, 'V Kavárně,' *Dikobraz*, 29 January 1959, n.p.

24 'Kulturu a umění prodchnout stranickým duchem,' unsigned article in *Život strany*, February 1959, 209–12

25 *Samožerbuch*, 125

26 Ladislav Štoll's speech 'Literatura a kulturní revoluce' took up a full issue of *Literární noviny*, 7 March 1959. It was published separately first as vol. 16 of the series 'Otázky a názory' (Questions and Views) by Československý spisovatel, then later in Štoll's collected speeches, *Umění a ideologický boj*, vol. 1 (Prague: Svoboda, 1972), 202–58.

27 Ladislav Štoll, 'Úkoly literatury v kulturní revoluci,' *Literární noviny*, 8:10 (7 March 1959), 7

28 Jan Otčenášek, 'K otázkám ideové činnosti Svazu čs. spisovatelů,' *Literární noviny*, 8:11 (10 March 1959), 3

29 Josef Škvorecký, 'Můj táta haur a já,' *Plamen*, January 1961, 146–52. Also Marie Majerová, 'Divoký Západ,' ibid, 155–75

30 All information regarding Škvorecký's publishing activities comes from entries in the *Bibliografický katalog ČSSR* covering the years 1957–64.

31 See 'Záběry z některých sekcí,' unsigned article in *Literární noviny*, 8:5 (1959), which refers to the activities at the Prague Conference of Workers in the Arts and Culture.

32 Schonberg, interview with Škvorecký

33 See Josef Škvorecký's article 'Pokus o chápání modernosti v literatuře,' *Literární noviny*, 6:17 (24 April 1957), 6–7.

9

IGOR HÁJEK

Last Jitterbug in Prague: *Konec nylonového věku* (1989)

The plot of Josef Škvorecký's novella *Konec nylonového věku* (1967; 'The End of the Nylon Age') is quite banal. A young couple attend a ball. The husband observes with dislike that another man, whom he has for some time suspected of having an affair with his wife, is once again paying too much obvious attention to her. When the lover does not heed a verbal warning to stay away, the husband leads him out of the building and, having punched him on the nose, leaves him lying in the snow.

Of course, the skeleton story is amply fleshed out with circumstances and characters. The circumstances are momentous. Communism, which had been creeping upon Czechoslovakia since the end of World War Two, finally leaped upon it in the bloodless political coup of February 1948. But the afterglow of the twilight postwar democracy was not immediately extinguished.

In 1945, still shocked by the Munich betrayal, a large part of the Czechoslovak population had seen in the Soviet Union its liberator and a guarantor of future security for the nation. Soon, however, it became apparent that the manners of the new and powerful ally were too coarse for the refined Central European taste. When Andrei Zhdanov launched his brutal attacks on Soviet writers and artists in 1946–7, even Czechoslovak Communists tried to dissociate themselves from such primitivism and vowed that they would never adopt this kind of cultural policy. (They did, only two years later.)

With Soviet culture compromised and Soviet lifestyle found unattractive, except to the Party's most faithful, the traditional Western orientation of the country asserted itself again. As happened in other European countries, it was American culture that replaced in influence that of France, in particular among young people. After all, jazz and Hemingway ruled in Paris, too. On the Saturday of the crucial week in February 1948, when a coup assured the

Communist Party absolute power in Czechoslovakia, Václav Irmanov still sang in English the latest American hits on the regular radio program of Karel Vlach and his big band. It was symbolic that a ball sponsored by the Association of the Friends of the U.S.A., where the same Vlach orchestra dazzled the dancers with its Glenn Miller sound, should have marked, a year later, the definite end of that brief gilded age.

The formal 'American Ball' is described in Škvorecký's forty-thousand-word novella, which was written in 1950, though not published until seventeen years later. In contrast to the closing scene of *The Cowards*, where Danny Smiřický plays his saxophone and watches his fellow zootsuiters dancing in front of the bandstand, the young gentlemen and ladies here are all in evening dress. The atmosphere is different as well. If there was a vague sense of impending change in *The Cowards*, now the change has already taken place and an undefined premonition has turned into a foreboding. The plot is a classic triangle but only in appearance: the illicit affair remains de facto unconsummated, but politics weighs on the husband's mind as much as jealousy. In varying degrees, it is beginning to affect everybody's life.

The novella is divided into twenty-nine sections; in each the scene is observed through the eyes of a different person. At the centre stand Irena Hillmanová, whose thoughts we are able to read in six sections; her would-be lover, Samuel Gellen, a medical student, whose mind we can penetrate also on six occasions; and her husband, Robert Hillman, who meditates on his life and marriage in only three sections, although at some length. Besides this trio with improbably cosmopolitan names, there are a few other characters endowed with names of such genuine Czech earthiness that they seem almost out of place in the surrounding splendour. Jiřina Kočandrlová, Sam's overweight cousin, reveals her mind, mostly tortured by visions of her impossible figure, on six occasions. Martin Bartoš, also known as Monty, muses four times on his unpromising future in a teacher's post one hundred miles away from the glitter of Prague. The mental anguish of Franci, in real life František Stodola, who struggles in vain to master the tenor saxophone, is represented in four sections as well.

The names seem to have symbolic meaning. The foreign-sounding ones belong to people who can be expected in the end to emerge as winners whichever side may win. Besides the three main characters, others can be glimpsed in the pages of the novella: Michal D. Holliner, Nora Hausman-nová, Bedřich 'Pedro' Geschwinder, Renáta Mayerová. Most of those with Czech names look destined just to muddle through. A certain symbolism, too, could be read into the story of the Hillman-Gellen love triangle itself.

On the way to pick up his fat cousin, whom he is to take to the ball, Sam Gellen notices in the tram a golden-haired working-class beauty in blue overalls, a messenger from a world that eludes him because of his bourgeois class origin. In the final scene, it is the same girl who contemptuously passes by as he is lying on the snow-covered pavement, having been knocked down by the fist of the irate Communist Robert Hillman. Victory of the Party and the working people?

Even if it is, it does not solve Robert's personal problems. 'When he parted ways with his [upper class] family, he believed that only the road to the future, the road of the revolution stretched in front of him. But where has it led him? Where is he today? He reads the works of socialist realists, but he is bored by them, because they do not answer the questions he is asking himself.'[1] Marxism can provide no cure for private grief. Where his wife is concerned, Robert finds himself just as undecided and decadent, he fears, as the detestable bourgeois dandies around him, almost like a character from a play by that depraved existentialist, Sartre. Does Irena really love him? She assures him she does, but why then does she remain so cool and aloof even during their most intimate moments? And what on earth does she see in that degenerate Sam Gellen, with whom she spends so much time and who, despite his and her protestations, is very likely at heart a reactionary who should have been expelled from the university long ago?

Irena's inner life is less complex. Most of the time she is preoccupied with girlish mischief, gossip, and nostalgia about love and youth, which she feels she has irretrievably lost. Considering that she is in her early twenties, her near obsession with time passing is slightly surprising. In fact, throughout the novella both she and Robert think and act as if they were much older people (Robert is still an undergraduate) and had been married for twenty rather than just two years. It is only the dialogues, often playful and reminiscent of those in *The Cowards*, that sound appropriate to their age.

Sam Gellen, by all indications not quite a mature personality, occasionally assumes behaviour that would also be more convincing in a middle-aged gentleman, in particular when he encounters Robert. In his case, the discrepancy between age and manners is less conspicuous, because he takes great care to look and talk as if he had stepped out of an American film. Just like Danny Smiřický four years earlier in *The Cowards*, when, with Irena watching, he was being marched by a German soldier across the town square with his hands above his head.

There are other aspects of Sam's character that he shares with Danny Smiřický: pretence, self-deception, studied cynicism, and the futile adoration of Irena. Some of Danny's other characteristics can be found in Martin

'Monty' Bartoš, who by a curious coincidence happens to come from
Danny's home town, Kostelec. There are strong traces in him of Danny's
sentimentality and intoxication with city life and things American. Monty,
we learn, even speaks English with the accent of a born New Yorker. He
does not, however, follow Danny in playing tenor saxophone. That is left to
the unfortunate, unmusical, but jazz-loving consumptive, Franci Stodola. For
him, the ball, where he plays in a sideshow band, marks the end of a dream
when he starts coughing blood.

It is not difficult to guess that in his second book Škvorecký split the
person of Danny Smiřický, whom he had introduced in his first novel, into
at least two characters, Sam Gellen and Monty Bartoš, with a tiny bit left
for poor Franci. Apparently he was tempted to experiment outside the
confines of the first-person narrative that he had used in the overtly
autobiographical *The Cowards*. The results are not quite successful, since
neither Sam nor Monty is entirely lifelike, the former being even less
convincing than the latter.

Robert Hillman is thus left without a strong and integrated opponent,
both in eroticism and in politics. Perhaps one is not required, as he carries
on a substantial struggle within himself. Sam occasionally comes close to
admitting that the class he comes from has passed its zenith, and Monty
Bartoš probably doesn't quite believe that his imminent departure for the
wastes of northern Bohemia is a personal tragedy caused by an act of gross
social injustice. But it is left to Robert to torture his mind not only with
Irena's suspected duplicity, but with his inability to decide how to cope with
the problem as well. This he regards as a political failure. Faced with the
problem of a potentially unfaithful wife, he needs to reassure himself
constantly that at least his Marxist faith is intact.

In the 1950s and 1960s the only way to voice any doubts about the
Communist system was to put them in the mind or mouth of a negative
character, or at least a wavering one such as, for instance, citizen Brych in
Jan Otčenášek's novel of the same name (1955). Authors, however, had to
be careful not to overdo it and not to make the 'erroneous' ideas more
plausible and attractive than the ideologically correct ones. Škvorecký had
pioneered this technique as early as 1950, before it became a trick. At the
time of his writing *Konec nylonového věku*, the repugnant show trials of the
early 1950s had not yet started and not every Czechoslovak thought of
communism and socialism as dirty words. There was enough of a sense of
guilt for prewar unemployment and poverty as well as disillusionment with
the Western powers to make it difficult for young liberal-minded intellectuals entirely to disregard the aspirations of the underprivileged and to

dismiss the initial advances in social equality made under Communist rule. Even Sam, the suspected reactionary, claims that rationally he is on the side of progress, even if emotionally he does not belong. On the other hand, there is much ambiguity and ambivalence, too, in the anguished debates that Robert conducts with himself. The author does not appear to have intended to present a clear case for or against Marxism through them. While Robert is treated with mild irony, his Marxist convictions themselves are not ridiculed.

In this respect the novella seems to reflect truthfully the state of mind of many young people in the first year or two of Communist rule, when the system was still being granted the benefit of the doubt. There are certain omissions. Conspicuously absent, for instance, is any mention of people who emigrated after the 1948 coup; perhaps the frequent references to girls marrying foreigners and to relatives living abroad allude to this. One has to wonder whether a conscious or subconscious self-censorship was already operating in the author's mind. Or perhaps he anticipated the position that Company Sergeant Major Danny Smiřický would find himself in in the next book, *The Republic of Whores*, where he makes fun of some of the questions that torment Robert Hillman here, but is himself secretly troubled by them.

Konec nylonového věku was published in Czechoslovakia only in the fairly liberal climate of 1967; it is improbable that some of the political references in it could have been tolerated earlier. Yet according to the author,[2] when he first offered the book for publication in the mid-1950s, the cautious publishers sent it for advance advice to the censors, who, incredibly, objected that the novel was pornographic. Škvorecký was in fact invited to a meeting with the censors, where a bashful young lady could not bring herself to read from a long list of allegedly pornographic terms such as 'bosom' and ' thigh' that she had found in the manuscript. This could have been the censors' way of avoiding notoriously unpleasant and tedious haggling about politically objectionable passages, during which they would inevitably have had to show their hand. In any case, they advised against the publication of *Konec nylonového věku*, but passed *The Cowards* without any difficulty. The latter was published in 1958, and the rest is history.

Had the novella been published as Škvorecký's first book, would it have changed the course of his writing? Depending on the response, it might have influenced the order in which he went on to release his unpublished manuscripts. But the author must have felt that the splitting of the narrative self and the use of the third person did not quite mark the road that he should follow. Before any of his writing was published, he returned in *The Republic of Whores*, written in 1954, to Danny Smiřický. *Konec nylonového věku* reflects a time of transition in the early history of Communist Czechoslovakia. A typical second novel, in which the author experimented with a new technique, it also seems a work of transition in Škvorecký's *oeuvre*. Being a good critic as well as a good writer, he must have recognized that the experiment was not promising.

NOTES

1 Josef Škvorecký, *Konec nylonového věku* (Prague: Československý spisovatel, 1967), 93. The novel has not been translated into English.
2 In a recording made for students of Czech at the University of Leicester in the early 1970s

10

ANDRÉ BRINK

The Girl and the Legend:
Josef Škvorecký's 'Emöke' (1980)

The eighty-odd pages of 'Emöke' (published originally in Czech in 1963 under the more significant title *Legenda Emöke*) is an evocation of a week's sojourn, years ago, by the narrator, in some obscure Culture Centre in an anonymous Czech town.

...thirty years old, still single ... a guy who didn't believe in anything any more or take anything very seriously, who knew what the world was all about, life, politics, fame and happiness and everything, who was alone, not from incapacity but of necessity, quite successful, with a good salary and reasonable health, for whom life held no surprises and with nothing left to learn that I didn't already know, at an age when the first minor physical problems begin to herald the passing of time, at an age when people get married at the last moment so as still to be able to have children and watch them grow up only to find out equally fast exactly what life's all about ... (66).[1]

Among all the loyal Czech Party members there was one outsider, a girl, Emöke,

...pretty and still young, with a child, Hungarian and hence a fairly novel being, relatively unfamiliar, but then again old enough at twenty-eight, but with a child which I supposed would mean an entirely different lifestyle, and a foreigner, Hungarian, not too intelligent, slightly warped by that parapsychological madness, out to proselytize, but heaven knows how holy, the ideal object for a vacation adventure, nothing more than that, and yet with that terrible look of a little animal of the woods, with that immense self-destructive defense mechanism against the world, in a fog of mystical superstition. (66–7).

Almost inevitably, the narrator fell in love with her, only to find that, after an early marriage to a sadistic brute and her wartime experiences, she refused all further involvement with men, devoting herself instead to the pursuit of a purely spiritual life. In spite of her diffidence, a significant bond of sympathy came into being between her and the narrator; but at the critical moment his roommate, a sordid and cynical middle-aged teacher, intervened to 'warn' her against the narrator's dishonourable intentions. She turned against the younger man, and on the return train journey he took his revenge by using a seemingly innocuous guessing game (in which a group of people identify a person or object that has to be guessed, through a process of elimination, by an outsider) to expose the teacher's obtuseness and helplessness. Since then, the narrator has lapsed into the trivialities of everyday existence.

And in time, very quickly, I was permeated with an indifference toward the legend, the indifference that allows us to live in a world where creatures of our own blood are dying every day of tuberculosis and cancer, in prisons and concentration camps, in distant tropics and on the cruel and insane battlefields of an Old World drunk on blood, in the lunacy of disappointed love, under the burden of ludicrously negligible worries, that indifference that is our mother, our salvation, our ruin. (114)

What transforms a charming romantic recollection into a masterpiece of modern world literature is Škvorecký's astounding manipulation of structure, including notably his exploration of syntactic patterns and possibilities. 'Emöke' is told as a triptych, with the evocation of the girl turned legend in the centre, preceded and followed by a brief, italicized, lyrical prologue and epilogue. Both of these are concerned with the 'life' of a story: with the fact that, after something has happened, it gradually dies with the deaths of those involved until apparently nothing remains. But in the prologue some redemption is found in the suggestion that places and buildings may retain memories after people have died, 'for a hundred, five hundred, a thousand years, perhaps forever' (33); in the epilogue the image of the building is superseded by something even more vague: 'But perhaps somewhere at least an impression is left, at least a trace of the tear, the beauty, the loveliness of the person, the legend, Emöke. I wonder, I wonder, I wonder' (114). This seems to indicate that the 'canonization' of the event can be achieved through what has happened between prologue and epilogue, ie, the narration, the narrative act, in itself. This act is a response to, and a comment on, the 'indifference' of the final paragraph: it turns the flat statement into its own opposite, creating a fascinating paradox.

The model of the broad structure outlined here (*prologue/narrative/ epilogue*) is repeated in the syntax of many of the key sentences in the narrative itself, where it takes the form of *initial statement / interpolation / completion of statement*. The most obvious implication of this system of narrative would be that Emöke herself functions as an interpolation in the life of the narrator: before her there had been a monotonous and self-contained existence, involving also the engagement with Irene and the affair with Margit; after Emöke comes the resumption of 'indifference,' including presumably marriage with Irene and a renewed affair. At the same time Emöke, as an interpolation, stands on an altogether different level of experience, offering at least a view on the possibility of the Other, of Something Else. (This is why it comes as such a particularly shattering discovery that Emöke should accuse him of being 'just the same as all the rest.')

The function of the system of interpolations offered by the text is also indicated by the rules of the guessing game as explained by the narrator to the teacher: 'Start out with something very general, the best is to localize the subject, and then get more and more specific until you determine, shall I say, the exact coordinates' (108). This directly involves the complicated relationship between Emöke the girl and Emöke the legend. But it proceeds from her to the level of the narrator himself: *through* an exploration of Emöke one is led to a discovery of the narrator. One becomes the subject, the other the object, connected by the subtle and intricate predicate of all that happens between them. (The guessing game, which leads toward 'identification' – and to the teacher's lack of identity – becomes a metaphor for the novel's complex pilgrimage toward a definition of identity.)

The semantic and syntactic patterns of the narrative are all set in motion by the opening sentences.

The room's ceiling slanted downward. It was a garret, the window high off the floor – you couldn't see out unless you pushed the table over to the wall and climbed up on it. And the very first night there (it was a hot night, August, the susurrus of ash and linden under the window like the distant rush of diluvial seas, the window open to let in the night's sounds and fragrances of grass and grass-hoppers and crickets and cicadas and linden blossoms and cigarettes and from the nearby town the music of a Gypsy band playing Glenn Miller's old 'In the Mood,' but in an undulating Gypsy rhythm, and then 'Dinah,' and then 'St. Louis Blues,' but they were Gypsies – two fiddles, a bass, a dulcimer – and the beat wasn't boogie but rather the weaving pulse of the Gypsy, the leader embellishing on the blue tones in a swaying Gypsy rhythm), the schoolteacher began to talk about women. (35)

The gradual lengthening of the sentences is significant: starting with the blunt statement about the sloping ceiling, enclosing the room in its suffocating, cramping way; and proceeding to the reference to the window, which is almost unattainable; and then to the sudden invasion of the room by the sounds and smells and the immeasurable space of the night. Between the phrase 'And the very first night there' and its completion ('the schoolteacher began to talk about women') lies a whole world of emotional, sensual, and spatial experience, insinuating itself into that confined area.

It is no accident that this first 'opening up' of the periphery of the factual statement to an immensity of space should be concerned with music: Škvorecký's fiction is conceived and born in music. Every significant new transition or movement is heralded and accompanied by music and/or dance. And the sentence quoted above does not simply offer a prose 'echo' of blues rhythms, but becomes, in fact, a *manifestation* of that music that intrudes into the narrator's space and enlarges and compounds it. The 'normal' syntagmatic, linear progress of the sentence is interrupted and dammed by the intrusion of a new signified world, a paradigmatic or associative expansion of the moment.

In this lies an early key, not only to the idyllic and paradisiac dimension embodied in Emöke, but also to the tragically inconclusive nature of the narrator's experience of her: in a stylistic interpolation like the one cited (which prefigures the interpolation of Emöke in the syntax of the narrator's life) the new information does not merely form an isolated pocket within the motion of the sentence; it also represents an intrusion from outside (the night into the room). And in his brief experience of Emöke much of the narrator's agony will derive from the fact that he can never be with her in her 'pure' or 'absolute' state but that the outside world continues to intrude and threaten their possible togetherness.

An examination of key sentences and passages in the novel containing striking interpolations and parentheses brings to light a broad spectrum of 'worlds' drawn into the inscape of the narrator and Emöke. (This in itself demonstrates Emöke's warning about the difficulty of liberating oneself from the flesh in order to become spiritual: 'I pity you. Why? Because you may have to live many lives before you become perfect' (44). Those 'many lives' are represented, to an important degree, by the intrusions presented by the series of interpolations. But one should bear in mind that it is a two-way process: in one sense the 'legend' is constantly threatened by intrusions from an impure world; but in another the texture of that inner world is immeasurably enriched by the 'amount and diversity of material' joined to it.)

Perhaps the most obvious sort of 'world' represented by the interpolations in the text is the social – not, however, the social *tout court*, but the social in a broader spatial or temporal context (socio*political*, socio*cultural*, socio*religious*, socio*historical*). When, for example, the teacher is described, it is in terms of his social condition, followed by an interpolation that adds historical perspective: 'Before the revolution a day-laborer on the estate of the lords of Schwarzenberg, in his blood the congenital defiance of forefathers who had sweated over soil they never owned, he had been driven here afterward by that very defiance, that hunger for land; now he had his land, and he sweated over it like all his sinewy and unshaven forefathers had done except that now the soil was his.' (Once again more is at stake than the information conveyed: this information is of another order than that in the rest of the long sentence; it is based on conjecture and fantasy, it is legendarized reality rather than fact.)

Variations on this model recur throughout the text. The significant excursion to Mariatal ('Vale of Mary,' in itself a name of peculiar significance for the 'legend' of Emöke) gives rise to a new extended interpolation conjuring up the rustic, mythical past of the place; and within this interpolation yet another is contained: 'She was silent and just said Yes (she was Hungarian, she spoke a strange combination of Slovak and Hungarian and some Gypsy or Carpathian dialect) or No' (40). This is a crucial construction, since it offers, in a nutshell, the entire precarious balance of Emöke's existence, and the narrator's, on the knife-edge between Yes and No, acceptance and rejection, unison and solitude; and, through the interpolation, a sociolinguistic experience is used to demonstrate the paradoxical centrifugal-cum-centripetal structure of the narrative.

Soon afterward, when the narrator inquires whether she would consider remarrying, another striking sentence marks the new stations of development. 'No, said Emöke' – then follows a parenthesis of seven lines, recalling her father and her youth, before the sentence is concluded: 'I'll never marry again' (42). This interpolation finds a motivation in her past for her present refusal; and in the intricate web of the narrative this motivational function influences other interpolations in other sentences; in addition, it insinuates a similar motivational function into the part played by Emöke as an interpolation in the life of the narrator.

Hardly any dialogue takes place, hardly a character is presented without this additional social dimension appended to the unique or the personal. In technical terms the unfolding metaphor of the legend of Emöke is constantly enriched, paradigmatically, through metonymic experience. In narrative terms it means that this bleak Cultural Centre somewhere in the heart of Czechoslovakia is not an isolated locality: upon it intrudes, within it lies embedded, the whole of contemporary Europe, the 'Old World' – and even, through music, America; and within one brief week in which we witness the tentative development of a relationship between one strange young woman and one worldly-wise young man, the whole history of man becomes relevant.

This results from the fact that almost every interpolation embodies some form of return, either to a personal or a collective history: to World War II, which had proved decisive to most of the characters, to memories of a more pastoral and also more burdensome past before the Revolution, all the way back to the primitive and the Paleolithic ('I began to talk about the Mesozoic Age and the Cenozoic Age and about Darwin, about the world's evolving, the blind and inevitable course of nature' [41]) – a return 'back to the animal that once was.' Even the 'sourish liquid of village dances' is traced back, in the imagination, to 'the earth which purifies the liquid and transforms it back into the crystal flow of the spring of the valley' (which is a precise metaphor for the narrator's attempt to distill the purity of the legend of Emöke from his memories, through the narrative act [77]).

A major reason for this preoccupation is that the meeting of this man and this woman represents a 'new beginning' for both, and for the world, grasping back to 'the primal cave couple' in an effort to strip themselves of 'the psychoneurotic dross of conventional sentimentality that has been sloughed off on the relationship of the human pair by centuries of war and thievery and perverse mysticism and male servitude and male dominance (*Frauendienst ist Gottesdienst*)' (84). It is, essentially, a groping, beyond the reality of the woman Emöke, to the absolutely pure legend of Emöke (while, simultaneously, the opposite is also taking place in the effort to distill the real woman from the conglomerate legend!).

In this process time becomes of as much importance as space: just as the rest of the world is involved in what happens in this remote Cultural Centre, time present, past, and future are focused on this still point of the turning world.

And do not call it fixity,
Where past and future are gathered. Neither movement from nor towards,
Neither ascent nor decline. Except for the point, the still point,
There would be no dance, and there is only the dance.[2]

In the one decisive moment on the dance floor when the narrator loses Emöke for good, he grasps the 'whole truth' – the whole legend – of this particular girl Emöke, expressing it in this musical, lyrical, ecstatic way:

'First time, first time, baby, last time, only time too. Short time, short time, baby, first and last time too' (81). This is the moment the narrative as a whole sets out to recapture. The novel as such may be seen as the narrator's effort to reach beyond the customary syntax of his prose life to the still centre of that innermost interpolation, that mythical first time, last time, only time too. The rest is silence; the rest is indifference.

The elementary logic of the archetypical syntactic model lies in the fact that the sentence strives for completion. This striving becomes even more urgent when the normal progression is interrupted by an interpolation. This touches the essential codes of 'Emöke.' Emöke has persuaded herself that she has been liberated from the physical. 'You're still a physical person, you're still imperfect,' she warns the narrator at a very early stage of their acquaintance (41). For her, 'significance' lies in striving to be mystically united with God: 'It is all aimed toward God, she said. Toward becoming one with Him. That is the significance, the meaning of all life' (43). The narrator interprets it as 'that tragically desperate poetry of a desperate dream that is to come to pass only in the hereafter of the utopian world of future wisdom' (46).

But the narrator experiences a totally different urge, directed not toward God or the future but toward the present, the presence of 'Emöke, that story, that legend, that poem, the past, the future' (73), convinced that the physical cannot be discounted or excluded (he is haunted by her delicate, small 'dancer's breasts,' by 'the womanly secret between the girlish thighs'): 'Longing needn't be exclusively and solely physical. It can be an expression of love, a yearning for oneness. Longing is at the very source of existence, insofar as people are born of love' (71). (There is an exquisite touch of psychological and poetic truth in the fact that, in the crucial dance scene, Emöke is untouched by the narrator and set free into pure spirituality by her diametrical opposite, the physical, lustful beast, the schoolmaster. This experience liberates her from the 'legendary' to the 'real': 'and this was she, not a legend, but the real Emöke' (62–3).

In other words, the inherent urge for completion in the archetypal sentence pattern is echoed, semantically, by the narrator's urge to be unified with Emöke – an urge interrupted and thwarted by all manner of obstacles. And the final obstacle is time itself. Looking after Emöke's disappearing train, he thinks of 'the voice of a woman who is being transformed into the image of time lost' (91). Small wonder that this new *recherche du temps perdu* should also involve a resurrected and revitalized Proustian syntax! It is this search (exemplified by the structure of separate sentences as well as by that of the novel as a whole) that predestines the recurrent cyclic patterns in the narrative: epilogue linking up with prologue; the constant returns to the conversation with the teacher in the dark room; the incessant excursions into social or historical space only to return to the present, the *here* and *now* of the narrative.

At the same time these patterns – sentences starting with factual, mundane, or sordid statements, then reaching out to the distant, the enchanting, the legendary, or the imaginary, only to return, by a *commodus vicus*, to the reality of the initial statement – suggest Emöke's own vacillations of mind and emotion. After all, her very spirituality appears suspect (at least to the narrator, who may, of course, have his own reasons for trying to 'contain' her by explaining her!): it often appears to be no more than a defence mechanism to ward off a reality she cannot otherwise cope with, 'as if she were afraid I wanted to rob her of something, of the certainty she possessed and without which she couldn't survive ...; it was the expression of an ensnared little woodland animal, begging you with its eyes not to torture it and let it go, to release it from your power' (51).

The enigma remains sealed. This spiritual woman, yearning for a utopian hereafter, becomes the embodiment of the small 'animal,' the primitive being: in her most quintessential experience, dancing herself into oblivion, singing with total abandon, she is united with primordial shepherds in a primitive world. The woman is this Emöke, this mysterious Hungarian girl spending a week in the Cultural Centre, with her personal tragedy; the legend is Emöke, who gathers into herself all of womanhood, from distant past to remote future. The two are mutually exclusive. Only in one context can they be united, and that is in the narrative, itself the desperate act of a desperate man, created in an effort to deny indifference, pain, sordidness, and suffering, and to affirm the one moment in his life in which the universe became visible in a grain of sand.

NOTES

1 Page numbers in parentheses refer to Josef Škvorecký, 'Emöke,' in *The Bass Saxophone: Two Novellas*, trans. Káča Poláčková-Henley (Toronto: Lester & Orpen Dennys, 1980).

2 T.S. Eliot, *Four Quartets* (London: Faber, 1947), 9

11

JOSEPH N. ROSTINSKY

Catholicity as Textual Function and Authorial Creed in *Miss Silver's Past* (1989)

Postwar Czech literature, produced under the auspices of the state-sponsored doctrine of socialist realism, does not have many authors devoted to the popular genre of the detective story. Nor does it teem with interest in religious themes. It is, therefore, all the most surprising to find in the work of Josef Škvorecký a combination of these two seemingly disparate concerns, one profane, the other sacred. To estimate for the purpose of a critical evaluation where the former begins and the latter ends in his *oeuvre* would be so difficult a task that one might as well not consider it. For, after all, it hardly matters whether the detective element serves in the text as a mere narrative framework within which the religious idea can develop, or whether it is the primary building block of a story written only to amuse. In either case, the reader could not avoid being imperceptibly instructed, taught, as it were, a moral lesson, both through laughter and tears. It is, thus, the moral aspect of Škvorecký's writing that warrants interpretation from the viewpoint or within the context of Catholicism. It should also be noted that Škvorecký has acknowledged that Catholicism has influenced the philosophical content of his work.[1]

An approach to Škvorecký's work by way of its 'philosophy' is justified both by its intrinsic merit as well as by the precedent set by his own literary criticism. In his 1968 volume of essays on American writers, *O nich – o nás* (About Us, About Them) he assigns a crucial function in his exegesis to the data concerning each author's philosophical beliefs. This insistence on examining the spiritual substratum of some of his favourite writers enables Škvorecký to deal with qualities usually absent in the adherents of socialist realism. Škvorecký views the quest for truth as the writer's ultimate responsibility. The truth, for which the writer is to sacrifice everything, is also the moral imperative propounded in all his major works.[2]

If we were to follow the often concealed spiritual affinities one author shows for another, we might be in a better position to postulate – albeit *cum grano salis* – the multiple influences exerted upon Škvorecký's thought and craft. Indeed, we could even begin to discern in the text 'the spiritual kinship' (*vnitřní spřízněnost*) Škvorecký admits having had at one time with Ernest Hemingway.[3] Or, by the same token, being more receptive to the statement he makes, in the interview for *Listy*, that Evelyn Waugh happens to be his favourite among the modern writers, there is a possible clue to Škvorecký's preoccupation with Catholicism.[4]

There is no doubt that some supporting evidence in this respect could be uncovered, even though it would be rather difficult to pinpoint the actual influence exercised on Škvorecký's writing. For one thing, little is known about the process of Škvorecký's growth as an author. An accomplished translator from, as well as a brilliant interpreter of, English and American literatures, he tends to foreground other novelists' achievements and ideas while reducing his own thought to an appropriate commentary. As a result the basic tenets of Škvorecký's viewpoint are revealed, while the structural relationships of his entire philosophical system remain obscure. And yet it is precisely this kind of information that could facilitate the reader's appreciation of the ideational or thematic complexity of Škvorecký's thought. As it seems at present impossible to reconstruct the philosophical system from the evidence available, all we can do in this essay is to examine scrupulously at least some of the structural functions contained in the text in order to establish the salient nodes in the complex network of meaning. To this end I have chosen to analyse one of his most characteristic works, *Miss Silver's Past (Lvíče)*.

Miss Silver's Past is the last novel Škvorecký published in Czechoslovakia before his writing was banned there in 1969. The English translation appeared in 1974. The discrepancy between the two titles shows that a semantic shift occurred in the interpretation of the text. (Graham Greene seems to say as much in his preface to the translation.) For the English version mainly stresses the diachronical, the impact of the past upon the heroine's present condition, whereas the Czech original (translated literally it is *The Lion Cub*) expresses the duality of infant innocence and the danger dormant beneath the surface. Thus, the Czech title reflects the primary concerns of the novel in a more poignant way. (Though for convenience I shall continue to refer to the novel by its English title, my text will be the Czech edition.)

The story is written in the form of first-person narration, and is narrated by Karel Leden, an ex-poet and present editor of the state publishing house in Prague. Among the several roles in this suspense drama of temptation and ultimate fall, that of a private detective is particularly appropriate. For, as Leden admits, he is fond of detective stories, and 'read them carefully even at the time when they had been placed on the index list of forbidden books, somewhere between Orwell and *The Imitation of Christ*' (166).[5] This purported interest in detective stories coincides with the real interest of the author of the text, which unfolds like a mystery. Are we, then, to conclude that Leden functions, to some degree, as an authorized agent of Škvorecký's views? After all, the author admitted on one occasion that he believes that 'our lives are in fact detective stories.'[6] Or, is it more likely that the authorial voice is more evenly distributed among the dramatis personae? This is an important point because it could alter our perception of the author's ethical code. Last, but not least, it could also add credibility to Vladimír Justl's assertion that 'Škvorecký, as novelist, writes exclusively about that which he experienced.'[7] Obviously, Justl should know since he used to belong to the immediate circle of Škvorecký's Prague friends. (Not by chance is *Miss Silver's Past* dedicated to Justl and other friends in the publishing world.)

As is well-known, one's experiences are delicately bound together, often in a manner of cause and effect, with one's ethical code. This never-ceasing interchange of the conditional present and the unconditional past, as it were, creates a field of tension, a space for a drama that is just about to develop. In *Miss Silver's Past* this drama is construed through the structural features of a detective story, which – as Škvorecký indicates – ought not to be confused with those of either a psychological or social novel.[8] What this also implies in fact is that real people are not depicted 'but only real attitudes in their rudimentary manifestations.'[9]

According to Škvorecký, 'consistent realism' (*důsledný realismus*) is out of place[10] in a detective story because it hinders the reader's attempt at creating his or her own imaginative world of dreams.[11] This is in effect another way of saying that the genre of a detective story belongs to the category of escape literature. That, in turn, means that Škvorecký has chosen as a medium of communication the type of writing that the ideologues of the Stalinist fifties in Czechoslovakia labelled as decadent, 'low works' of art that were unsuitable for socialist culture. The argument brings us to yet another problem. It involves the concept of opposition in conceptualizing reality. Forced to choose between the officially protected ('high') and the officially rejected ('low') types of literature, Škvorecký shows a pronounced tendency to be on the side of the stigmatized. To support individuals and views seen as contrary to the interests of the state requires indubitably a great amount of resolve and belief in the righteousness of the persecuted. And this, conversely, implies a religious position.

It is at this point that we should pause and reflect on the function of the motif of sympathy for or empathy with another human being. This is of some importance especially in *Miss Silver's Past*, but it can also be found in such major works as *The Miracle Game*, *Sedmiramenný svícen*, and 'Emöke'.

A succinct description of the story of the novel – as Antonín Měšťan offers it in his study on Czech literature[12] – inevitably simplifies the complexity of the text. For the purposes of summary, it may suffice to say that the novel 'depicts the situation of the sixties in a Prague publishing house.'[13] And yet, though accurate, this is misleading in the sense that it does not explicitly point to the moral function the author emphasizes in his preface. He warns his readers to 'stop trying to identify your friends and foes with the villains of my fictitious story, and start searching your own conscience.'[14] The stress put on the concept of self-examination is obviously biblical. It is advocated in Scripture, and is often found in Škvorecký's writing. (Cf. *Povídky tenorsaxofonisty* [Stories of the Tenor Saxophonist], whose epigraph is taken from the Gospel of St John.[15])

The problematic nature of the individual value judgment is closely related to the concept of sympathy for another human being. In *Miss Silver's Past*, the author tackles the problem through the episode involving the editor of the state publishing house, Blumenfeldová, and her young protégé, Cibulová, whose unconventional approach to writing causes much commotion, ill-humour, and resentment. Due to the combination of racial prejudice and her unique experience of survival, Blumenfeldová, a remnant of Prague's Jewish population, typifies the iconoclastic extreme. Keeping ties with her foster parents in the West, she even looks different from the usually monotoned and monotonous others on the editorial staff. In order to have Cibulová's first novel approved and published by the authoritative lectors she is willing to use 'everything, including her vagina' (213). However, all her 'female' strategy ends in fiasco, in a sort of punishment, because her sympathy for the frustrated Cibulová is tinged with hypocrisy, which, in turn, negates the good she is trying to do. Thus, despite her effort and apparent self-sacrifice, she emerges, in principle, as a negative character because the contempt she has for the opportunism permeating all the strata of the state publishing house can be extended to encompass herself.

It is taken for granted that every attempt at categorizing things and people inherently contains the Procrustean danger of discarding that which cannot be accommodated within the given format. Therefore to minimize this danger in a textual analysis means essentially to make use of contextuality.

In this particular case it amounts to looking for a sort of concordance as to the distinctive characteristics of Blumenfeldová. There is no doubt that her action on behalf of Cibulová is based on deceit. She merely pretends to be affectionate in order to outwit the dogmatists, whose timid mediocrity rejects every literary talent. (As Procházka, the chief of the state publishing house, rhetorically asks: 'What the hell do we need the talent for?' [112].) We find the same idea of deceit emanating from a somewhat different premise in Škvorecký's *Sedmiramenný svícen*. In the story of 'Mifinka and Bob, the Killer,' Father Meloun tries to save the life of a young Jew by means of arranging a marriage with a Christian. This, however, violates Nazi law, as marriages between Jews and Christians are strictly forbidden. Nevertheless, the Catholic priest musters enough courage to oppose the inhuman treatment of the Jewish people. The cowardice of the others, however, interferes with his good intentions, and the priest is accused of deceiving the Nazi authorities. Father Meloun answers the accusation with 'dear sir, deceit – under certain circumstances – can turn out to be an act of Christian mercy.'[16]

The theme of deceit, as presented in the two texts, functions to reflect the author's moral convictions. He chastens, as it were, Blumenfeldová's excessive involvement with the men voting on the fate of her protégée's novel. Hence chapter 13 of *Miss Silver's Past* deals with the events surrounding the end of Blumenfeldová, that is, the termination of her job with the state publishing company after she fails to have Cibulová's novel published. As far as Father Meloun is concerned, his deceit is without consequences, and, as a result, he partakes in no further scheme that might save the young Jewish man. The episode is, in fact, presented as hearsay. As the reader has at his disposal insufficient information about the author's moral evaluation, he is compelled to pass his own judgment even on an act that exists only as a thought. He may thus raise a number of questions as to where the line distinguishing the positive from the negative, the moral and immoral, actually runs. And, how relative are the moral values at issue? Škvorecký does not provide easy answers, and, indeed, there is no need for him to do so. As previously mentioned, his intention to view social malice through the prism of humour and criticism implies deep moral ramifications that ought to corroborate the reader's awareness of the universality and permanence of ethical principles. Hence the problem of deceit is to be resolved with regard both to the circumstantial evidence and the pragmatic function of the story.

Justl, in the essay previously cited, refers to Škvorecký as a 'modern satiric moralist' who is in essence romantic.[17] Although we have already mentioned the moral aspect of Škvorecký's text, it will be prudent to elaborate on the subject in connection with humour. Since humour and criticism are the two essentials of satire,[18] humour in its various forms permeates almost all of Škvorecký's writings. This is one of the reasons for their immense popularity both in and outside of his homeland. Indeed, humour enhances the impact of social criticism, and amplifies the resultant meaning. That is why it deserves special attention in an analysis of *Miss Silver's Past*.

The proverbial 'traduttori traditori' connotes the inevitable harm that is done to the original text by rendering it into another tongue. Sometimes the item most obviously damaged is the character's personal name. In *Miss Silver's Past*, for instance, some minor characters carry such punning names as Kopanec ('Mr. Kick'), Dudek ('Mr. Hoopoe'), Cibulová ('Miss Onion'), and comrade Kaiser (comrade Emperor'). Even the so-called ordinary names, whose incidence is rather rare, evoke grotesque associations. Take, for example, the protagonist Leden, whose name translates as January. Hence the connotation or suggestion of a cold disposition. And indeed, in more than one respect, Leden is emotionally cold and always non-committed. As Ela Procházková, the wife of his boss who knows Leden intimately, tells him: 'Forget the whole darned thing, and go and fight for something worthwhile' (133). His indecisiveness in matters of principle, however, is offset by sensual desire. In other words, there is hardly anything cold about him when he follows his predatory instincts. At such moments, his surname is rather ironic.

The critical tenor of the novel is manifested especially through its depiction of the senseless destruction of the Czechoslovak cultural heritage and the Communist administration's malignant bureaucracy. Editing (or rather 'correcting') classical literature for the purpose of propaganda and indoctrination, damaging in the most barbarous way religious objects, desecrating sanctuaries of worship, these are some of the evils Škvorecký points to in the novel. He makes no direct comment on the actual situation; instead, he treats each individual problem by presenting an appropriate episode, a parable, as it were, aimed at the reader's moral judgment. Occasionally he quotes or paraphrases Faulkner and Hemingway. Particularly important in this respect is his use of Schopenhauer's comment that life is a sort of tragedy that in details shows the features of a comedy (204).[19] The statement could also be taken as referring to Škvorecký's idiosyncratic approach to the genre in which detective fiction is combined with satire.

Since the novel's title refers implicitly to Leona Stříbrná (Lenka Silver in the English translation), it is clear that she embodies the text's mystery. From the viewpoint of Leden, the narrator of the story, she is the only figure of the text whose characteristic features can be in a large measure defined by means of Catholic symbols. To begin with, her last name (Stříbrná or Silver) stands for purity and chastity. As Psalm 12: 6 states, 'The words of the Lord are pure words: as silver tried in a furnace of earth, purified seven times.' The symbolism of the number seven, the lucky Jewish number, as Škvorecký reminds the reader, is intrinsically connected with the succeeding happenings in which she is to take part.

Her mystery is her Jewish past, which she keeps secret as if afraid of being recognized as a survivor of the Holocaust. In the solution of the detective story we learn all the significant details which justify the story's murder. They also explain why she changed her name from Silberstein to Stříbrná, why she had the concentration camp prisoner's number surgically removed from her arm, and why she never mentioned her sister's engagement to an Aryan (Czech) poet who had backed out of his promise at the time of Nazi occupation. Leona's sister had been betrayed, and died in the concentration camp. She blames the unfaithful fiancé for this, and looks for an opportunity for revenge. This comes at the moment of an impromptu party where the traitor, the present chief of the publishing house (Procházka), and Leona meet, and take a ride on a boat named the 'Charon.' In a manner of speaking, the boat is crossing the imaginary Styx with a dead load. Procházka's death is described as an accident, and Leona, the executor of vengeance, remains unsuspected. That is, unsuspected by the police investigating the case, but Leden, in the 'elementary' manner of Sherlock Holmes, deduces the truth (262). He then uses it to blackmail the heroine.

Distinguishing Leona from other characters of the novel is her association with the sun or heavenly light. She is the symbolic recipient of the power of the sun that suggestively endows her person with spirituality. 'The whole surface of her body was receiving the sun like the Sacrament,' comments the narrator (11). The way she sunbathes is compared to the Eucharist consecrating the bodily elements that make her so beautiful (12). The water splashed around her forms a sort of halo (28), and the sun's rays expire on the surface of her dress in a vivid burst of colours (32). Indeed, this is a poet's description, the poet who rests underneath the mask of an opportunist moulded by the circumstances. It is Leden's portrayal of the *ewig Weibliches* that he tries in vain to reach. 'In my vision she was shining like an engagement ring,' confesses the poet, imbued with the unsatiated passion of a medieval *Minnesaenger* (60). He surrounds the object of his worship with epithets modifying the mundane and transposing it onto the level of the divine. 'She was beautiful, light brown, composed of symbols, the moon, a mystery, the baritone timbre of saxophone' (189). Leona thus emerges from the poeticizing as a series of metaphors. She is seen as having the attributes the Church usually reserves for the Virgin Mother. This becomes especially obvious in the following scene involving Leden. 'I set to writing a poem about the girl standing in the bowl of the crescent, about the snake, the Virgin comprising all the Catholic symbols, about Miss Stříbrná' (218). The above image needs no further interpretation, as it is a well-known topos of Catholic writing. It projects both infant innocence and the power-crushing evil.

Although Leden draws heavily on the imagery of the New Testament, he is a cynic whose viewpoint is rooted in the teaching of Ecclesiastes. Since he thinks that 'nothing is new under the sun,' there is very little reason for him to strive for a substantial change in the status quo. Everything comes out as déjà vu. Hence the motto tacked to his office desk, *festina lente*, which also captures the essence of the foot-dragging bureaucracy in the state publishing house. It is significant that in the initial stage of his quest for a kind of mystical union with Leona, Leden describes himself in Biblical terms. A typical example is the simile, 'Like the apostle, I left my finger in the scar' (13). He also compares himself to the Pharisee expiating his trespasses (70). To assume from this evidence, however, that Leden is a covert believer in God would be misleading. For in spite of the use of the Catholic symbols, he is essentially a product of the official atheism propagated in his Communist society. Hence, too, the certain amount of cynicism that can be detected in his use of Christian imagery in scenes of sexual frustration such as the one in which he is invited to Leona's apartment and attempts to force himself upon her. Being painfully rejected and finally told that he is only a scribbler who is not even fit to be a sincere lover, Leden objects with the commonplace, 'Oh God, don't say that!' whereupon he gets the rest of Leona's opinion, 'You do not believe in God, so don't take His name in vain' (189).

In the Czech text, the distinction between the two diametrically opposed ways of conceptualizing reality is remarkably expressed in the orthography of the utterance 'God.' When Leden speaks, God is persistently spelled with the small letter in order to indicate an ideological conviction. In Leona's speeches, the capital is used to indicate a humble and reverent attitude. It is the function of humility, especially as exemplified by Christ's deeds, which conveys the notion of a dramatic change of inner awareness. It signifies a stage of spiritual awakening that strengthens one's power of moral discrimination. In *Miss Silver's Past* the concept of humility assumes an important role in that it starts to modify, as it were, Leden's outlook on the real world. This gradual metamorphosis is simultaneous with the poet's quest for some sort of mystical union that involves Leona and the truth embodied in her mystery. Before the poet is endowed with the new vision, he has to pass through the stage of spiritual catharsis. Refused and humbled, Leden experiences the feeling of emptiness. This is his Passion week, and he realizes for the first time in many years that he is actually all alone in this world (139).

Since alienation is said to have disappeared under the socialist system, it is striking to see its effect upon a protagonist representing the state-sponsored culture. For readers indoctrinated by official ideology, it must seem almost bizarre to see the narrator described in Catholic images and symbols. As Leden compares his situation to that of Jesus Christ facing all the stations of the Passion events, he should, logically, take upon himself the suffering of the martyr, and the responsibility of the prophet. Yet Leden is not the martyr or *vates* in the strict sense of the word. He is above all a detective story fan enlightened by the knowledge of unreciprocated love. That is why his vision is directed toward the immediate present, but it is averted from the future, from the process of realizing the ideal. Since he lacks both the self-esteem and the confidence to pursue an ideal or to help in reforming the state, he only stands next to the crowd of would-be reformers, always doubting the efficacy of yet another cosmetic change of the political system, which does not reach deep enough to alter significantly its substance. Leden is aware of the spiritual devaluation of the times in which he lives and that he helps create (207). He is critical of the ubiquitous pretence and dishonesty infecting the entire nation, which is perpetuated by the poets and writers swearing by the dogma of socialist realism (243). Nevertheless, his ultimate observation sounds a pessimistic note.

The melancholy, amplified by the distant sounds of saxophone music, permeates a good portion of the novel. It surfaces particularly in the scenes where both Leona and Leden perform their parts, and functions as a leitmotif in the setting. Through the rhythm of jazz, the author introduces into the text the motif of sex, which is usually seen as an act of primeval spontaneity. It is as if the very etymology of the word *jazz* sensuously evoked the circumstances of its origin, so vibrant is its impact upon the text.

Melancholy is also evident in the questioning of the extant moral values that superseded the supposedly obsolete ethics of the outlived capitalist system. Leden realizes that the socialist society has become spiritually impoverished by its dismissal and negation of everything that smacks of the values of the past. Perhaps 'some old virtues' should have been preserved, he thinks, so that the brutality and hatred generated by racial and political prejudice could be avoided even at the boxing match taking place in Prague (136). This motif of the retrospective evaluation of the things past, of looking back at the irretrievable *aurea prima sata est aetas,* recurs frequently. In the chapter entitled 'Editorial Conference,' for example, through a concatenation of episodes depicting the intrigues in both the state publishing house and Leden's private life, the narrative culminates in the moment of the poet's aroused self-awareness. As if engaged in a sort of inner monologue, he addresses himself: 'And where do you actually want to go to on this path of your life without the Ten Commandments?' (165). The ethical teaching formulated in Scripture has a pivotal function in the narrative. It is stressed time and again at different points of the story, and foregrounded as in the above quotation by means of stylistic devices that form a kind of counterpoint in the composition of the text.

The evocation of the past for the purpose of comparing it with the present has as its corollary a gamut of symbolic associations that implement the meaning through an elaborate network of imagery. Some of the salient motifs presuppose throughout that the reader discriminates among the ethical values embodied in and articulated by the protagonists. However, some difficulties arise when it comes to the point of exemplifying the ideological mechanism by which the meaning of an utterance is turned upside down often to emerge in a grotesque form.

An example of the visual representation of this grotesque effect of the semantic reversal is to be found in a scene set at Procházka's luxurious house. The scene is brief enough to be easily overlooked, yet it illustrates the point mentioned. In the house of his boss, Leden suddenly notices that the cuckoo bird coming out of the clock door has instead of its own funny head the little head of the infant Jesus with a tiny gilt crown (249). The episode, referred to by Leden as a 'requiem,' links the grotesque with the tragic, which is in this case the death of Procházka (unmourned by wife and colleagues). Viewed from the angle of the author's attitude toward so-called historical happenings, the scene with the cuckoo clock only epitomizes the tenet previously mentioned, namely that life is a tragedy, but in its details it has the character of a comedy. This truism applies equally, on the level of macrodimensions, to communism, as the author points out not only in the story of *Miss Silver's Past,* but also in his *magnum opus The Miracle Game.* The question asked in this connection concerns the problem of the deified status of the Communist Party in power. Once the act of merciless subjugation of the entire political structure to the interests of the Party has been accomplished, the full-fledged dictatorship can proclaim its infallible and provident role as the sole arbiter of values, supplanting the function of God in society. Thus the displaced image of the Church is superseded with the image of the state, which merely executes the power of the Communist

Party. As a result, the hierarchy of moral values undergoes a corresponding process of semantic reversal. Hence the top stratum trades its position with the bottom, and vice versa. In *The Miracle Game* one of the protagonists puts it as follows: 'Do you want me to believe that the Party is God and that's why it may keep people under its absolute control? Do you want me to believe that mankind was created by Communists?'[20] The answer to the question suggests the function the Party assumed in society. It is the new Saviour, Messiah, as it were, and has the indisputable right to exercise his will, and rule over everything and everyone forever. Structured like the Church, the Party, too, has its rituals, martyrology, symbols, and myths – most of them borrowed from religious sources. It also assumes the rise of the low and the fall of the high, although only in terms of the social class. It erects its own sanctuaries of ideological 'invocation,' but at the same time destroys the consecrated edifice of the Church. The truth becomes inconvenient and is simply discarded in the name of a much nobler goal vaguely placed in the distant future.

The finale of *Miss Silver's Past* consists of Leden's lengthy explanation of Leona's crime. The scene takes place Thursday night and can be interpreted as Leona's Gethsemane, the night of her mental anguish: the chapter title is appropriately 'Black Mass.' Indeed even the moon is missing, and in its place there are the city lights devoid of religious connotation. Leona is thus deprived of her scintillating attributes. Trapped, she is full of scorn for the poet who is anxious to possess her body if not her love. As if written in the tradition of Minnesang, or through the symbolism of Joseph Roth's *Job* (*Hiob*), the rain in this final scene also signifies the fulfilment of carnal desires. 'I revenged myself on you, little lily-of-the-valley, forgive me, it was nasty of me, but I love you terribly' (269). Leden's soliloquy does not represent atonement. It resembles far more the momentum of stepping over the demarcation line separating the man of character from the real bastard, to borrow Ela Procházková's classification of humankind (135). Leden's attitude toward Leona thus exemplifies yet another aspect of the dehumanizing process that disintegrates the moral fibre of people in the totalitarian society.

However, the symbolic complexity of the text offers an additional, equally plausible interpretation of the story. In order to arrive at the meaning essentially complementary to the reading suggested above we need to read the novel within the larger context of Škvorecký's *oeuvre*, which, for our purposes, can be represented by *The Miracle Game*. Published abroad, it expresses in a more explicit way what the author meant to say through the symbolism of *Miss Silver's Past*, which was published in Czechoslovakia.

Both novels deal with the religious problem in a society advocating, even at the cost of violence and moral decay, universal atheism. Both novels have as their principal heroes young men (Karel Leden and Danny Smiřický), who search for an unidentified ideal, for the constancy of values in the world marked by the misconceived notion of societal relativity. Since each protagonist looks for clues that could help explain the mystery unfolding in the text, he de facto takes upon himself the role of a detective. The narrative then proceeds in the tracks of a detective story.

In *The Miracle Game*, the author reiterates that 'life is a detective story, the offender is the truth. It is a bad detective story. The offender always escapes.'[21] This aphorism, as the author terms it, actually provides the key to the text. Therefore, *Miss Silver's Past* could be also understood as a mere metaphor of the recurrent mystical quest of the Romantic for the ideal blue flower. Thus, the colour symbolism is as important as the topos of nature in the story. When Leden meets Leona for the first time, for example, she is wearing a blue bathing suit. Indeed, she personifies both the power and danger of the truth. That is why Leden can tell her, 'I am not myself any more because of you' (118). She is the truth that Leden can only identify and temporarily violate, but he cannot ultimately possess it because his quest lacks sincerity and the will to sacrifice oneself. In this respect, Leden, the poet of mediocre qualities, the non-committed observer, unpartisan opportunist, and so on, epitomizes the type of man against whom Škvorecký's satire is aimed.

What remains to be elucidated is the pragmatic approach toward the issue of faith. In the previously mentioned interview in *Listy*, Škvorecký states, 'For me, Christianity is the beautiful and deepest democracy' because it contains the idea of equality of all the souls before God, and leaves to each individual human being to decide what one wishes to do with one's life and soul.[22] The pragmatic function Škvorecký singles out from the concept of belief is also reflected in the choice of textual devices employed in his work. Back in Prague, the choice seems to have been made along the axis of binary opposition. On the one hand, it was the Party with its atheism, and, on the other hand, the persecuted Church with its traditional ethics. While Christianity stands for the perfect democracy, the social order advocated by the Party is a dictatorship. The positive or the negative – that is the choice the real writer, the genuine poet, has to make; it is the crucial idea embedded in Škvorecký's *oeuvre*. The zero of non-commitment as portrayed by Leden is a meaningless option, albeit precarious, as more often than not it helps the evil continue its destructive work.

Miss Silver's Past clearly documents the consistency of choice Škvorecký has made in his life. Travelling the rough road, he has entered the narrow gate that leads to life, and 'How few there are who find it!' (Matthew 7: 14).

NOTES

The translations from the Czech are by the author.

1 Antonín Liehm, 'Hovoří Josef Škvorecký,' *Listy*, 3 (16) (1986): 193–8
2 Josef Škvorecký, *O nich – o nás* (Hradec Králové: Kruh, 1968), 37
3 Josef Škvorecký, 'Ještě o kritice vraždící,' *Host do domu* 7 (1967), 73
4 Liehm, 197
5 Josef Škvorecký, *Lvíče* (Toronto: Sixty-Eight Publishers, 1974). Page references in the text of the essay are to this edition.
6 Josef Škvorecký, 'Cesta (s překážkami) za Egonem,' in *Egon Hostovský*, ed. Rudolf Sturm (Toronto: Sixty-Eight Publishers, 1974), 56
7 Vladimír Justl, 'O nich – sobě,' in Škvorecký, *O nich – o nás*, 194
8 Josef Škvorecký, *Miss Silver's Past*, trans. Peter Kussi (New York: Ecco, 1985), 11
9 Ibid
10 Josef Škvorecký, *Nápady čtenáře detektivek* (Praha: Československý spisovatel, 1965), 159
11 Ibid, 151
12 Antonín Měšťan, *Česká literatura 1785–1985* (Toronto: Sixty-Eight Publishers, 1987), 374
13 Ibid
14 *Lvíče*, upozornění (n.p.)
15 Josef Škvorecký, 'Povídky tenorsaxofonisty: Malá pražská Matahara,' *Host do domu* 4 (1967): 20
16 Josef Škvorecký, *Sedmiramenný svícen* (Zürich: Konfrontace, 1974), 62
17 Justl, 205
18 Peter Petro, *Modern Satire: Four Studies* (Amsterdam: Mouton, 1982), 8
19 Cf. 'The Troublemaker,' *New Republic*, 7 March 1988, 38.
20 Josef Škvorecký, *Mirákl*, vol. 2 (Toronto: Sixty-Eight Publishers, 1972), 201
21 Ibid, 254
22 Liehm, 197

12

JAN KOTT

The Emigrant as Hero: *The Engineer of Human Souls* (1984)

After spending the first year of my two-year leave from the University of Warsaw at Yale, I spent the second, and what was to have been my last year in the United States, lecturing at Berkeley. I was supposed to return to Warsaw in the fall of 1968 at the latest, but as early as the winter of 1967–8 the news from Poland was getting grimmer. Friends warned me not to return. 'Stay as long as you can!' In the letters that got by the censors, they wrote about an anticipated 'night of long knives,' about what was almost outright anti-Semitism in the Party apparatus, and about the increasingly brutal attacks on revisionists. At the same time, in Czechoslovakia, the system of oppression was slowly crumbling. Letters from my Czech friends were full of optimism. It was then, probably in December 1967, when people were beginning to write about 'socialism with a human face,' that I was invited to lecture at Charles University in Prague, and I accepted. I thought that I would be close to Poland in Prague, and that if I could wait out the storm, I might be able to return to Poland in time for a renewal.

The 'Prague Spring' did not even last three months. In August 1968, Soviet tanks rolled into Prague, and 'fraternal' Polish armies crossed the Czech border to defend socialism. In Warsaw, there were 'anti-Zionist' marches and rallies. Friends feared pogroms. In 1968 I became an 'emigré.' Josef Škvorecký became one in January 1969.

The word *alien* derives from the Latin *alienus, alius*, meaning 'other.' An 'alien' is someone transplanted to foreign soil. An 'alien' is an exile, a refugee, an émigré, or an emigrant, whether by his own will or by dint of necessity. For fifty years the predicament of the emigré has become almost the universal experience of the second half of the twentieth century. How many of these 'aliens' are there in the world? Not even the High Commissioner for Refugee Affairs at the U.N. is capable of giving an approximate number. Are there ten, fifty, or a hundred million of them? Of these millions of refugees and displaced persons, the emigrés from Central Europe (which was also geographically displaced to Eastern Europe after Yalta) make up only a small percentage. But it is not everywhere that history reveals its destructive force and is let off the leash (as one of my old teachers was wont to say) at the same time. The Hungarian emigrés of 1956, the Czechs of 1968, the Poles of the 'infamous March' of 1968, and the Poles who left Poland after the defeat of Solidarity in 1981, all bring with them experiences which, for the lucky non-aliens of Western Europe and America, are a history lesson as bitter as it is instructive.

The oldest of these emigrés were born at the beginning of the World War I and were already in their twenties at the outbreak of World War II. In many cases they experienced both Nazi occupation and Stalinist terror on their own soil. For the younger emigrés, the first history lesson came in 1968; for the youngest, in December 1981. But young or old, all of these refugees from Hungary, Poland, and Czechoslovakia had behind them three months (or even just three weeks) of hope. It was only when the renewal turned out to be an illusion that they decided to emigrate, often to a country where there was also no hope, but in which life was at least free from fear.

The Toronto skyline is more beautiful to me than the familiar silhouette of Prague Castle. There is beauty everywhere on earth, but there is greater beauty in those places where one feels that sense of ease which comes from no longer having to put off one's dreams until some improbable future – a future inexorably shrinking away; where the fear which has pervaded one's life suddenly vanishes because there is nothing to be afraid of.[1]

Thus the first-person narrator of *The Engineer of Human Souls*, the Czech writer Danny Smiřický, who left his country in 1968 and who, like Josef Škvorecký, teaches English literature in Toronto. Except for the fact that the name of the college has been altered (from Erindale to Edenvale), the incidents and dates connected with the main character and the author are identical. Škvorecký's novel does not seem to fit into the category of either autobiography or novel, which accounts for its originality. Yet the communication of an experience and its scope is far more important than artistic innovation.

In *The Engineer of Human Souls*, there is a present time and many past times. The present time takes place in the mid-1960s in a suburb of Toronto called Edenvale. The past times encompass the forties, fifties, and sixties in Czechoslovakia. But these pasts do not organize themselves chronologically, nor are they rendered as a steady stream of reminiscences. Instead, the book unexpectedly cuts away, like a camera, to foreign landscapes and other times. The constant jumping back and forth from one time to another seemed to me, at first reading, to be an overwrought narrative sophistication, a needless obstacle for the reader to overcome in following the vicissitudes of the characters. Later I realized that the author was right. The past always remains in the memory in a tangled synchrony. And an emigrant's past, more than anyone else's, is a second present time. It keeps opening, like a badly healed wound.

The past also returns in another way: in letters. The narrative in Škvorecký's novel, from the first chapter to the last, is constantly being interrupted by letters from Czechoslovakia and from the four corners of the earth to which all his old friends and acquaintances have been scattered. These letters, too, seemed schematic and superfluous at first, an interference with the narrative; again, about halfway through the book, I had to admit that the author was correct in including this minor epistolary novel in his work. The biographies of each of us emigrants – and this is even more true of emigrant writers – are discontinuous, as if they were cut off midway and made up of two sections that do not want to grow together. And the biographies of our friends, of those friends who remained behind and of those who left, are also discontinuous. They are full of blank pages, empty years. It is only in letters that the stories of their lives merge and form one collective destiny.

But past time returns not only in letters. Acquaintances come to visit, sometimes only the acquaintances of acquaintances: musicians or actors on tour; the Czech, Polish, and Hungarian wives of foreigners; *provocateurs*; informers; police agents of both sexes on special assignment. The past of the political émigré is never quite closed or written off as a loss once and for all. There are always some unsettled accounts that are usually quite personal and quite common. Each letter from the homeland fills one of these blank pages, as does each encounter.

At all those emigrant gatherings in all the vales of Eden, the New Havens, or Stony Brooks, the conversations are carried on in the native tongue of the particular group. In the first hour, before the bottle of slivovitz or vodka is emptied, every second sentence is patiently translated into broken English for the Canadian husbands or American boyfriends. (What for? They don't understand a thing, anyway!) The emigrés talk about nothing but their native land – how it was there, and how it will be in the future. You really think that it could happen one more time? In *our* lifetime? Each person tells his own story; the life stories of the emigrés are a chapter out of the collective history of that country, the weaving of a collective destiny from incoherent and astigmatic scraps of reminiscences, pieces of paper, and eternal conversations: these are the only things that make up the 'recovered time' of the emigrés.

In *The Engineer of Human Souls* Prema Skočdopole was the narrator's colleague in the small city of Kostelec, not far from the Polish border. He formed a group of saboteurs to resist the Nazis, and in the third year of the war it destroyed a German warehouse. In 1948, after Beneš' death, when the Communist dictatorship became an obvious fact and the prisons were quickly filling with old members of the nationalist group Sokol and then the Social Democrats (all labelled 'agents of imperialism'), Prema formed a new underground group in the same town. He was, it turned out, incorrigible. The narrator visits him:

I had come from Prague just for a visit, with no idea that they'd set up any kind of organization ... It was the same as the one I'd got mixed up in four years before simply by taking pictures of Prema's heroic act of sabotage against the Nazis. Only the adversary was different. This time it was the Communists. The decisive factor in each instance was the circumscription of freedom, but with my smattering of university Marxism I could not really understand what a worker from a tobacco warehouse, like Prema, needed intellectual freedom for. (216–17).

The group prints leaflets and sets up clandestine radio transmitters. Everybody gets caught. Prema is the only one to escape being captured during a raid. He flees abroad. In 1952 he sends his first letter. He writes of being kept in a transit camp for the displaced near Regensburg in West Germany. He cannot get out, he knows no foreign language, and there is no one in the whole world who can vouch for him. He is recruited into the Foreign Legion. He runs away when a transport ship is moored off Spain. He is captured and sits in various prisons until he is sent to a camp for stateless persons in Sicily. In the camp there are SS men and Fascists from the Croatian police. They beat him to a pulp when they find out who he is. He applies for a visa to the United States, but is rejected because of a decayed tooth.

The next letter is from Sydney in 1956, four years later. He has made it to Australia and then illegally to New Guinea, where he gets work at an oil refinery. He sleeps and eats in barracks, saves every penny, and after a year returns to Australia, where he buys a piece of land. In March 1968 he sells the farm because he cannot stand the loneliness. He sets the money aside. He wants to return. 'The word here is that this Dubček is giving amnesty for political offences' (418). He finally gets to Czechoslovakia in October. This is after freedom and after Dubček. He is given forty-eight hours to pack his bags. The last letter is from Australia once again. He works in construction. He earns a good salary, but is alone. 'I tell you, buddy, it's no place for us to be any more back home, we aren't used to holding our tongue all the time and sitting tight in one spot, it's just not the place for us any more' (526). He dies in a hurricane in 1977, in the city of Darwin on the northern coast of Australia.

The blank pages are slowly filling up. Even on the boundless expanses of Russia there is always a trace that remains of the millions of camp victims: a creased card with a few words for loved ones, a few exchanged words when transports pass each other, a remembered face or handshake. Hungary, Poland, and Czechoslovakia are not large countries. But the emigrés, refugees, and exiles from Central Europe are in all the countries of the world.

And still another fate: Rebecca Silbernáglová. Before the war, she and the narrator used to go swimming together. It is likely that she had a crush on him. In the novel, we read only her letters. The first is in January 1944 from a camp, Terezín, before she is transported out. She asks that he keep a miniature portrait of her mother. After the war, she is brought back to Czechoslovakia on a stretcher, an expiring skeleton. She had been in Auschwitz to the very end, but had somehow survived. The next letter is from Braunau in 1953. Her husband has been arrested on charges of being a Zionist, and she works in a textile plant, the new labour camp. She cannot take a day's leave and has no money. She asks for Swiss medicine for her ailing son. The next letter, seven years later, is from Israel. Rebecca is living with her son in a kibbutz. And after another seven years, in 1967: 'Daniel, I only hope the peace lasts ten years at least. But our Slavonic brothers will certainly do their best to ensure that it won't last that long. So I'll hope for at least five years. At least five' (467). Her last letter is from Tel Aviv in 1974. Her son and daughter-in-law die when a bomb planted in the centre of the city explodes: 'For the first time in my life I've said to myself what the women in Auschwitz would say when their husbands, their children, their families, everyone was killed: Why couldn't I have gone up that chimney too?' (563).

In *The Engineer of Human Souls*, individual fates make up the common lot. They are instances of the Great Mechanism: the steamroller crushing the ants. Škvorecký is interested in exemplary lives. He is shamelessly real, like Solzhenitsyn. The most astonishing thing in this epic novel about the annihilation of people, however, is the laughter. It is not 'black humour' or 'laughter through tears.' It is plain, ordinary, and hearty laughter – Švejk's laughter, which rings out in Škvorecký as it does in Kundera. When there is no hope or consolation, there is still laughter – bawdy laughter. This slightly archaic word *bawdy*, bawdy but never indecent, seems appropriate here for Škvorecký. Bawdy laughter is good medicine, as the old carnival wisdom teaches. And it is not an accident that many scenes in *The Engineer of Human Souls* take place, as in Jaroslav Hašek's *The Good Soldier Švejk*, in the latrine. In 1936 when I was in the army, I was taught: 'Only the house is peaceful evermore, which has never known the state of war.' Conversations in the army, camp, or factory latrine, are always full of civilian wisdom. In times of war and terror, the only refuge of civilized conversation is the latrine, the only place free from fear.

The most characteristic feature of Polish theatre and Czech prose of the past quarter century is the presence in them of a menace that is nevertheless ludicrous. This is not the comic terror so often invented by Western writers of the absurd; it is an observed fact. It is not surrealism; it is super-realism. Kundera, and Mrożek in Poland before him, are peerless in their demonstrations of the absurdity of the menace; but no one will be able to outdo Škvorecký.

The last of the emigrants to show up in Toronto is Dr Todt, a decent, kind-hearted, and non-Party electrical engineering specialist. A year earlier he is officially sent to attend an international conference in London. He returns according to plan, sleeps off the trip, and the next day, after a hot bath and coffee with milk, he puts on his slippers and opens the newspaper *Rudé právo*. On the first page is an article, 'The Story of a Traitor' (301). The article is about him, about how he had gone to London for a conference, how he had met each day with the head of the Soviet delegation to get instructions for the following day, how he had read two papers. Everything was accurate except the claim that he had not returned and that he had had an interview with the capitalist press about his not returning. Sweet, honest Dr Todt wipes his glasses and rereads the article. He keeps telling himself that this could, conceivably, be about someone else, but his name and titles stand out in very bold print.

He runs quickly over to the newspaper's editorial offices. The editor looks at him and then very carefully at the front page of his newspaper, as if he were looking at it for the first time. Then he says, ' "Aha, I have nothing to do with this, Comrade Doctor. This came from the Ministry. I only put it in this particular issue of the paper. If you have a query about it, you'll have to go to Interior" ' (303).

Dr Todt then runs over to the appropriate ministry. This time he waits longer, but is eventually received by the man who wrote the article. From him he learns that 'the mistake had taken place in London because they had received the news from the embassy there' (303). In the end he advises Dr Todt to return to work and pretend that nothing has happened.

At the Institute where Dr Todt works no one will speak to him. Only his faithful secretary occasionally sneaks him a glass of pale, already cooled tea. His phone is bugged, and it seems that someone is always following him. And perhaps someone is. After six months of this, he applies to go abroad on a skiing trip to the Austrian Alps. He uses all of his savings to buy two pairs of skis, a knapsack, sleeping bag, and ski jacket. He never uses the skis, but within a month's time he finds himself in Canada.

The story of the Prague electrical engineering specialist who was declared a defector before he defected is straight out of Kafka's world, in which 'the cage seeks a bird' and the punishment is proof of the guilt. Yet in Škvorecký's work one hears Gogolian laughter (as in *The Inspector General*, where the sergeant's widow beaten by police has 'whipped herself') more than one hears Kafka. That absurd Gogolian dread, which strikes even though it never stops being ridiculous, is not only a characteristic of a specific literary genre; it is also a characteristic of a specific system of repression, in which contempt for the party apparatus is stronger than fear, and those in power are grotesque and ridiculous because they have come to believe their own lies.

Among Škvorecký's literary affiliations, we should name one more: Nabokov. Nabokov was also an emigrant writer, even though he belonged to another epoch, and hailed from a separate cultural sphere. He was a great emigrant in two literatures: Russian and English. He wrote about Russian literature from a Western literary perspective and about English and French classics from the perspective of a Russian writer – a comparatist in the fullest sense of the word. Škvorecký's hero reads Poe's 'The Raven' to his students, but first in Russian, in Yesenin-Volpin's well-known adaptation: 'Kak-to noch'yu v chas terrora ... / ... Karknul Voron: Nevermore!' (6–7). And then in his own translation: 'Once at night in time or terror ...' And he concludes with a surprising, startling interpretation that equals Nabokov in its mastery of style: 'We have always been surrounded by terror and by the beauty that is an inseparable part of it' (11).

In this Canadian present time of the novel there is also the narrator's romance with his twenty-year-old pupil, who is fascinated by his lectures on literature. These are not the best pages of *The Engineer of Human Souls*. The girl is the daughter of extremely wealthy Swedish emigrants and has the beauty of a Northern goddess. The first love scene takes place on her parents' yacht, which is moored at lakeshore: '... she seems made of alabaster. She glows like the white goddess in *Trader Horn*, and around her head a golden halo of blonde hair and in the female centre of her body a magnificent golden thicket ...' (341). She loses her virginity a little later, on the folding seat of her father's Cadillac. The whole romance abounds in clichés, which range from the unbearably sentimental to the even more unbearably vulgar, and its model seems to be the worst of American soap operas. The flatness of these episodes is even more apparent when compared with the wartime love scenes, in which there is tenderness and harshness, the smell of flesh and earth, real landscapes and feelings. Long after one has shut the book, one recalls Nadia, a worker in the same military factory in Kostelec, in oversized men's boots and raglan, the latter probably sewn long before she was born. Nadia is always hungry, and kisses with a mouth still full of the pancakes that the narrator's mother sends him from home.

Of all the times past that are evoked in *The Engineer of Human Souls*, the fullest is the last year of the war, and of all the places recalled, Kostelec is the most distinct. Emigration is always (and not just metaphorically speaking) an emigration from the land of one's childhood and youth. *The Engineer of Human Souls* is a settling of accounts with all the past times of the emigrant. Yet since Josef Škvorecký and Danny Smiřický, author and narrator, emigrated not from Kostelec in 1946, but from Prague in 1968, the absence of the Prague Spring in this novel written by a political emigré may seem somewhat odd. But the Prague Spring only *seems* absent from Škvorecký's novel. It is not there in description or in action, but it is always present as an undercurrent in the narration, in the hope and despair of the refugees. 'We need them both, Prague and freedom,' says Veronika, the youngest of the refugees, 'but the way things are, we can't have both. It's either-or' (455).

Prague returns for the last time, via Paris, at the end of the novel. Paris is the first stop in the flight from Soviet tanks.

I remember Paris in 1968. We were standing in front of *Les Deux Magots* like poor relations whose house had just burned down and Milan Kundera said, 'I only hope I die soon. There's been too much of everything. How much longer do you think we can last?' I too had felt the longing for death. The Death Wish. The tanks had suddenly turned a theoretical Freudian concept into a real feeling ... (533).

One of the most anguished poems in Polish literature was written in the 1830s by the Polish poet, Adam Mickiewicz, in exile in Paris:

While my body sits here among you,
Looks you in the eye and talks aloud,
My soul leaves and wanders far, o far away,
It roams about and wails, o how it wails.

The Engineer of Human Souls, written 150 years later, is a novel about the same experience.

NOTE

1 *The Engineer of Human Souls*, trans. Paul Wilson (Toronto: Lester & Orpen Dennys, 1984), 5. All page references are to this edition and are included in the body of the text.

13

PETER PETRO

The Engineer of Human Souls in Czech and in English (1991)

Josef Škvorecký, together with Milan Kundera and Bohumil Hrabal, belongs among the best writers that Czech literature produced in the second half of this century. Unlike Hrabal, Škvorecký and Kundera also became part of another, wider literary context when they left their country. While Kundera, triumphantly installed in Paris, became an internationally acclaimed novelist and a spokesman for the cause of Central Europe, Škvorecký – without losing any of his own Central European status – became a Canadian writer.

A formidable figure on the Canadian literary scene, Škvorecký's reputation as a Canadian writer was amply confirmed when his *The Engineer of Human Souls*, subtitled *An Entertainment on the Old Themes of Life, Women, Fate, Dreams, the Working Class, Secret Agents, Love and Death,*[1] received in 1984 the Governor General's Award for literature, the highest honour a writer can aspire to in our country. It is a country, to be sure, where perhaps as much as one-third of the population are immigrants like Škvorecký, and where the word *immigrant* lacks pejorative connotations.

The immigrant theme is naturally present in the novel. It is part and parcel of the narrator's, Danny Smiřický's, Canadian experience. The action of *The Engineer* moves between Canada in the mid-seventies and Kostelec in northern Bohemia during the Protectorate (Nazi occupation) in the mid-forties, with shorter parts devoted to some episodes in the fifties and sixties with the important exclusion of the key year of 1968. Apart from these two main locations – Canada and Bohemia – there are episodes in France, Germany, Australia, and other exotic locations. Many of these are mentioned in the letters that further enrich this rather complex work.

While I am moved by those sections of the novel where Danny fantasizes about Irena and Marie, but sleeps with straightforward and saintly Nadia – that is, flashbacks from Kostelec as we have known it ever since *The*

Cowards (1958) – it is the Canadian experience, that heretofore lesser-known dimension of Škvorecký's work, which is of particular interest to me. Following the translation of the novel in 1984, it was this aspect of the novel that inspired some controversy among the Canadian critics.

For Škvorecký, who knows Canada better than most Canadians, Canada in the novel means Toronto, or more precisely its suburb, Mississauga, the site of his Edenvale College (a fictional version of Škvorecký's own Erindale College of the University of Toronto, where the author has taught for the past twenty-some years). If Danny cannot be found at the college, he is in his car, his apartment, or one of Toronto's watering holes, such as the Czech Benes Inn restaurant, or Mr. Zawynatch's bar. In Edenvale College, Danny is surrounded by his students, in the restaurant and bar, by his countrymen, fellow immigrants.

Edenvale College stands in a wilderness. In a few years the nearby town of Mississauga is expected to swell and envelop the campus with more variety and colour, but for the time being the college stands in a wilderness, two and a half miles from the nearest housing development (3).

The wilderness surrounding the college is both literal and metaphorical. Such isolation is rather common in Canada: college and university campuses are often built away from the hustle and bustle of the city, which eventually catches up with the campus. But Canadian wilderness is something that in this novel surrounds even the Toronto skyscrapers: 'It is dark; the huge radiant beehives of downtown Toronto stand like luxurious lighthouses of a wild civilization' (321).

Here, the native civilization itself is wild. And what of its literature? In another context, Škvorecký speaks of the 'literary wilderness of Canada' (518), which seems to suggest an acute case of alienation. However, both Danny and his author are perfectly at home here. In the much quoted opening passage the narrator leaves no doubt at all where he stands:

Often, as my thoughts flow, I conjure up again the many wonderful things I have seen in this country of cities of no past. Like the Toronto skyline with its black and white skyscrapers, some plated with golden mirrors, thrusting their peaks into the haze, glowing like burnished chessboards against the evening twilight above the flat Ontario landscape, and beyond them a sun as large as Jupiter and as red as an aniline ruby sinking into the green dusk. God knows why it's so green, but it is. The Toronto skyline is more beautiful to me than the familiar silhouette of Prague Castle. There is beauty everywhere on earth, but there is greater beauty in those places where one feels that sense of ease which comes from no longer having to put off one's dreams until some improbable future – a future inexorably shrinking away; where the fear which has pervaded one's life suddenly vanishes because there is nothing to be afraid of.

I feel wonderful. I feel utterly and dangerously wonderful in this wilderness land. (4)

The beauty of this wilderness land is among the most frequent comments made by visitors and immigrants to Canada. The sheer size of the land, its relatively unspoiled countryside, particularly its North, is something of a shock to a European. And yet the lyrical evocation of the Canadian landscape can also serve as an example of the transformation that took place following Paul Wilson's translation.

There is nothing but praise in the many reviews of the translation, as the authors invariably mention the difficult original. I agree and would like to add that one facet of Paul Wilson's originality is the inevitable homogenizing of the original. For in the lyrical passage above, Škvorecký uses in Czech a self-deprecating register that undercuts the lyricism, as if he found the straight description too maudlin. The English 'Prague Castle' of the above quoted passage is a rather formal rendering of the down-to-earth colloquial Czech 'Račany' instead of 'Hradčany,' while the 'high, narrow and gothic' window of the first sentence of the novel is actually *skleněná gotická nudle* (14): 'glass, gothic noodle.'

The general effect of this self-deprecating style is the creation of a persona that is the very opposite of a pompous preacher. This was understood by a number of reviewers, whether or not they read the Czech original. A reviewer with political blinkers, that is, one who was not particularly well disposed to Škvorecký's criticism of totalitarian ideology, would read Danny as a pompous preacher. But even such a reviewer, Terry Goldie, who found Škvorecký 'derisive towards Canada,' and who speaks about the 'racism of the novel,'[2] which he found 'generally anti-anything which smells of leftism,'[3] is forced to pay a compliment:

The Canadian reviewer would probably know no Czech (as I do not) but could note that the excellent dialogue *seems* right and that it *seems* like a good translation by Paul Wilson. The structure hopping back and forth from the Second World War in Czechoslovakia to the present in Canada, with various stops in between, is confusing but appropriate, recalling the discontinuity of the central character's life and also his devotion to jazz. Most characterizations are a bit thin but that can be justified by the first person narrative and the narrator is often fascinating. The only significant literary misjudgment is the length. The novel displays sufficient imagination for only about half of its 571 pages.[4]

Well, things are looking up when the worst you can say about the novel is that 'the excellent dialogue *seems* right' and 'it *seems* like a good translation.' As for Goldie's charges of racism, the derision towards Canada, and being anti-leftist, those were admirably dealt with by Marketa Goetz-Stankiewicz and Josef Škvorecký himself.[5] However, this review proved to be the exception rather than the rule in the Canadian press.

'Is it then a Canadian book at all?' asked Goetz-Stankiewicz, answering that 'indeed, it is,'[6], adding that it is a 'truly international work but also in a deep sense a work of Canadian literature,' and 'a major landmark on the Canadian cultural scene,'[7] as was clearly understood by other Canadian critics. Sam Solecki, who considers *The Engineer* one of 'the most important novels ever written in Canada,'[8] sees it as the culmination of the series that starts with *The Cowards* (1958) and continues with *The Republic of Whores* (1969) and *The Miracle Game* (1972). Together, they 'constitute one of the major achievements in contemporary Eastern European fiction and together with the work of Miłosz, Solzhenitsyn, Kundera and Konrad are indispensable accounts of modern life in Eastern Europe.'[9]

This double character of the novel – important in Czech literature as well as in Canada – was also noticed by Kundera's American translator, Michael Henry Heim, who believes that 'the novel belongs equally to Czech and to Canadian literature.'[10] 'On the one hand, it is the high point of one side of Škvorecký's prodigious Czech output and shows him at his sparkling best; on the other, it places him in the forefront of the cultural life of the new, "ethnic" Canada, which has acknowledged its gratitude.'[11] The paradoxical, though logical, outcome of this is that the success turned the unwilling exile into a happy emigrant. In Heim's words, 'by combining the Czech and Canadian worlds so deftly, by molding them in such a way that they complement each other and work together, Škvorecký demonstrates emblematically, as it were, the *value* of emigration.'[12]

Far from suffering, and unlike the stereotypical exile whom Škvorecký partially preserved in the character of Veronika, the protagonist is full of praise and gratitude for his good fortune. Danny Smiřický loves to immerse himself in the multi-racial, multi-ethnic world of Canada:

I am in bliss. At the Jarvis Street exit, the three-lane column of cars separates smoothly into two, one of them continuing along the Gardiner Expressway, the second, with me in it, no less smoothly descending the curving ramp and passing through the green light. My eye is caught by an immaculately luminescent bill-board for 'Breggfast' with a freckled turnip-faced brat stuffing himself with eggs done sunny side up. On an impulse I decide to consummate my feeling of well-being with supper at the Benes Inn, where they cook the best sauerbraten north of the United States border. So I turn onto Richmond and from there onto Universi-ty Avenue. A few blocks later I stop for a red light, and a group of young Chinese girls in knitted woollen caps, obviously medical students, cross the street in front of me. They have faces like oriental dolls. The green light comes on. A black medical student hurries across after the Chinese and, dazzled by the headlights, she blinks the huge whites of her eyes at me. I feel as though I'm in Paradise. Nothing can unsettle me. I don't remember ever experiencing such an evening back home. (34)

Is it quite clear why Danny feels so blissful?

The passage communicates something of the freedom of choice, the openness, the possibilities, and the tolerance Danny found in the new country. Danny is happy to be there with the Chinese girls and a black girl: they make him feel not an immigrant, an outsider, but a person integrated into perhaps a higher order of world citizenship. At least this is what some Canadians like to think of themselves: they picture themselves as more fortunate than people in countries with racial and ethnic tensions. They see themselves as citizens of a country that already exhibits in reality the features of the 'Spaceship Earth,' or McLuhanesque 'global village,' that is a microcosm of our planet minus its most vexing problems. One could perhaps criticize it as a somewhat selective picture of Canada, but after all, with its cars and good roads and services, the tolerance, and the high standard of living, life is so convenient and there is even the sauerbraten to celebrate this feeling of being one with the world! Finally, this passage comes after the wartime Kostelec section. It provides a magnificent contrast, as Canada avoided the two world wars in the sense that there were minimal privations and no physical occupation or destruction of the country (although a horrendous number of Canadian soldiers died in World War I, and Canadians were used without much regard for losses by the Allied Command in World War II). Apart from the service men and women, as well as the families who suffered the loss of their loved ones, most Canadians have not experienced any war in this century. This, too, forms a subtext of the blissful moment and thus – for Danny who cannot help remembering the war – the paradise.

The possibility that by marrying the two literatures (the Czech and the Canadian) Škvorecký had created something of a landmark of modern literature is present in the review by Canadian Mark Czarnecki:

As an exhaustive, insightful document of modern society in both East and West [this book] has no equals. Škvorecký easily keeps company with Joyce, Barth, and Pynchon.

The Engineer of Human Souls will become a milestone in the evolution of world literature.[13]

Czarnecki's enthusiastic interpretation presents a possibility of reading Škvorecký as an experimental novelist, which would line him up with the rather unlikely group of authors. However, this is a possibility lost to those who could not overcome the ideological hurdle. If Terry Goldie represents one pole in the field of the Canadian response to Škvorecký, Mark Czarnecki would represent the opposite.

Certainly, few Czech critics would agree with Czarnecki's interpretation, if only because reading the novel in Czech one gets enmeshed in the multitude of voices and perhaps also quite vexed with the distortions in the sections dealing with the Czech Canadians. It is this 'untidiness' that Paul Wilson's translation softens.

I well remember the effect on me of that mixed Czech-English when I first read the book in Czech; how in the world was this going to be translated, I asked myself, and then asked Josef Škvorecký, after he told me Paul Wilson was working on it. I did not anticipate the effect such homogenizing would have on a non-Czech, English reader like Czarnecki. Škvorecký probably did not, either.

A question arises then: Is the novel better in English than in its original language? This is not at all as silly a question as it might seem. If the Canadian reviews quoted are anything to go by, Škvorecký's *The Engineer* is more appreciated in English than in Czech. Peter Schubert, reviewing the Czech original for *World Literature Today* was quite critical: 'His [Škvorecký's] Czech, however, leaves much to be desired. This fault is accentuated by the mutilated language as spoken by the characters.'[14]

Reviewing the translation of the novel for the same journal, Peter Kussi, instead of finding fault with the language, accentuates it: 'as the ironic title suggests, it is a book about communication and language itself.' (15) He reminds the reader that in the original, 'the novel was written in a variety of languages: proper Czech, uneducated Czech, macaronic Czech, and, to a large extent, the Canadian-Czech of émigrés.'[16]

Whatever is preserved of the first three varieties, the Canadian-Czech of émigrés (the most shocking of the four mentioned by Kussi) cannot be rendered in translation. This is rather unfortunate, because in the Canadian-Czech of the émigrés we have a priceless piece of Canadiana accessible only to Czech-speaking Canadians. We stand before the fact of two versions of the novel: the shocking original with its 'untidy' or even 'mutilated language,' and the 'homogenized' version. And although I enjoyed the first more, I really prefer the second version, the translation. It is, to me, more philosophical, more meaningful – perhaps because the medium does not distract me from the message. And I say it despite the fact that Danny Smiřický is an enemy of 'meaning.' He says: 'How beautiful life is when everything loses its meaning and one begins to live simply for life itself.' And also: 'I have not lost the meaning of life, merely the illusion that life has a meaning' (533). And again: 'Meaning is a compulsive neurosis. It is only when the neurosis goes away, or when we are cured of it, that we can live' (534).

I believe the same could be said about politics. And Škvorecký assures us, somewhat tongue in cheek: 'I am not an ideological novelist, I am a photographic realist.'[17] It is not too far-fetched to suggest that the political charge of the novel also comes from a clash of values, or rather, as an incident in the novel suggests, from a clash of Veronika's values against the often expressed view that there aren't any values worth fighting for in Canada (230). Škvorecký reminds his Canadian readers most emphatically that there are values worth fighting for: indirectly through his flashbacks to wartime Kostelec, directly through his blissful experiences in Toronto.

Written after the publication of *The Engineer* in Czech, but before the translation, the following excerpt from Škvorecký's article is a fitting explanation of the role of the Canadian experience in the novel:

Oh my! I wanted to write about this beautiful land; about its golden skyscrapers silhouetted against the skies of the Indian summer; about the joy of its libraries; about the sweet charm of freedom I and my wife and all my good old countrymen found here, under the protective umbrella of the Yanks. But damn politics got me like the blues, and the naïveté of so many of my fellow Canadians does not help me out. I am far from being the stuff that Sisyphus was made of, and yet, again and again, I push this boulder up the steep slope of incomprehension. How silly of me![18]

Life has its surprises. It may well be the case that the *The Engineer of Human Souls* will end up being more appreciated by Škvorecký's Canadian readers than he expected. That would be an ample reward for his Sisyphian labour and a proof that his Canadian experience, creatively interpreted by Paul Wilson, contributed to this success.

NOTES

1 Quotations are from J. Škvorecký, *The Engineer of Human Souls: An Entertainment on the Old Themes of Life, Women, Fate, Dreams, the Working Class, Secret Agents, Love and Death*, trans. Paul Wilson (Don Mills: Totem, 1985) or from the original, *Příběh inženýra lidských duší. Entrtejnment na stará témata o životě, ženách, osudu, snění, dělnické třídě, fízlech, lásce a smrti* (Toronto: Sixty-Eight Publishers, 1977).

2 Terry Goldie, 'Political Judgments,' *Canadian Literature*, 104 (1985), 167

3 Ibid, 166

4 Ibid, 165

5 Marketa Goetz-Stankiewicz, 'Literary Mirrors,' *Canadian Literature*, 110 (1986), 165–71; Josef Škvorecký, 'A Judgment of Political Judgments,' *Canadian Literature*, 110 (1986), 171–6

6 Goetz-Stankiewicz, 165

7 Ibid, 171

8 Sam Solecki, 'The Laughter and Pain of Remembering,' *Canadian Forum*, 64 (August–September, 1984), 41

9 Ibid, 39

10 Michael Henry Heim, 'Dangerously Wonderful,' *Nation*, 4–11 August, 1984, 87

11 Ibid, 88

12 Ibid

13 Mark Czarnecki, review of *The Engineer*, *Quill & Quire*, 50 (May 1984), 30

14 Peter Schubert, review of *Příběh inženýra*, *World Literature Today*, 52 (1979), 655

15 Peter Kussi, review of *The Engineer*, *World Literature Today*, 59 (1986), 287

16 Ibid, 288

17 'A Judgment of Political Judgments,' 172

18 Škvorecký, 'Are Canadians Politically Naïve?' *Canadian Literature*, 100 (1984), 296–7

14

GEORGE WOODCOCK

The Unforgivable Sin of Ignorance: Notes on
The Engineer of Human Souls (1989)

Blessed ignorance! The unforgivable sin of trans-Atlantic civilization!

Veronika said, 'I guess we need them both, Prague and freedom! But the way things are, we can't have both. It's either-or.'[1]

If I were asked to judge a competition for the most interesting novel published in Canada during the 1980s, my first choice would undoubtedly be Josef Škvorecký's *The Engineer of Human Souls*. It is not a novel presented in either of the two major Canadian languages, for Škvorecký wrote it in Czech (and in Toronto) and it was Paul Wilson who rendered it so subtly into English. It does not emerge out of an awareness of the Canadian past, or from an experience of the Canadian land in all its vastness and grandeur; it is Canadian only in the sense – though that is by no means unimportant – that it gives ample expression to the immigrant experience, which in Škvorecký's case, as in that of many of his predecessors of many races, is an experience of both uprooting and liberation. Indeed, what makes *The Engineer* so significant in the context of Canadian writing is not that its present is set in Canada, but rather that its exploration of the past of Danny Smiřický, before he flees to the tranquillity of Canada, links us to world experience and helps to break down what, at one point of encounter with the innocent Canadian youth he tries to teach, the protagonist describes as 'blessed ignorance! That unforgivable sin of trans-Atlantic civilization!'

The Engineer is in some ways a classic Central European novel, using the same type of realism with a romantic overlay as appeared in Thomas Mann's novels, a realism that, apart from the massive and imperfect works of Frederick Philip Grove (another displaced Central European) did not in the past strike very deep roots in Canada. It fits quite well into the specific

European category that the Germans call *Künstlerromanen*, stories of the development of artists; yet as well as being an account of personal integration and liberation, *The Engineer* is also a remarkable portrait of a people – the Czech people – living in the storm centre of the repeated political crises of twentieth-century Europe.

Daniel Smiřický, the not especially heroic protagonist and narrator of *The Engineer*, is a Czech writer now teaching English literature in a Toronto college; he fled from Prague, like Škvorecký himself, shortly after the Soviet invasion of his country in 1968. The immediate action takes place in Canada, where Smiřický lives and carries on his double vocation of writer and teacher (or moral and intellectual guide). The past happens during the Nazi occupation of Czechoslovakia in World War II and the period of Communist rule, following the tortuosities of the Party line from 1945 to Dubček's 'socialism with a human face' interlude in 1968. That past is shown partly in flashbacks irradiated by the shifting lights of the narrator's memory, but partly also by interspersed letters from old associates, which not only tell us how things have changed in Prague after his departure, but also offer somewhat different recollections of events from those he projects, which suggests how far one must distrust the ability of the human memory to give objectively reliable evidence about the past.

Writers not only hide their humdrum everyday selves behind the striking personae which they and their publishers and reviewers create for the benefit of the public. In an age when academic categorization has permeated the literary world, they are tempted, in self-defence, to forestall the scholars by offering not merely a creative persona, but also a creative method that an examination of their writings does not always support. Thus, in a very interesting and already much quoted 1983 interview with Geoff Hancock, the editor of *Canadian Fiction Magazine*, Škvorecký presented himself in high camouflage as essentially an autobiographical novelist of a rather simple kind, as one can see by isolating a series of quotations.[2]

I just belong to those writers who base their writings on personal experience. I never have any trouble finding my subject matter. I just described episodes in my life. That goes for what I may call my serious fiction ... I never looked for subject matter. That's probably due to life in Czechoslovakia where everybody went through so many different experiences within a lifetime that it's not hard to find something to write about. (67)

I simply described the events as they appeared to me, and as they appeared to most people. (70)

If I should characterize myself, I am a simple realist. I try to capture my life experiences, and it so happened that I lived under dictatorships, so they are always in the background. (77)

But when we begin to live in the writer's mind through these personal experiences that have been given a character similar but not identical to those of the author, moving among people similar but not identical to the author's friends and acquaintances, we recognize that they are experiences lived out within a powerfully overshadowing situation, and that the shadow is not, as it might be in a Canadian work, the geographical one of an overbearing landscape, but the historical one of a land set in those unfortunate political verges between empires where world forces clash. Škvorecký tells us in the same interview that all his 'major' novels, as he somewhat ironically calls them, 'are based on important historical events, or set at a time when something historically important happens.' And he continues a little later to remark that *The Engineer* is 'a re-examination of the past thirty years in the life of Czechoslovakia, which is framed by Nazi occupation and the year 1968.' Of course, as we shall see, it is a great deal more than that, but the period and place where in the past of the novel the characters survive and develop is perhaps what distinguishes *The Engineer* most strikingly among novels written in Canada, and links it to European more than to North American traditions, even though the present of the novel is enacted in Canada.

It belongs to a kind of fiction that long flourished in Europe east of the Atlantic and south of the English Channel but has rarely been naturalized in English-speaking literatures, and then usually among writers whose background, like Joseph Conrad's, is European. This is the novel in which the effects of political events and systems shape the lives of the characters. Its moving impetus lies in the interaction between the domineering state and the individual who sets out to resist or evade it.

This kind of fiction dates far back in the nineteenth century, to Turgenev (*Virgin Soil*) and even before him to Stendhal (*Le Rouge et le Noir*). It became particularly important during the 1930s, with totalitarian systems rising up everywhere on the European continent from Russia to Spain. Such writers as André Malraux and Ignazio Silone, Arthur Koestler and Albert Camus, made the struggle between the collectivity and the rebel the central preoccupation of their novels, giving their work a remarkable prophetic power. Only one writer in England had the same kind of political prescience at that time; he was George Orwell, who acknowledged the foresight of his Continental contemporaries, and evoked the totalitarian threat in *Coming up for Air* (1938), even before he wrote his better-known *Animal Farm* and *Nineteen Eighty-Four*. And Orwell made virtually the same accusation of 'Blessed ignorance! The unforgivable sin ...' against the English of his time and their writers as Škvorecký would make against the Canadians half a century later.

For me the great virtue of books like Malraux's *La Condition humaine* and Silone's *Bread and Wine* and Orwell's last three novels is that they insist by implication that the heart of a piece of fiction is not its style or form, which are the skin and the skeleton, but its content, the moral or intellectual core. *The Engineer* has this vital core of content, a vision of freedom perpetually imperilled, and a parallel collective vision of the Czech people, separated yet united, some carrying on as best they can in their own country, and others living in exile among bewildering Canadians, an exile they find sometimes as unbearable as they found the enslavement of their own country. 'I guess we need them both, Prague and freedom!' says the sad girl Veronika. 'But the way things are, we can't have both. It's either-or.' (She is one who returns.)

The Engineer is thus not only a remarkable political novel, presenting an era of totalitarianism a quarter of a century long, seen through the eyes of those who elected for life and music, like Danny and his fellow jazz players: 'We were sixteen, we were young and free in that awful dictatorship, and we had no respect for its glories.' It is also a fascinating study of the way cultures and traditions change yet continue in exile. Danny has become a Canadian professor, and his links with Canadian youth lead him into recollections of the young people he lived among and loved a generation ago. The book is largely structured on these parallels between the young in different times and places, for, as Škvorecký says in the Hancock interview: 'Danny is teaching young Canadians, including young Canadian girls, and suddenly he realizes young people are not very different in different countries; they are in fact similar. They go through the same emotional upheavals and they even act in similar ways. So that reminds him of his own young years, when he was young and the girls who [are now] fifty were eighteen. So the putting together of episodes which in actual life were divided by thirty years has a logic. It forces the reader subconsciously to compare' (80–2).

Yet in spite of this tendency to synthesize the two backgrounds and the two lives that he had acquired by the 1970s, Škvorecký's general attitude still places him in that central European tradition that came early to the encounter with the regressive forces of recent history and that Škvorecký's friend and fellow writer in exile, Milan Kundera, has so well described in his most recent book of notes and essays, *The Art of the Novel*. The novelists who inhabited the disoriented fragments of the Austro-Hungarian Empire advanced beyond the interior monologue that occupied so much of the attention of early twentieth-century novelists in the West to a more alarming dialogue with the forces that assault the individual from the shadows of an increasingly irrational world. As Kundera remarks, at the 'peaceful time' of the great modern masters of the West, like Joyce and Proust, 'man had only the monster of his own soul to grapple with. But in the novels of Kafka, Hašek, Musil, Broch, the monster came from outside and is called History.'

Kundera writes at length and very interestingly on Kafka and also on that dark, obscure genius, Hermann Broch, whose trilogy, *The Sleepwalkers*, is perhaps the greatest unrecognized masterpiece of modern times. Kundera stresses an important neglected truth about Kafka when he pushes aside the attempt to explain *The Castle* and *The Trial* as works of religious allegory, which they clearly were not, and sees them instead as feats of prophetic insight into the direction in which European society was developing. Kafka, he asserts (and I believe rightly): 'does not ask what internal motivations determine man's behaviour. He asks a question that is radically different. What possibilities remain for man in a world where the external determinants have become so overpowering that internal impulses no longer carry weight?'[3]

Such a situation Kafka knew only in prophetic imagination, for apart from a job in a bureaucracy he had no experience to go on. But what Kafka imagined, Kundera, Škvorecký, and their Czech associates were forced to live through when the ancient western culture of Bohemia was overwhelmed by the 'totalitarian universe.' They found they were living in a world hostile to the very concepts on which the novel had traditionally been based.

Kundera sees a situation developing in which the novel, product of 'the great illusion of the irreplaceable uniqueness of the individual – one of Europe's finest illusions' – will in fact die because the world has 'grown alien to it.'[4] But Škvorecký has declared his belief that even if the liberal values 'are now almost forgotten or not respected or not valued' (and here he is talking about the situation of people in the West who have not experienced life in a totalitarian regime), a writer must stand up for them and if necessary 'go against the tenor of the age.' The point is that he still believes the going against is possible, and so, while he shares Kafka's perceptions about the perils of the future he resists the condition of Kafka's characters, who in the end offer the crime to fit the punishment and whose ultimate desire becomes to be accepted by the irrational powers that destroy them. From his beginnings as an adolescent saboteur to his present as an exiled writer, Danny Smiřický continues to 'go against.' In the final analysis

Škvorecký is a writer of comedy rather than tragedy, of humanity surviving through its virtues rather than dying through its faults, and if he has a master in the generation of Central European writers who preceded him it is probably Jaroslav Hašek, with his *Good Soldier Švejk*, rather than Kafka. Though *The Engineer* differs in many ways from Hašek's marvellously anarchic book, it also is a story of evasion and survival rather than of acceptance and destruction.

I use the word *story*, which is one Škvorecký is constantly using to describe his fiction. For him the story comes about through the mingling of actuality with imagination, and then what the reader perceives becomes, as he said in another interview (with Barbara Leckie in Peter O'Brien's collection *So to Speak*), 'more powerful than the actual event.'[5]

The emphasis on a powerful narrative is connected with Škvorecký's idea that the first purpose of fiction is to entertain, and that its artistic qualities are emergent from its success in doing that. *The Engineer*, though perhaps his most complex and ambitious novel, is called 'An Entertainment on the Old Themes of Life, Women, Fate, Dreams, the Working Class, Secret Agents, Love and Death.' They are the themes that would probably seem most important to the average Czech who had passed through the years of Nazi occupation and Communist domination. Secret agents personified for many people – and for all intellectuals – the political realities of Czech life over this long period, no matter what kind of totalitarianism dominated the country. Many Czechs were thrust into the working class by labour conscription during the Nazi period; and afterwards, under the Communists, to pass as a worker was useful protective colouring. And yet – and this is perhaps the great point of the novel – the universal themes of 'life, women, fate, dreams ... love and death' are still what most concern people even in times of great repression. In a rather foolish way Danny becomes a saboteur against the German war effort, and therefore a potential martyr of the resistance, but he does not abandon his everyday life of a moony adolescent, comically failing in his efforts to woo pretty girls of his own class.

There is a grasping after life, in what to outsiders seemed a regime dominated by fear and death, that is moving and inspiring for those who want to keep their faith in humanity. It finds expression with mingled comedy and pathos in Danny's first real affair, with the working-class girl Nadia. Nadia shares his bench in the factory, making parts for Messerschmidts, and it is with her that he concocts his sabotage plot to drill brackets in such a way that the ammunition drums will tear away from the guns on the planes. They are saved from discovery by the Gestapo because the factory is honeycombed by a resistance network that includes at least one of the German supervisors. Danny impatiently loses his virginity to poor emaciated Nadia with her fiery eyes that haunt him ever after; she is consumptive and soon she is dead. It is a story that could have been made mawkish rather than moving, as it was in so many nineteenth-century operas with tubercular dying heroines, but it is saved and humanized by comedy suffusing the melodrama. Nadia is doomed, and we are saddened for it, yet the awkwardness of Danny's lovemaking and Nadia's unashamed greed when food confronts her, and the naïveté with which the two of them embark on their perilous adventure of sabotage often draw one's laughter; it is this subplot that most illuminates Škvorecký's point that life can be all the more vivid in the shadow of death and that dreams still do their work no matter what fate holds in store.

Škvorecký is setting out to show us that the human condition at any time in history is something different from the political structure superimposed on the lives of ordinary people. That, as he has remarked at various times and in various ways, is his message. For, in spite of what he chooses to tell us, Škvorecký is a great deal more than entertainer. He also believes that what he has to tell can carry a message and a warning. True, ordinary people can to a great extent continue to live private and enjoyable lives even under a dictatorship, but such lives are mentally circumscribed, and it is the creative people who are most affected by the circumscription. In such circumstances one learns about life at its starkest and brutally simplest, and perhaps learns more; the difficulty is in communicating what he has learned. As Škvorecký said to Barbara Leckie, 'It's always easier to become a readable writer if you live in a dictatorship. Provided you get out and publish what you know' (32). But the message – the distillation of that experience lived under pressure – cannot be overtly stated by the novelist, as a pamphleteer might do. It has to emerge from the narrative and the dialogue, and here lies the skill of the novelist that makes him something more than an entertainer as well as something more than a pamphleteer.

The Engineer is in fact a cunningly collaged book whose action unfolds between two societies: democratic Canada where – despite an ominous growth of puritanical interferences – we still enjoy much real freedom; and the totalitarian realms where freedoms are few and furtive and the liberty to speak and write as one wishes is perennially precarious. The sense of two worlds interflowing despite their apparent separateness is increased by the fact that Danny takes part in a lively Czech émigré society as well as having found a safe place in Canadian academia, and also by the reader's awareness that though the book originated in Canada it was both written and first published in Czech. The message that seems to emerge out of this process of cross-culturalism is that while there are still places where people are often imperfectly free, the tyranny of the totalitarian world can never become complete. During the Nazi regime and the early Communist years, for example, jazz was a liberating influence among the young, and one of the best and most significant scenes in *The Engineer* is that in which a group of young people, aware of the Gestapo presence in their little town of Kostelec, hold a party at which they extravagantly parody that sacred theme tune of the German invaders, the Horst Wessel *Lied*. Thus, instead of dividing the book, the juxtaposition of its Canadian present and its Czech past serves as a unifying factor. By opening its doors to the fugitives from the events of 1968, Canada made itself a part of Czech history, but at the same time the arrival of Czechs like Smiřický (and of course Škvorecký) has added to the pluralist richness of Canadian literature and of Canadian culture in general. *The Engineer* is in this way a manifestation of the cohesion of Western civilization.

Neither in intent nor in practice is Škvorecký an avant-garde writer; Czech writers, including Kafka, have mostly stood aside from the kind of meta-fictional experimentalism that stemmed from the modernism of the period of World War I and still in changing ways remains so important a factor in Western literature.

Like Škvorecký's other novels, *The Engineer* is realistic in the sense of aiming at a verisimilitude that can create a convincing image of 'things as they are' (Godwin's classic desideratum for the realist novel) in the reader's mind. He is detailed and evocative in his description of places: the factory where Danny works in the 1940s and the college where he teaches in the 1970s, the forested hills where Nadia lives. He dwells on the look of people, not only their physical characteristics and especially the eyes of women – Nadia's sapphire-blue eyes, Nadia's dark burning depths, Canadian-Scandinavian Irene's grey northern remoteness – but even their clothes, so revelatory of character and circumstance. With this building up of an intricate authenticity of surface, Škvorecký combines a sense of the distinguishing qualities of speech, which Paul Wilson's translations of his novels have felicitously rendered, so that, as Škvorecký clearly intends, each of his people – even down to minor factory workers or members of Danny's classes in Canada or habitués of the Benes Restaurant in Toronto – is distinguished not only visually but also in his or her idiosyncratic speech pattern. Mostly we are aware of his characters through Danny's present perceptions or his shaping memory, but a diversification of point of view is offered by the letters from the friends of Danny's youth, the young people of Kostelec whom history has scattered over the world.

But the use of letters is as well-tried fictional device, dating back into the early days of the English novel with Aphra Behn and Mary Manley and used even before that in France, and the alternation of scenes from the present with memory flashbacks has been current in films and fiction for half a century. One judges the use of both these devices for effectiveness rather than originality. Škvorecký uses them effectively.

But their effectiveness tends to confirm his somewhat conservative realism. And here we may find the reason for his relatively rapid acceptance among Canadian readers, despite the political connotations that stand outside Canadian experience and that have made him condemn our unforgivable innocence. For realism has been and remains the dominant mode of Canadian fiction, and it is interesting here to consider where Škvorecký may have affinities among the writers of his adopted country.

He is unashamedly didactic, yet the didacticism of *The Engineer* is both more firmly based in experience and more thoroughly assimilated into the world of human feeling than is the case of our leading native didactic, Hugh MacLennan. Of pedantic realism, displayed most assiduously by Robertson Davies with his relentless display of esoteric areas of knowledge, Škvorecký fortunately has none; he is in such matters an informed but self-effacing man, though his fiction is based on its own special area of knowledge, that of an experience few Canadians share.

If there is a Canadian writer with whom the author of *The Engineer* would seem to have a true affinity, it is surely Margaret Laurence. Laurence was not only like Škvorecký concerned with time and memory in human lifes; she also placed emphasis on visual surface, and on the relationship of speech to character. And in a way she, too, was an exile, for she had been a stranger in strange lands, and though her memories were rooted tenaciously in the small prairie towns of her childhood, experience had so far alienated her that she could not return to live in them. And so, in the ultimately nationless world of literature, Laurence's Morag Gunn and Škvorecký's Danny Smiřický, both coming to terms with themselves in the middle ground of Ontario, can be seen as siblings under the skin. In more ways than its having been written here, *The Engineer* observes the archetypes of the Canadian novel.

NOTES

1 J. Škvorecký, *The Engineer of Human Souls: An Entertainment on the Old Themes of Life, Women, Fate, Dreams, the Working Class, Secret Agents, Love and Death,* trans. Paul Wilson (Don Mills: Totem 1985), 65, 455. Subsequent page references are included in the body of the essay.

2 *Canadian Fiction Magazine,* no. 45–6, 63–96
3 'Dialogue on the Art of the Novel,' *The Art of the Novel,* 26
4 'The Depreciated Legacy of Cervantes,' ibid, 8
5 *So to Speak,* 15

15

EDWARD ROTHSTEIN

New World Symphonietta: *Dvorak in Love* (1987)

If we are ever to understand the course of American music there are three things we must know about Antonín Dvořák's visit here during the 1890s. (1) He was brought to New York to direct a new conservatory – founded by the wife of a wholesale grocer. (2) Two of the most important black musicians of the following decades were his pupils. (3) During a night out at New York's watering holes, Dvořák drank the influential critic James G. Huneker under the table. (We might include with the third item Dvořák's passion for pigeons – he visited Central Park to observe them at least once a week – and his love of locomotives; he would hang out at 155th Street just to watch the Boston trains come in.)

What do trains, whisky, grocery stores, and Negro musicians have to do with the course of American music? Well, Old Borax, as he was called by the natives who couldn't quite get that 'zha' sound in his name, arrived here at a most propitious moment, bearing propitious gifts. (1) This was a time of *nouveau* money in the arts. Dvořák's patron had no investment in the weightiness of the European heritage; her passions were for what could be made of the land whose fortune she shared. (2) There seemed to be no 'given' American musical culture, but Dvořák – himself an explorer of his native Czech folk music – found that culture in the music of the blacks and Indians; he argued passionately for its inclusion in concert hall music. (3) Dvořák was eminently suited to his time and place – an earthy, ordinary man who happened to be a composer.

I confess that I would not be as convinced about Dvořák's centrality had I not read Josef Škvorecký's *Dvorak in Love*. This historical novel about the composer, written by a fellow Czech who emigrated to these shores on a more permanent basis and for more profound reasons than did his subject, is robust, exuberant, affectionate – like Dvořák's attitude toward the 'New

World.' In fact, it may be the best novel about a composer since the book that is its precise opposite in spirit and tone and subject, Thomas Mann's *Doctor Faustus*. For here, instead of Adrian Leverkuhn's high modernist piety, there is Dvořák's devout innocence; in place of Germanic brooding, there is folkish glee; instead of syphilitic sickness, there are episodes of bittersweet romance; in place of European *Sturm und Drang*, there is this book's subtitle: *A Light-hearted Dream*. And if the decline of European civilization inspired Mann's dour brilliance, here the inspiration is the explosive rise of a peculiarly American culture.

But the comparison is unfair to Škvorecký. He doesn't mean to be solemn or even profound. He never lets us see the world through Dvořák's eyes or lets Dvořák become too real. He doesn't care; he is too much in love, dizzyingly so, as is everybody in this book. 'Intoxication' is everywhere. Dvořák loved drink. So did his compatriots in Spillville, Iowa, a small town of Czech immigrants where the composer and his family spent a remarkable summer during their sojourn here; the conjunction of drink and well-told tales provides some of the book's most wondrous concoctions. Every chapter, in fact, is a story, recalled or imagined by one of the players in this drama, drawn from various periods of the composer's life, relating to the American visit. It is a chorus of voices: they include the critic Huneker, who disliked much of Dvořák's music; one of Dvořák's black students, Harry T. Burleigh, who later brought the spiritual into the concert hall; Dvořák's wife's sister, Josephine, who, in the author's compelling interpretation, was the love of Dvořák's life; and a rather robust tuba player in a New York saloon, who convinced Dvořák to put a part for his instrument into the *New World* Symphony.

Despite the occasional haze of overly crafted variety (and some precious-ness), even the extravagant inventions of this book have a hold on the imagination. But it would be hard – even in the interest of tall tales – to improve on the facts of American musical life during the nineteenth century. In 1817, for example, Anton Philip Heinrich, also a Czech-born composer, led the first American performance of a Beethoven symphony – in Lexing-ton, Kentucky; he later had an audience with President Tyler, and journeyed hundreds of miles through rugged country in quest of native music. He wrote epic, grand pieces, now thankfully lost to time, with titles like 'Pushmataha, a Venerable Chief of a Western Tribe of Indians,' 'The Treaty of William Penn with the Indians: Concerto Grosso,' and the resounding 'Rhapsodia Majestica ad Maiorem Gloriam Rei Publicae Americanae Transatlanticae.'

And there was the French-born maestro Jullien, who came to New York in the 1850s with his orchestra to present 'Monster Concerts for the Masses' and conducted fifteen hundred performers under the auspices of P.T. Barnum; his jewel-studded baton was usually brought to him on a silken cushion. A successor in monster concerts was one Patrick Sarsfield Gilmore, who may not have had Heinrich's dedication to accounts of Indian treaties and tribes, or Jullien's bejeweled baton, but he did intend to bring to these shores Europe's biggest and brightest. After the Civil War, Gilmore planned the 'Grandest Musical Demonstration that the world has ever witnessed.' A new coliseum was constructed in Boston, and in 1869, 10,000 choral voices joined an orchestra of 590 to present for the delectation of 20,000 listeners two movements of Schubert's Symphony in C, 'The Star-Spangled Banner,' and the 'Anvil Chorus' – the last two by request of President Grant, who was in attendance. This was no mere show, of passing import. The report in the *New York Sun* read:

Heretofore America has had no standing in the musical art world. England has looked down on us. Germany has supposed that no festival could be given here except by her Sangerbunds. Italy and France have recognized for us no higher possibilities than the production of their operas. At one step, without any prelimi-naries, without more special preparation than could be crowded into a few weeks, we have lifted ourselves, so far as great musical gatherings are concerned, to an artistic level with these nations ... The enterprise has been conceived and executed on a scale in keeping with the vastness of the country, with the breadth and large-ness of the American methods, and with the expedition and fearlessness that characterize all our attempts in untried fields of efforts.

'Only in America' Škvorecký's Dvořák says in wonder, hearing of these men and their dreams – immigrants and operators whose taste for enterprise and breadth and expedition and fearlessness matched their Bunyanesque personalities. The quest for a native American music inspired all the devotion of the quest for the lost grail or an unsullied natural state; but it was spiced with a certain anxiety about measuring up to the highest standards of artistic achievement while still obtaining the highest possible return on investment. Showmanship mixed with kitsch and warm-hearted good faith.

It is another of the paradoxes of America's culturally democratic past that these extravagant and ludicrous enterprises had serious ramifications. Jullien's imported orchestra brought to America players and virtuosos who later had an important impact on native musical education and performance. The grandeur that was Gilmore's helped inspire interest in the endowment of new philharmonic orchestras across the country. As for Heinrich, his quest for a native American music among the Indians was echoed more than a half century later when, in 1892, Dvořák came.

He was lured by a fifteen-thousand-dollar salary offered by Jeannette M. Thurber, herself an extraordinary American musical figure, who used great sums from her husband's wholesale grocery business to found the American National Opera – a company that lasted just long enough to lose a small fortune – and the National Conservatory of Music, whose directorship Dvořák accepted. The conservatory was created to help establish a national musical culture; Dvořák was to play a crucial role. He was thus Heinrich's well-schooled heir, turning the grand-scaled public extravaganzas of Jullien and Gilmore inward, in the service of art. Would that Mrs Thurber's husband had not suffered in the crash of '93 – Dvořák might have stayed, the conservatory might have flourished, and the course of American music might have been different.

But Dvořák's entrance into phantasmagoric American musical life was still quite profound, for Dvořák himself represented a music not of false epic grandeur but of folk intimacy – the sort of music that made Smetana, Tchaikovsky, and Sibelius national heroes back home. Dvořák had already attempted to combine the symphonic culture of Western Europe with the folk-songs and musical culture of Middle Europe. He once offered a toast in Russian to Tchaikovsky, praising him for the glory he had brought to the Slavic people. Dvořák himself received similar toasts here for what he had done for the New World.

For what he saw when he arrived was that the national musical culture did not need to be invented; it needed to be discovered. In 1893 he wrote in the *Chicago Tribune*: 'Every nation has its music. There is Italian, German, French, Bohemian, Russian; why not American music?' He reminded the *New York Herald* of the source of this music: 'All of the great musicians borrowed from the songs of the common people.' And he revealed what he had found: 'The country is full of melody, original, sympathetic, and varying in mood, color, and character ... America can have great and noble music of her own, growing out of the very soil and partaking of its nature – the natural voice of a free and vigorous race.' In fact: 'I am now satisfied that the future music of this country must be founded upon what are called the Negro melodies ... These are the folk songs of America and your composers must turn to them.'

These were principles with which Mrs Thurber agreed. Dvořák found evidence of these American musics among the students at the conservatory – including Harry T. Burleigh and Will Marion Cook, a black violin prodigy who studied with Joachim in Europe before he turned to musical comedy, producing the first Negro musical-comedy Broadway production, 'Clorindy, or The Origin of the Cakewalk' (he also appears in Škvorecký's novel). Dvořák found Indian songs and Negro spirituals in New York and on his trip to Spillville, which helped inspire his *New World* Symphony, his *American String Quartet*, and even an arrangement of 'Old Folks at Home.' Škvorecký's characters also remark on another lineage of American music that Dvořák may have fathered: Ruby Goldmark, one of his students at the conservatory, later went on to teach George Gershwin, that quintessential 'American' figure for later generations.

This influence didn't come, ironically, from the particulars of Dvořák's 'New World' music, but from his ideas and temperament. Only the great Largo melody of that clearly named symphony seemed to have a concrete heritage: it was so authentic in its Negro inspiration that it fathered a spiritual, 'Coming Home.' (There have even been arguments about which came first.) But Dvořák's music served as an icon for his followers, a sign of what was possible when a composer attempted to sound deeply a people's spirit. Similar musical solutions were worked out generations later in the great American symphonic music of the 1930s and 1940s.

The currents of musical traditions, of art musics and folk musics, run together, with Dvořák at a sort of vortex. But the result is a mixture of styles and attitudes that have yet to be sorted out. During the 1920s American composers (like Copland and Gershwin) actually reversed Dvořák's path, travelling to the Old World, to Paris, in order to become more truly American. And whether talking about jazz and swing, the WPA, Leonard Bernstein, rock, or minimalism, the quest for an American music in its various incarnations continues. It is a quest that, in controversy and contradiction, is the inspiration behind *The New Grove Dictionary of American Music* – one of the most ambitious and conflicted attempts to document American musical culture.

Given all this, Škvorecký's novel, despite its sometimes gnomic wanderings, is a stunning success. For it turns the quest into a matter of temperament and spirit rather than issue and achievement. The book – to step away for a moment from the musical musings it has instigated – is a romance, in which the characters perform dances of love and desire; Dvořák's love for his sister-in-law, his daughter's love for the composer's American amanuensis, the book's various movements of seductions and flirtations – all create a spirit of unrequited yearning found by the author in America itself (and in Dvořák's music). Škvorecký is himself a jazz musician and, as his earlier work has shown, he is quite ingenious at finding high seriousness in low comedy, and vice versa. The gentle and affectionate imagination at work makes the composer seem at once vital and imaginary, a creature of body and of spirit. As in his music, nothing profound is demanded, much that is sweet is offered, and something rich and pleasing is received. That must have been the way Dvořák was welcomed here; it is the way he is still heard. The author comes down heavily on Dvořák's side, sharing his vision of an American music growing from popular and folk roots. This is too simple – as Škvorecký's robustly brilliant novel *The Engineer of Human Souls* showed, he would hardly take the same view of literature – but no matter. 'Deo gratias!' proclaims an epigraph at the close of this novel. For all the qualifications, yes indeed.

16

MARKETA GOETZ-STANKIEWICZ

A World Symphony in a Scherzo: *Dvorak in Love* (1986)

Imagine a panel discussion on Josef Škvorecký's novel *Dvorak in Love*. Meet the panelists: a historian, a musical theorist, an anthropologist, a sociologist, a literary critic of Jungian archetypal persuasion, and a literary theorist. As you listen to an imaginary discussion between them you hear entirely different opinions: the historian is impressed by the 'thorough research' that has gone into the novel. The musical theorist counters this with the remark that research is inconsequential in a work of art, that the novel is valuable because it 'synthesizes two of the dominant musical cultures of our time – the classical European tradition ... and the jazzy American tradition.' 'Sure, the book is about a composer,' snarls the anthropologist, as the discussion gets more heated, 'but its real feat is that it touches on language, cultural barriers, and social alienation.' At this point the hitherto silent sociologist raises his voice: 'What do you mean by cultural barriers? This is a meaningless cliché. The novel deals with Dvořák's encounter with the New World and at the same time with the American Dream.' 'Dream as such is right,' mutters the archetypal critic, 'but your comment about "the American Dream" is superficial. The novel's dream theme is multi-levelled and reveals an ever-changing kaleidoscope of dreams.' 'I still believe the background research is important,' remarks the unshaken historian. 'If you tackle something like a biography, you must make sure that you've got the facts right.' 'Dwelling on facts hinders the discovery of the subtext,' says the literary theorist. '*Dvorak in Love* lowers a probe into the past and allows the reader to share this probe in an "act of collaboration" as analysed by Roland Barthes.'

Just as the members of the audience (the panel is held in public) realize that this is obviously an extremely complex and demanding book if it elicits such radically different and obviously well-founded reactions from specialists of various persuasions, a student in the sixth row leaps to his feet. He is in high spirits because he has just successfully defended his dissertation on the 'arrangement of ontological space' in *Moby Dick*. 'Ladies and gentlemen, please don't forget that *Dvorak in Love* is, above all, a pleasure to read! You see, at last I'll be able to read for pleasure again. This is a rare feat in our profession. The novel is funny and sad, it's real and fictional, it's learned and yet has preserved the wondrous gaze of a child. It throbs with music like ...'

But it is time to silence our imaginary panel, only to admit that it is not imaginary at all. It reflects, for the most part verbatim, what was written in, say, a dozen reviews that appeared in 1986 when *Dvorak in Love* was published in English.[1] Critics, scholarly or not, were trying to cope – each in his own way – with the fact that the novel is a treasure house of literary, historical, psychological, musical material, held together by the author's artistic vision, wide learning, and knowing humour.

Scherzo capriccioso, the novel's original Czech title, is perfect for this formidable text, woven from familiar as well as freshly discovered historical material and the teeming imagination of a writer who is endowed not only with a deep ironic sense of what a human being – outstanding or average – is all about, but also with an uncanny musical sense. This is why the tentative label 'historical novel,' which some reviewers have used, sits on this text as poorly as the label that its theme brings readily to mind, 'musical biography.' *Dvorak in Love* is neither, both, and much more.

As with nearly all of Škvorecký's works, this 'light-hearted dream,' as he calls it in the subtitle, contains the germs of several other novels. Just a single example shows how far this work goes beyond a cliché novel about nineteenth-century composers (Chopin, Schubert, Schumann, Tchaikovsky, Liszt, Wagner, even Brahms) in and out of love: embedded in the very centre of Škvorecký's tale – the thirteenth of twenty-six chapters – is a chapter called 'Exodus,' in which a prosperous farmer of Spillville, Iowa, tells the story of his emigration from a Bohemian village and his journey to the new world. He made the voyage with his wife and half a dozen children, the first of whom was born 'before they abolished serfdom'[2] in 1848. Two others died on the gruelling, three-month sea voyage, during which a seventh was born. Once landed in New Orleans, the brave new American settler was dismayed to discover that blacks were tough competition for working wages. Hoping to make thirty-five cents a day, he found that the shipowners' unwillingness to hire him was caused by the blacks working a twelve-hour day for twenty cents. Later he made another discovery: their masters got the twenty cents. 'What I didn't know at the time was they really was slaves' (176). Dvořák, who hears this tale while spending a summer in that same village of Spillville two generations later, in 1893, has been shown a thread from the rich historical tapestry of nineteenth-century America, which is unravelled before his eyes. And the reader suddenly realizes that he has been taken to Spillville – an important place in the action of the novel – not on Dvořák's relatively comfortable and safe journey, but by another way, tortured, hazardous, and darkened by fear.

As in Škvorecký's previous novel, *The Engineer of Human Souls*, there is no linear storytelling in *Dvorak in Love*, no streamlined development of character. There is no reflection by the biographer on the composer's psychology. There is also no sketching in of suitable selected facts to illuminate the creation of individual works by the composer, with a couple of notable exceptions – the two pieces of music whose origin is related to Dvořák's psychological experiences, the Cello Concerto in B minor and an aria 'To the Moon' from his opera *Rusalka*. The inspiration for the latter is seen in a comic light (drifting along the midwestern Turkey River for a little night fishing, Dvořák became the innocent witness to heiress Rosemary Vanderbilt's unclad moonlight dip in a secret cove); the former is shrouded in a delicate but sustained theme of sadness (the loss of Dvořák's first love, Josephine, whose sister, Annie, became the resolute wife, common-sensical companion, and energetic pianist who saw him through life).

In fact, this book about Dvořák does not say much directly about its main character at all. The other figures talk about him, and their thoughts, hopes, and cares move around him, coming from all directions. This aura that Dvořák radiates to others and that elicits a large spectrum of moods – from ironic amusement to impatience and irritation, from worried care to impassioned admiration, awe, and love – is the only way through which we are allowed to approach the central character of the novel. But we never get too close to 'the master,' as he was called by many, or 'Borax' (125) as he was nicknamed with an appropriateness that stems from envy (the nickname was invented by New York's pedantic musical personality James G. Huneker). Though all the facts are there – from Dvořák's position as teacher to the Čermák sisters, starting in 1865 to his unwillingness to come to New York a third time in 1895 – the reader is always kept at arm's length from the composer's psyche. As Škvorecký said, with typical modesty, during an interview: 'It would have been preposterous for me to have tried to imagine what went on in his head ... I decided to do him through the mediums of time and milieux, so that,' he hopes, 'a kind of composite picture emerges.'[3]

Those who wish to read a pre-packaged romantic tale about the man whose melodious music moves their spirits might find this book disappointing. Like life itself, *Dvorak in Love* tells its tale with interruptions. It coils playfully around the mind that strives to impose order on the material too early on in the novel; it teases the reader with echoes of half-remembered events picked up many pages later by another character in whose mind the same events are seen in a different context and hence are given a different meaning. We must submit to this novel and let it guide us until, at a given moment, the motley scenes suddenly reveal the essential pattern beneath.

Dvorak in Love accomplishes, above all, two literary feats. The first one is the way in which the author has breathed life into historical facts, or, as he puts it himself, 'used poetic licence where historical reality does not rule out historical possibility.'[4] Most of the events described or referred to did actually occur. Škvorecký even said, in an interview, that he played with the idea of footnoting events and dates.[5] He wisely decided against it, but such an experiment would have revealed the historical precision that underlies the seemingly wilful tale.

This happy union of fiction and reality can best be illuminated by a brief look at one or two of the 'historical' characters that fill the novel's pages. There is, for instance, Mrs Jeannette Thurber, the charming, tough-minded lady impresario who used – and largely lost – her devoted husband's flourishing wholesale grocery business to found the National Conservatory of Music in New York, and who was responsible for bringing Dvořák to the new world. In this capacity Mrs Thurber is, of course, mentioned in practically all books about Dvořák. But there are other aspects of Mrs Thurber's activity that bring the figure to life here in a quite unique way. For example, Škvorecký describes how she, a gutsy innovator on all levels, was the first to run her brave new, but ill-fated opera company as a co-operative venture by selling 'shares to the stagehands' (71). He also points out that she offered free tuition in her new conservatory in New York with the prerequisite that, after graduation, students should give back one-fifth of their professional earnings to benefit the school. Since most of them earned their living from quite unmusical enterprises, the noble plan turned out to have been utopian. However, far from being treated as a cliché figure of an early liberated woman, Jeannette Thurber, before 'spreading her net for Antonin Dvorak' (70), is also seen as comically, indeed farcically, presiding over the fiasco her opera company experiences in Toronto. Not only clergymen organize a boycott against her staging that 'godless piece of American decadence' (73) *Don Giovanni* in their virtuous city, but also – worse – the orchestra's flautist has his front teeth knocked out in a fight with the tuba player just before the performance, and the leading baritone, a man of considerable proportions, gets stuck in the trapdoor that was to carry him off to eternal damnation. It is a moot point where the author's touches of fictionalizing occur in these by-and-large real occurrences. The luminous colours of 'historical possibility' enliven the original historical events.

Or there is Adele Margulies, the attractive young music teacher originally from Vienna, sent back to Europe by Mrs Thurber in order to convince Dvořák to come to New York. On the piano and during her diplomatic mission, resourceful Adele can manage practically any situation. Her only moment of embarrassment occurs when she has to face the waiter serving breakfast on a hotel terrace in Prague. She knows he has seen handsome Will Marion Cook, the black virtuoso violinist travelling with her, sneaking from her room at the inappropriate hour of 7 a.m. Fiction? Reality? What does it matter? Again, the 'historical possibilities' are all there. Or, as Nabokov says: 'I parted the fabric of fancy, I tasted reality.' Other real figures pop in and out of the novel: there is the composer Harry T. Burleigh, for whom the second movement of Dvořák's *New World* Symphony was his 'ticket to immortality' (97); there are Joseph Joachim and Steele MacKaye, whose Buffalo Bill Ensemble Dvořák went to see in Madison Square Gardens; there is Sigmund Freud, who logically concludes that the pattern of repetition in Dvořák's music is the sign of 'some subconscious obsession' (308); and there is the Master himself, listening intently to Will Marion Cook's violin and 'grappling with the mystery encoded in Will's diminished thirds' (19) and those new sounds – from where? – 'grated onto the polka sounds' (20).

This brings me to the second feat the novel accomplishes: it merges in an entirely new way literary and musical creation. Someday it will join in the annals of literary history those eminent novels of the twentieth century that have been called 'musical,' albeit for different reasons; for what this work accomplishes is the rendering of musical experience by words and the finding of a linguistic expression for musical culture. The author's lifelong love for music pulsates through the pages of *Dvorak in Love*, informs its most memorable scenes, and lingers most succinctly in the reader's memory. Having listened intently to Harry T. Burleigh singing a Negro spiritual, Dvořák suddenly grasps the pencil sharpened for him by his daughter Otylia, writes in bold letters 'Corno inglese' over the seventh bar of the *New World* Symphony's Largo movement, and calls out: 'The English horn, Burleigh ... I knew those flutes didn't belong there ... it needs a feeling of distance to contrast with that forlorn timbre – just like you, Burleigh' (98). Or else we learn from an inebriated conversation in a restaurant – but by now we are in the twentieth century – that Dvořák had woven twelve bars of a tuba part into that same symphony because an enthusiastic tuba player wanted to participate in bringing the work to the public. A tall tale told after the sixth beer by a Dvořák fan? Well – as another character who listens to all this muses – the tuba player is not likely to invent such a story from the past just when the news of Dvořák's death has reached the world.

Perhaps the best example of the way music – the rhythmic sound of related cultures – permeates the novel is a passage about the bells of Prague:

It was two o'clock: from the tower of the royal castle on the hill came a deep, resonant chime, the reverberation of a huge mass of bell-metal; then, from some-where across the river to the south, rang out two strokes a fifth lower, and while these were still echoing in the air the same melody, but in a different key, sound-ed from the spire of the Church of the Knights of Malta, while from the north, bells in a third key interposed themselves between the first two. She felt as though she were inside a gigantic celesta on which an inebriated Johann Sebastian Bach was improvising a cacophonous counterpoint. More and more bells now entered the fugue in cruel, clashing couplets, a gigantic polyrhythm beating the air above a city submerged in sleep. (53)

This is perhaps as close as literature (not merely lyrical words) can come to music. Colours and sounds, as Rimbaud said, answer each other. The passage can also serve as an illustration of the superb quality of Paul Wilson's finely tuned translation.

Dvorak in Love, Škvorecký tells us, is his first attempt at writing historical and biographical fiction. It is also a text that reveals from a new angle his quality as a contemporary writer. If Dvořák, by integrating jazz into his compositions, turned music in a new direction, Škvorecký, by writing about him in his inimitable artistic idiom, has perhaps moved musical biography as well in the intimate and intricate history of human creativeness in a new direction. Through the medium of Dvořák's music (The Slavonic Dances – 'typically Czech?' The *New World* Symphony – 'typically American?') the author explores the unfathomable mysteries of artistic inspiration. Through the figure of a little black boy who, his ear flattened against a frozen window, ecstatically listens to Rafael Joseffi playing the pianoforte to assembled guests inside, Škvorecký explores the socially troubled yet amazingly creative scene of American jazz born of anguished Negro spiri-tuals and an intuitive sense of rhythm. Through the medium of many personal letters, stories, and conversations he explores with the sensitivity of a seismograph,[6] the intricate patterns of cultural differences and proxim-ities. A 'light-hearted dream'? Perhaps. But within it is the whole spectrum of voices of an Old and New World symphony.

NOTES

This essay is an expanded version of the review article 'A Literary Scherzo,' which appeared in *Canadian Forum* 67, no. 771 August–September 1987.

1 Phrases from the following reviews are quoted: Jonathan Keates, London *Observer*, 5 October 1986; Vera Blackwell, *World Literature*, 59: 4, Fall 1985; William French, Toronto *Globe and Mail*, 25 October 1986; Ken Adachi, Toronto *Star*, 8 November 1986; George Galt, *Books in Canada*, November 1986; Thomas Shapcott, Sydney *Morning Herald*, 21 February 1987; Rhoda Koenig, *New York Magazine*, 9 February 1987.

2 Josef Škvorecký, *Dvorak in Love*, trans. Paul Wilson (Toronto: Lester & Orpen Dennys, 1986), 169. All subsequent references are included in the body of the essay.

3 James Adams, 'Škvorecký Feels Canadian,' *Edmonton Journal*, 15 November 1986

4 *Dvorak in Love*, Author's Acknowledgements

5 Adams, 'Škvorecký Feels Canadian'

6 An expression used by Helena Kosková in her book on modern Czech prose, *Hledání ztracené generace*, (Toronto: Sixty-Eight Publishers, 1987) 143

17

PETER HRUBÝ

Meeting Josef Škvorecký (1989)

Literary historians and critics will comment on and evaluate his novels. His close friends will tell us about his life and human qualities. All I can do, looking out of my window into an Australian winter garden as green and full of blossoms as if it were July in northern summer, is just add a few remarks as a distant observer and reader of an author without whom Czech literature and cultural life of the past thirty years would have been immeasurably poorer. My short report is about meeting him – and also about not meeting him.

The first time was long ago, in 1948, after the Communist *coup d'état*, during my last months in Czechoslovakia. In order to help two of my closest friends to escape safely, my father, my brother, and I helped to organize a voluntary work brigade to an abandoned village on the Šumava frontier, under the pretext of digging peat for fertilizer. After a few months of work, my two friends – a young married couple – were sent off by the whole voluntary brigade to the other side of the border.

Only years later did I discover that serendipity had played one of her tricks. The group digging peat on the border had a great time. They didn't work much, were paid quite well, and enjoyed themselves, since all were compatible students from Prague's higher institutions. Among them was Josef Škvorecký. Lasting friendships were made, at least one marriage followed, and literary co-operation was encouraged. However, I missed my chance of meeting Škvorecký because by then I had left for Switzerland. That was my penalty for leaving the country too early.

In my long life I have met Škvorecký three or four times, once visiting him in his home and only once more intimately, during a dinner party where we sat next to each other discussing and disagreeing about religion. I have often met him, however, through his manifold activities. So often, indeed, that I could not imagine my adult life since the 1950s without him.

Between 1956 and 1958, I enjoyed his editorial work in bimonthly issues of the journal *Světová literatura* (World Literature), which among the Communist regime's publications looked like an apparition from another world. Its cover pages were visually attractive and the thick volume contained a good selection of well-translated stories and poems from otherwise forbidden foreign countries, such as the United States, Great Britain, France, and Italy. Photographs and reproductions were included in a typographical display unlike any other in Czechoslovakia. I read the journal in Munich while obligatorily going through many unpleasant and uninteresting Czech and Slovak publishing products. How much more unusual it must have appeared to Škvorecký's readers at home.

Then in 1958 came the miracle of his novel *The Cowards*. There was just one copy available in the New York editorial offices of Radio Free Europe, where I happened to be working, and it went from hand to hand. Very much like the later samizdat publications, it could be borrowed for just a short period of time. At home we read it aloud in order to rejoice about the marvellously recreated, fresh and re-invented literary language. The style and vocabulary shocked many people who were used to much less candid expressions, but I soon began to think that without this revolution in literary communication the Czech intelligentsia could not have won the protracted fight against the pseudo-revolutionaries in power. It was a necessary part of the liberation.

It was not just a question of form and language: it was also one of a radically different attitude to life, to power, to great public and small private politics. It was, or to many seemed to be, cynical; but it was frank, open-minded, gently human, and quietly heroic. It was realistic, modern, and up-to-date in a regime of hypocrites who, though petits bourgeois themselves, pretended to be progressive proletarians.

In disagreement with purists and moralists who were shocked by the book (and continued to be shocked by future novels), I still think that the extent and the glory of the gradual liberation from the strait-jacket of Stalinism would not have been possible without the daring abandonment of linguistic and literary clichés, and without the guts to feel and talk truthfully and openly, disregarding moralistic and linguistic prejudices. Škvorecký started the process.

It is necessary to mention that not only Communists felt offended and enraged. *The Cowards* attacked both the pseudo-socialist pretenders and the bourgeoisie from which they came. Škvorecký's picture of the ineffective Sokol-type 'preparation for fighting' that never gets over its formal exercises into an actual battle also embarrassed many. The author began what several other writers then continued exploring, namely the question of a soft national character, of cowardice masked as bravery. Courage to see clearly, without illusions, was a necessary precondition of the victory of the sixties.

Later Škvorecký devoted several other books to young people who in time would be called beatniks but who already during the Second World War in *Protektorat Böhmen und Mähren* and then in the 'people's democracy' showed their contempt for official incantations with a home-grown 'popular surrealism.' At least two generations of young people found themselves on these pages.

Reading one of the author's other major successes, *The Republic of Whores*, many people were shocked again by the number of 'dirty' words associated with bodily functions, but that was exactly the way soldiers (and not only soldiers) were expressing themselves. Škvorecký had to write it down that way if he wanted to provide a realistic picture of the Sovietized armed forces. One of his major gifts has always been an acute ear for the variations and nuances of the spoken word. As one reader wrote, he is a first-rate 'slangster.' His army novel was often favourably compared with another anti-militarist saga of Czech literature, Jaroslav Hašek's *The Good Soldier Švejk*. But in Škvorecký's newer version of Czech pacifism almost all the subordinate conscripts are Švejkian and try to turn the stupid drill and brainwashing into fun, and so keep intact their individualism and sense of values. And the main hero of the comedy is not an idiot of genius but rather a well-educated and very shrewd young man ably coping with all the official silliness he has to face and survive. He is also much gentler and more emotional than Švejk.

Beginning with his first novel and through a whole series of stories devoted to young people's lives, Škvorecký showed his pro-Western, especially pro-American orientation, not so much politically as culturally. A sense of clean fun, love of jazz, admiration for Hemingway, Faulkner, Salinger, Chandler, and other American authors mark the character and style of his writing from the start. It comes as no surprise that at the Charles University in Prague he studied Anglo-American literature; later, in his exile, he taught it in Canada.

During his demanding teaching career Škvorecký continued publishing numerous novels. He also somehow found time and energy to pursue the two other great loves of his life, film and jazz. His pages devoted to jazz belong among the best ever written on it in any language. The author of several film scenarios for Czech films, and an accomplished if minor actor in a few, he wrote an enchanting 'personal history of the Czech cinema,' *All the Bright Young Men and Women*. Published at the beginning of the seventies, it is an extremely well-documented story written in his usual breezy and witty style. It came out just at the time North Americans were getting interested in the directors of the Czech new wave of the sixties, who were beginning to produce their American works. It remains a scholarly, though very readable, source for researchers into a corner of the threatened but flourishing Central European culture.

Until recently, almost all the author's stories (his detective fiction is the exception) were highly autobiographical. Other characters than the perennial Danny were also often based on actual persons, in spite of the usual disclaimer about 'any resemblance to any persons living or dead being purely coincidental.' No one seems to know as much as Škvorecký about important or interesting Czech literati, and no other novelist helps us understand and feel as well the atmosphere and attitudes of people involved in the tragicomedy that has taken place in twentieth-century Bohemia. He should write his memoirs, but for obvious reasons they would probably have to remain unpublished for another twenty or thirty years.

So for the moment, we have to be content with his memoirs disguised as novels, which have enraged many contemporaries who do not enjoy as much as he does a satirical and lovingly sceptical humour. *The Miracle Game*, which deals with 1968, was written with the same sceptical sadness as he displayed in *The Cowards*, which treated the legendary events of the liberation in 1945. Those of us who left the country in 1948 welcomed his penetrating reports on people involved in developments at home that we were able to follow only indirectly from the outside. I must admit that I was surprised by his rather mocking description of the reforming Communists of 1968, the 'heroes' of that memorable year. While I was impressed by their growth from silly 'fools' of the late forties and early fifties into daring anti-Stalinists and quasi-democrats, he disliked the renewed revolutionary fervour of 'the painful playboys of Marxism-Leninism' and saw it as a madness dangerous to the laboriously achieved 'kadarization' of Novotny's Czechoslovakia. Although they helped to soften the dictatorship throughout the sixties, he proved to be at least partly right. Legends about lost battles are silly, but I still believe that the experience had positive results for the nation's psyche and self-confidence. To a large degree, the haunting national anxiety about Czech cowardice was replaced by a more positive outlook. Even previously contemptuous neighbours – Germans, Hungarians, and Poles – began to take the Czechs and some Slovaks more seriously. And who can measure the degree of Dubčekism's beneficial influence on the Russian intelligentsia and soldiers? Would Gorbachev's program of glasnost and perestroika have been possible without the eight months of 1968? The dispute about whether progress can be achieved by systematic small nibbling at power structures or by more decisive actions will surely go on.

Škvorecký's long novel *The Engineer of Human Souls* is enjoyable reading. He allowed us to enter his classrooms and observe his teaching methods. The seven authors of Anglo-American literature, whose names provide chapter titles, were used not only to wake up and enlighten his young students about the mysteries of literature but also to connect them with the problems of the contemporary world. He does not treat these as dead authors of books from and about another age but as living testaments of the beauty, misery, and crises in personal and public life. The novel is written with his typical sadness, satiric scepticism, acute ear for nuances of many variations of the spoken and written word, and, let me finally say it, wisdom. The motto of his favourite song expresses the mood: 'When you see me smilin' I'm smilin' to keep from cryin' ...' Škvorecký's democratic pluralism and tolerance, sentimentality, and a tempered idealism based on Christianity shine through the pages.

The cynicism that some of his critics see in his work is, in my opinion, just the disguise of a very sensitive man in an environment in which a benefactor's goodwill is often suspected of being hypocrisy and is considered to be a silly weakness in practical or realistic men. Neither Škvorecký nor his semi-autobiographical hero, Daniel Smiřický, is really a cynic. For one thing, a cynic would never have committed himself to founding and managing an expatriate publishing house in order to keep his country's culture alive. The two hundred–odd books that Škvorecký, together with 'the girl he met in Prague,' has published at the Sixty-Eight Publishers they established in Toronto is an incredible success story, comparable only to Ludvík Vaculík's samizdat editions, Petlice (Padlock), in Prague.

What would Czech readers have done without the hundreds of thousands of copies of these books, sent all over the world for more than sixteen years? What would researchers and literary or social historians have done without the publication of so many novels, collections of poetry or of short stories, important memoirs, and, what is even more daring, literary studies, including even a dictionary of Czech writers? For many years, I have been meeting Josef Škvorecký in his highly autobiographical books and, several times every year, obtaining packages of books co-published by him in Canada. They are nicely produced with carefully selected reproductions of paintings often on their title-pages – as artistically and lovingly produced as was his journal

Světová literatura more than three decades ago. Since then he has himself become part of world literature.

Josef Škvorecký and his wife, what an unbelievable couple! From a faraway continent: many thanks to both of you and my thanks and congratulations for your excellent work.

18

GEORGE GIBIAN

The Poetics of Prague: Literary Images of a City (1989)

The action in Josef Škvorecký's most famous novel, *The Cowards*, takes place not in Prague, but in a small town very reminiscent of his own Náchod. Nevertheless, the presence of the capital is very palpable. For the young heroes of the novel, Prague is a magnet gleaming somewhere in their future. They look forward to going to Prague now the war is nearly over and the Germans are gone. Prague is the focus of their yearnings and aspirations, as Moscow was for Chekhov's three sisters. But the Prague of *The Cowards* holds very different promises from those of Moscow in the Russian play: the young Czech boys look to Prague for the fulfilment of their dream of a marvellous girl and of marvellous jazz. The last words of the novel read: 'I played for them, and thought of all those usual things that I always thought about, about girls and jazz and that unknown girl I am going to meet in Prague.'[1]

In this article, however, I am not concerned with the images of Prague in the works of Škvorecký; I shall leave this fruitful and enjoyable topic to others to pursue. Rather, I shall examine the lyrical literary image of Prague as the words of generations of Czech writers have shaped it.

I base this essay on the supposition that in the writings about any city it is possible to discern patterns of frequently found themes, images, and attitudes. Moreover, these structures – this poetics – result both from the actual physical and other 'facts' of a city as well as from the tradition of generations writing about it (including chroniclers' accounts, the textbooks used to teach children in schools, and many other sources). There exist traditions (or poetics) – though very different ones – of Petersburg, Vienna, Paris, and other important cities. Within the Prague tradition, one may discern several subcategories: there was a conception of Prague constructed and favoured by the romantic period, and there may have been peculiarly naturalist, symbolist, and expressionist images of Prague.

I shall concentrate here on one particular 'Poetics of Prague,' the lyrical, and I shall draw my chief examples from the extraordinary late poetry of Jaroslav Seifert. The lyrical Prague is not merely one variant of many. While its core may be the particular images and poetics of the group that called itself Poetism, this twentieth-century lyrical Prague is also the dominant poetic tradition. Contemporaries and members of other literary schools continued to react to its ways of patterning feelings, concepts, attitudes. Subsequent writers about Prague have taken it into account, some have tried to accommodate themselves to it or partially to repudiate it, others to qualify it or quarrel with it – yet this image has remained the compass by which most writers have defined (perhaps tacitly, perhaps even unconsciously) their own approaches. This perennial image of Prague exerts a strong force that rivets, focuses, and guides the imagination of Czechs thinking about Prague.[2]

What assertions can we make about Prague as a presence in the minds of generations of Czech writers affected by this dominant model?[3] Let us first give a short account of the main characteristics of Prague's lyrical image in Czech culture, and then illustrate it with passages from the poems of Jaroslav Seifert.

First, Prague has been and continues to be dominant in Czech culture and consciousness as few towns have been elsewhere. Perhaps only Paris occupies a similar position in France, or Kyoto in traditional Japan. As early as medieval Czech chronicles one may find passages that demonstrate that Prague is more important than, and has primacy over, the entire Bohemian kingdom, above the Czech lands.[4]

Second, a love affair has been going on for many centuries between Czechs and Prague. There is a constant stream of books of photographs and of historical and topographical books about Prague; other symptoms of adulation also abound. Moreover, this tradition of affection for the capital is not limited to the inhabitants of Prague itself, but Czechs outside of Prague participate in it as well.

Third, there are certain physical aspects of Prague that have imprinted themselves firmly on the Czech consciousness. References to these – transformed by an imaginative tradition and through such clichés as Golden Prague, Mother Prague, and the Hundred-Towered Prague – recur often in Prague aesthetics. Thus we are looking not merely at a topography and an architectural ensemble, but at a mythology of a topography and architecture.

The physical items include, first of all, the river Vltava (Moldau). Writers tend to describe it as meandering, and this meandering, in turn, suggests slowness, delay, not hurrying to a goal. The many bridges that span the river also play a dominant role in this physical poetic of the city.

The bridges crisscross the river and tie Prague together like a sloppy shoelace, not drawn very tight and straight, but tied nevertheless. The river does not divide, separate, or split the city into fragments; instead it links, it embraces, it hugs. Here as in other important respects, the image of Prague contrasts with that of St Petersburg where the recurring floods of the Neva and the destructiveness of the natural elements, harnessed and conquered by its creator, Peter the Great, are always close to the literary consciousness. The Vltava is felt to be and is spoken of as a friendly, cuddly river.

The dominant views of Prague depend on its hills – chiefly Hradčany, Vyšehrad, and Petřín. These provide sweeping long-distance panoramas. But there are also the antithetical, close-range views – those of little alleys and lanes where you cannot see far. Yet both are positive, amiable, benevolent: they do not contrast with each other but function instead as parts of a unified whole. Thus insight does not compete with blindness to preside over Prague aesthetics. Instead the long-range panorama suggests freedom, while confinement evokes the sense of a shelter. The exhilarating vistas contrast yet coexist harmoniously with the protective, close crookedness, darkness, of corners, multi-angled tiled roofs, and studded gates.

What does all this yield in terms of emotional attitude and how is this attitude expressed in literature? The literary image of Prague is above all associated with women and with beauty. Physically adorned by the river and its bridges, Prague culminates in one overriding dominant: the aesthetic reactions to the beauty of the feminine city. They may have become stereotypes, but we must not be afraid of platitudes: Czech writing about Prague plays on these banalities – it uses them as a known common denominator, as clichés to which it sometimes gives a little twist, from which it flies off into a small orbit or at a tangent.

Fourth, there are certain historical periods that literally created Prague (built it, brought it into actual material existence); these periods also stamped associations and feelings on the Prague tradition.

The great, in the sense of most influential, historical periods of Prague consist of four key historical moments – four peaks that formed Prague and accumulated the materials from which imaginative minds created a conception and a structure of what Prague means:

1 Fourteenth century – the age of Charles IV, who was the son of a Czech mother and French father, and was a great builder of streets and castles and the founder of Prague institutions[5]
2 Seventeenth century – the age of Rudolf II[6]

3 The second half of the nineteenth and the beginning of the twentieth
century
4 The First Republic (1918–39)

The age of the great dramatic events of the twentieth century (1939–91) –
Munich, German occupation, liberation, Communist takeover, Prague Spring,
Soviet occupation, the 'velvet revolution' – drew on the four great earlier
periods and became superimposed upon them in literature.

The four ages were periods of building and of artistic achievements, as
well as climactic moments when Prague achieved wealth and power. They
were also the times when Prague had the greatest influxes of foreigners –
not only artists but also bakers, alchemists, astronomers, astrologers,
magicians, con men, moneylenders, money changers, importers, mystics,
merchants, craftsmen. Many of these foreigners settled and continued to live
in Prague – Jews (very early), followed by Germans, Italians, and others.
The milieu tolerated them and benefited from their presence. Cross-fertilization of cultures and nations led to the moods of irony and to multiplicity in
culture, both baroque and modernist.[7] This traditional multi-ethnic Prague
no longer exists: now it is a pure Czech town. The Germans were deported
in 1945, the Jews were murdered by the Nazis or left, and many of the
Jewish survivors were driven into emigration by the Communist regime.
Compared with the thousand years of Prague history before 1939, a great
impoverishment has taken place. Now Prague culture is purely Czech –
perhaps the fulfilment of a few nationalists' wishes – and less rich.[8]

What are the qualities writers attribute to Prague in their works? As
we have already seen they are – to name a few – associated with the
feminine: love, sensuality, as well as farewell or parting. (And it is often felt
that an earthy language [zemitý] is particularly appropriate for describing
these.)

Our first illustration, from an unusual source, is by an exiled statesman.
The BBC Christmas message by Jan Masaryk, Foreign Affairs Minister of
the Czechoslovak government in exile in London in 1942, was broadcast
from abroad to an occupied country:

I bring you my Christmas and New Year's wishes. But first I must confess what I
wished for myself. It is a little selfish, forgive me.

My wish is to walk through Prague. To start best of all at the Wilson Railroad
Station, go down Wenceslas Square, walk down National Street, past the theatre,
then turn and go down the embankment. Stop in front of Trnka's mills, take a
peek at Hradčany, a slow but good peek at Hradčany. Maybe it will be at sunset

or maybe not. Across the Stone Bridge to greet the statues. The beautiful gilt cross sticks in my mind. Along Bridge Street and under the colonnade on Small Side Square. Past Fragner's Pharmacy. Poor Karel Fragner is now in God's glory too. Up Thun Street past number 9 where we used to live, and where the Germans later had their embassy. Up the New Castle steps to the Castle. Not inside the castle, that does not interest me, but to the second and third courtyard. To stroke St. Vitus' Cathedral and the Golden Lane. Down the Old Castle steps, along Klárov and Carmelite Street. The late Šamal lived there till they dragged him off to be tortured. In front of this house we must take our hats off. We Protestants used not to take our hats off in front of churches and statues. Now we must take our hats off in front of the houses where our saints live. Not low, the way ministerial counsellors used to do, but just a little bit, with embarrassment, and then in a sort of whisper, 'Chancellor, forgive me that I am still here.' And on past Tyrš' house ... And then maybe I'd go back to the Wilson Railway Station to have a paprika and a roll and a Pilsner or a Smíchov beer. I wouldn't like anybody to recognize me. I have changed a lot in these hellish years. I definitely haven't become better looking.[9]

Jan Masaryk's message is light and full of gentle, understated pathos. His imaginary, wished-for walk through Prague is circular. His tone, his attitudes are very familiar, informal, close, intimate, physical. He wishes to look, to stroke the stones, and to include in his sentimental walk some typical, average food and beer, alongside his sorrow over the fate of the nation – the occupation, subjugation, tortures. So he wants to look, to keep on looking, and stroking – caressing – the familiar. The mood and the tone are tender, gentle, self-deprecating, modest, but firm.

Jan Masaryk's message was of course a very special one, an unusual one. He spoke as a statesman at a historical moment. The walks that Prague normally suggests are for lovers,[10] not for the metaphysical or desperate purposes to which Petersburg or Paris lend themselves in literature. Masaryk's walk is typical of the frequent association of Prague with a return – with a backward look, serpentine movements into the past, associated with close feelings (and tactile contacts with familiar, beautiful old stones).

Let us now turn to some examples from the works of Jaroslav Seifert, to illustrate the general points stated above. Seifert's short poem 'A Song about Girls' exemplifies several aspects of Prague poetics that we have been speaking about in general terms:

In the middle of the town a long river flows,
seven bridges tie it together,

along the embankment a thousand beautiful girls walk
and each one is different.

From heart to heart one goes warming one's hands
in the beams of their great, warming loves,
along the embankment a thousand beautiful girls walk
and all of them are the same.

In the brief compass of this charming poem we notice the association of
Prague with femininity; the tying together rather than isolating by the
bridges and the river; the link with beauty; lightness of touch; the mood of
contentment, happiness; and warmth.

In other poems (in *Býti básníkem* [Verses from a Tapestry]), Seifert
similarly links Prague with the feminine, the beautiful and aesthetic. For
instance, he identifies Prague with two forms of art (music, weaving):
'Prague! ... She is herself a song woven in time.' In another passage, Seifert
starts with banality – roofs – and then introduces a startling simile drawn
from the contemporary world:

My first still happy dreams
sparkled above her roofs
like flying saucers.

Or:

Once I pressed my face
on the stone of an old wall
somewhere under the courtyard outside the Castle
and a gloomy roaring
suddenly sounded in my ear.
Long gone centuries were thundering.
But the moist soft cupola
from White Mountain
whispered amiably in my ear
Go, you will be enchanted.
Sing, they are waiting.
And don't lie.

I went and I didn't lie.
To you, my loves,

only a little

...

I was foolishly young
and sometimes I would come home late.
I'd wander around a little longer
in the alleys of the Old Town.
While prostitutes shouted
on the sidewalks
I spoke verses of love.

In the poetry of Prague there are many stanzas about roses, parks and gardens, and the green slopes of Petřín. For urban poetry, Prague lyrics speak surprisingly often about nightingales and bushes, and trees in bloom. We do not find expressions of deprivation, or of contrast, antagonism, between the urban and the green world of nature. Prague includes the vegetable kingdom. Her writers speak of the pleasures of parks, shrubs, trees, flowers, grass, as an integral part of the Prague cityscape.

Like Masaryk, Seifert also finds tactile pleasures in his city:

Hat in hand I step from foot to foot
in Prague's little streets
I touch her stones
They are rough
but a poet kissed them.

He again associates love for Prague with love for a woman as well as with plants. The speaker of the poem, feeling unhappy,

stroked the silky darkness
of enchanting nights.
They smelled of women's hair
and sweet jasmine.

After a deceptively commonplace passage about how time flies, Seifert surprises us with the originality of what follows: he no longer tears up his poems in order to stuff them inside the 'hungry gargoyles on the cornices of the cathedral.'

We can conclude that the poetics of Prague emphasizes the sensual and the physical – not aspiring too high, or settling for too little. The purely rational and intellectual elements are few and slight. Instead the poetics of this city belongs in the realm of the legendary and the mythic, often the myths of origins, which can be unusually expressive. There is a favourite Czech legend that ties in amusingly with my suggestion that writers have represented Prague with a strong emphasis on feminine beauty and on the aesthetic in general. The legend of the founding of the Czech lands has it that the ancestral leader, the Ur-Father Czech, could not decide where to allow his migrating band to settle. But when the advance scouting party reported from Říp, a hill or mountain in Central Bohemia, that the view of the land below was unusually pretty, their leader suddenly consented to settle in that region – Central Bohemia. Generations of Czech schoolchildren have commented, cynically perhaps, that choosing a land to settle in merely because it was beautiful showed a deficiency of rational calculation and an excessive weighting of the aesthetic factor. After all, the Germans were on one side and the Russians on the other. Precisely such a preference may be thought to have entered into the combination of the lyrical image of Prague.

We can also suggest some absences. What is it that is not present in the lyrical image of Prague? What we do *not* have is a sense of the town as the centre of an empire (as in old Vienna and other capitals) or the impression that it may vanish (something Petersburg reportedly threatens to do). This is a town where flesh is part and parcel of what is suggested, strongly associated with the very firm, very real stones, trees, bushes, lawns. There is no sense of unreality, insubstantiality. Often there is a mist or a veil, but behind the mist and veil, or in it, we are made to realize, there definitely is a very, very old, long-lasting, solid, physical Prague.

In Prague there is little or nothing of the other-worldly. We find no search for the metaphysical – no supercelestial strivings. Instead there is femininity, sensuousness, magic, and mystery. And if there is nothing supercelestial, there is nothing demonic either. Prague is not a New Jerusalem, nor is it thought of as a Babylon. We do not find the devils and apparitions of Gogol's or Pushkin's Petersburg. Instead we encounter the spirit of Mozart, a storytelling Mozart.

It is also worth noting that fantasy is not merely tolerated in the garden or kingdom of Prague, it is encouraged and welcome. Surrealism took root here. There is freedom to leap from one level of diction to other, very different ones. There is also the storytelling, the palavering, of Hašek, Hrabal, and others. The leaps from one story to another do not have to make sense, and logical connections are not obligatory. Nonsense and mystery are admitted and sought after. But these considerations would take us too far afield, away from our subject and into the realm of another – Czech narratology.

One must insert parenthetically, however, that there also exists a literary anti-Prague. Its negative characteristics re-emphasize what I have been saying about the lyrical, positive Prague. This anti-Prague has its own poetics or antipoetics – that of the huge new prefabricated housing developments. Věra Chytilová, in her film with the un-Czech title *Panel-Story* (known as *Prefab Story* in its English version), has shown the patterns of life in these huge settlements where one cannot find one's way; all is numbered, the same, muddy, raw – and its qualities are the opposite of those associated with lyrical Prague. The geometry in this new anti-Prague is that of the straight line and the right angle; the materials are mud and reinforced concrete; the movement, that of elevators that stop between floors and won't go any farther. The predominant psychology at home there suggests exploitation or self-barricading behind closed doors. The typical vehicles are a pretentious baby carriage and a back-hoe. The characteristic emotion is fear; aggressiveness prevails, not a sense of being cozily sheltered. There is no room for the lovely crooked lines of the poetic Prague. There is a raw, new, inhospitable town. This is the Other, the antinomy, against which the Prague of our lyrical poetics is now defining itself, whereas in the past it defined itself *vis-à-vis* the countryside, the country village, or against other cities like Vienna. Chytilová's prefab Prague could be anywhere (not located on the Vltava, meandering and oxbowing, with the bridges tying it together). Jaroslav Seifert, in his *Praha ve snu* (Prague in a Dream) also evokes this anti-Prague, speaking of housing developments, satellite towns (sídliště), with their jaws and canine teeth (animal, predatory), wanting to swallow inner Prague, chestnut trees, lawns, and flower-beds.

After this brief excursion into the poetics of anti-Prague, let us in conclusion recapitulate the traits and patterns of Prague poetics. In a fine article Maria Banerjee argues that the poems of Seifert's contemporary Vítězslav Nezval are a surrealist celebration of Prague.[11] She discusses the sensuousness of Nezval's Prague and goes on to argue that there is a secret at the centre of Prague, and that the city has a mysterious order or arrangement. The poetic patterns characteristic of Prague ask to be divined rather than reasoned out; they recall and seem to explain the alchemy of Rudolf II's court, the meandering of the Vltava, and of the crooked lanes in the old parts of the city.

This collective artistic creation is a structure of sensuousness and mystery belonging to the realm of feeling, not the world of reason. It looks backward through the many layers of the past. Its energy is created by intensity of narration, by story following story, image after image, with emphasis on the medium, on how it is expressed: whether through a phrase, or a striking image. The poetics of Prague can be thought of as baroque[12] and also as akin to the surrealistic, yet down-to-earth, too. The poetics of Prague embraces hedonism and *joie de vivre*, while avoiding both the depths of gloom and lofty heights of intellectual or religious speculation.

NOTES

1 *Zbabělci* (Prague: Československý spisovatel, 1964), 353. (My translation.)
2 In classical Japanese literature, the term *utamakura* gives recognition to the cultural fact that a place can become defined in terms of successive poetic usages of it and associations thus created. See Earl Miner et al., *The Princeton Companion to Classical Japanese Literature* (Princeton University Press, 1985), 302, 433–5. Originally applied to phrases or images codified for poetic use, in later usage the term referred to names of famous places. The special features and the resonance of particular places celebrated in poetry were recognized for their special associations and evocative powers. Lists of these *utamakura* (used for convenience, hence 'poetic pillows') were compiled.
3 The surrealistic reaction to the image of Prague is presented in Maria Němcová Banerjee's pioneering article 'Nezval's "Prague with Fingers of Rain"': A Surrealistic Image,' *Slavic and East European Journal*, 23, no. 4 (1979).
4 See František Kavka, in Jaroslav Pěšina, ed., *České Umění Gotické, 1350–1420* (Prague, 1970), 7–18.
5 Ibid
6 Thomas DaCosta Kaufmann, *The School of Prague: Painting at the Court of Rudolf II* (Chicago: University of Chicago Press, 1988), 3, quotes Karel van Mander, 1604, who worked in Italy and lived in the Netherlands: 'Whosoever nowadays desires has only to go to Prague (if he can), to the greatest art patron in the world at the present time, to wit, the Roman Emperor Rudolf the Second: there he may see at the imperial residence, and elsewhere in the *Kunstkammern* of other great art-lovers, a remarkable number of outstanding and precious, interesting, unusual, and priceless works.'
7 Sometimes this was so even when artists of various nationalities lived side by side but were unaware, or little aware, of the others' existence. There was enrichment even when the world of Hašek and that of Kafka touched very little. Many Czechs knew nothing of Kafka till long after his death. The various subcultures, subworlds, of Prague, constituted autonomous circles – the German world, the Czech tavern world, and so forth.
8 Will some future historian disagree and claim that the culture of Prague of the

mid- and late-twentieth century was also ethnically impure, after its different fashion? That the Soviet Russian influence was the alien element corresponding to the Jews and Germans and others of previous centuries and cultural epochs? I doubt it. That would be the only possibility: to regard the cross-fertilization, the alloy-making quality, of forcibly imposed Soviet social and political ideology to be the foreign aspect. Or would perhaps the influence of German and Austrian TV and tourists – and VCRs – constitute the alien element? In one art form foreignness is present, electronically: in jazz and in rock.

9 23 December 1942, reprinted in *Československé listy*, New York, 16 December 1988. (My translation.)

10 When Franz Kafka's young man in 'The Judgment' ('Urteil') is sentenced to death by drowning by his father, he runs through a city and leaps over the side of the bridge to his death in the river. He is not persecuted or murdered by the city, but by his inner neurotic fears and anxieties. Similarly in the case of Gregor Samsa in *The Metamorphosis* (*Verwandlung*), Prague is not only the locus of his nightmarish terrors, but, at the end, when he is dead and gone, the whole family goes for a happy walk through the outskirts of Prague – in the green yet urban setting – and it is then that, rid of him, the parents become aware of the nubility of their now marriageable, healthy young daughter. In *The Castle* Kafka is describing not a Prague castle but a rural structure, similar to that of Count Clam-Gallas' castle in Friedland in northern Bohemia, for his hero's attempt to establish connections with the authorities. There is a fine illustration of this northern Bohemian castle, to which Kafka made a business trip in Jan.–Feb. 1911, as an insurance official inspecting a textile factory, in Klaus Wagenbach, *Franz Kafka: Pictures of a Life* (New York: Pantheon, 1984), 122.

11 Banerjee, ibid.

12 Roman Jakobson, in a postscript to Milada Součková, *The Baroque in Bohemia* (Ann Arbor, MI: Ardis, 1980): 'The baroque cast of Czech thinking belongs among the interesting problems of modern characterology. Perhaps the greatest and freshest humorous novel of our century, *The Good Soldier Švejk*, by Jaroslav Hašek, is an embodiment of the unshakeable national world view – in a baroque spirit. It was also the baroque of the 17th century that developed the most militant and the most effective literary weapons against every foreign interference and invasion' (201).

19

The Girl from Prague:
A Conversation with Zdena Salivarová (1989–92)

SOLECKI I have the impression that while for most Czechs, both at home and abroad, you are known as a novelist and short-story writer, most Canadians probably associate you with Sixty-Eight Publishers and have an image of you based on those photographs of you and Josef that appear in newspaper and magazine articles about your publishing house. That split is probably reflected in your two names: you are Salivarová the author, and Škvorecká the publisher.

SALIVAROVÁ I think that's generally true. But you know, when Czechs want to flatter me about something that Sixty-Eight has published they always write me or phone me as Salivarová. Although I don't mind Škvorecká, because I don't mind being in Josef's shadow at all. And it doesn't surprise me that Canadians know me only as a publisher of Czech books and as the wife of Josef Škvorecký. They wouldn't really know me as a writer.

SOLECKI But anyone who has read your fairly autobiographical novels *Summer in Prague* (*Honzlová*, in Czech) and *Ashes, Ashes, All Fall Down* (*Nebe, peklo, ráj*) would also realize that you have had a remarkably varied career as singer, dancer, actress, student at the Prague Film Academy, writer, and publisher. When you sang with a folk-song group you travelled to Paris; the folklorist group you worked with seems to have travelled far and wide in the Communist world.

SALIVAROVÁ You know I was with the Folklorist State Ensemble for ten years, and I left because I was really fed up with singing the same folk-songs over and over. I hated it. Also the atmosphere in the collective was really unpleasant. When I quit, four of us put together the Incognito Quartet to sing in nightclubs. I was really longing to sing jazz. Unfortunately, my colleagues in the quartet wanted something different. They wanted to sing polkas and waltzes with brass orchestras, something that was quite easy, required little rehearsal time, and would pay well. We were hired by a small Czech theatre with an orchestra whose musicians made arrangements for our four voices. At the same time we were able to make money working outside the theatre. So the actual singing or what we performed wasn't what I had in mind when I left the folklore collective.

But I must tell you, these ten or twelve years of my life or my career, from 1952 to 1962, were completely unplanned – they were caused by necessity. It was the only way of making a living and supporting my mother and sister. Singing in a folklore choir was easier than working in a factory and I was happy to have a job, and I had no ambitions to become a soloist or star or whatever. Even though I had a fairly good voice, I knew my limits.

When I was admitted to the Film Academy in 1965, *that* was what I had wanted ten years before, but there was no way that I could have been admitted in the 1950s. In the sixties, I was Škvorecká, and Josef had a fairly good name among writers and artists as an editor at *Světová literatura*, as a translator, and as the author of *The Cowards*. So he knew people.

I was also already writing in the sixties and published my first stories and novellas, and that showed, I guess, that I had some talent as a potential scriptwriter. Three of the novellas were later collected as *Pánská jízda* (Gentleman's Ride). In Czech the title refers to when men go off by themselves and women aren't allowed to come along. It's funny, but I was provoked into writing the book by Milan Kundera's *Laughable Loves* (*Směšné lásky*), which upset me for various reasons, and I answered it with *Pánská jízda*.

SOLECKI You knew Kundera in the sixties, didn't you?

SALIVAROVÁ Yes, he was my teacher at the Film Academy, but I had known about him from his writing. Anyway, *Laughable Loves* made me so mad I felt like a feminist and decided that I had to pay him back in some way and try to write something from a woman's point of view. And that's how the three novellas came to be written. They were published by the state publishing house, Československý spisovatel, which was in the sixties a very good publisher. They had a special series that published only new writers, and that's where *Pánská jízda* appeared in January 1968 in an edition of ten thousand.

It was my first published book, though, as I said, I had published various stories in magazines. The first appeared in Brno, and its title was 'Why Did I Play Bruch's Violin Concerto So Well?' It was about a young violinist whose father comes back from prison. He enters the house, and without even taking off his coat he asks her to play the violin so that he can see whether she has made any progress in her technique. She plays beautifully, very emotionally, because her boyfriend has just left her.

Then in 1968 I had a script accepted by the Barrandov Film Studios. It was scheduled to be filmed in 1969, even though we were already in Canada. I even received a contract. The script was about a mother's visit to her son, who is in a concentration camp. It was based on my own experiences, my family's experiences, since my father and brother had both been imprisoned. Whenever they got permission to have visitors, my family would go by train across the country to see them, and the trains were always full of people like ourselves, going to the same place, but nobody would ever talk to anybody because they were all too scared. It was sad. The script was about that whole world.

SOLECKI You said a moment ago that Kundera was your teacher at the Film Academy. What did you actually study with him? What kinds of courses did he teach?

SALIVAROVÁ He taught one in the history of world literature and he based it primarily on French literature, of course. He was already well-known, handsome – no, let me take handsome back, he was charismatic, and he was the best teacher at the academy. He was often very arrogant and ironic but he could also be very nice. Don't forget that I was ten years older than the other students because I had been accepted very late, after years of performing. I was already thirty, and they were twenty-one or twenty-two. And they were all in love with him. I'm not exaggerating. And they shook and trembled when they had to take an exam with him. The examinations were always taken individually with the student answering the professor's questions in his office. Kundera was very, very tough. He would do things like tell a student to her face, 'Go away, you don't know your work, you're stupid.' But he could do that because he gave a lot to us as a teacher. He was one of the best.

SOLECKI Other than Kundera's course, what else did you do at the academy?

SALIVAROVÁ Well, every year those of us who were in the scriptwriting division had to get together with some people in directing and the other groups, to make a film. And each year the film had to be longer. Instead of writing a dissertation we made a movie. So there was that kind of practical studying. Of course, we also had to do courses on Leninism and Marxism and socialist economics, and there were all sorts of restrictions and rules, but looking back on it I think it was a very good film school, and you can still see that if you look at the films of the 1960s and at the individuals who came out of it. There were excellent teachers who knew their craft very well.

But you know I also learned a great deal about film by working in films during the period which is now known as the Czech New Wave. In 1966 I had a part in Jan Němec's *The Party and the Guests* (*O slavnosti a hostech*), and in 1968 I was in Evald Schorm's *The End of a Priest* (*Farářův konec*).

SOLECKI What was it like to work with Němec and Schorm?

SALIVAROVÁ Schorm was my favourite. Němec was a neurotic, hysterical, he was terrible. He shouted at people, foamed at the mouth, got heart attacks. It was terrible to work with Němec, but he's a good director.

Schorm was the complete opposite, a sweetheart. So quiet and gentle. He smiled all the time, but even as he was smiling he'd say, 'It's all going to end badly. This movie is going to be awful.'

SOLECKI Josef was also involved in those films, wasn't he?

SALIVAROVÁ Yes. He had a bit part as a guest in *The Party and the Guests*, and he wrote the script and had a slightly larger part as an expert of some kind being interviewed on television, in *The End of a Priest*. There are some stills from both films in Josef's book *All the Bright Young Men and Women: A Personal History of the Czech Cinema*.

SOLECKI Did the two of you ever work together in any other films?

SALIVAROVÁ No, not in films, but we did do a lot of work in the theatre in the early sixties. There was a weekly show called 'Textappeals' and it was made up of new work, usually short, by popular writers who appeared on stage and read it to the audience. In fact, because they knew the audience you could say they wrote the pieces for it. The same people came regularly to the show so that there was a rapport between the writers and the audience. Josef was a regular reader and would present something written for the occasion, and I would interrupt once in a while with a song.

From 1963 to 1968 was a golden age, the best time of my life, the best time of our lives.

SOLECKI Let's return to your writing. How did your novel *Summer in Prague* come to be written?

SALIVAROVÁ My editor at Československý spisovatel, Marie Vodičková, a wonderful woman, had always encouraged me to write a novel. She kept saying, 'You must write a novel, you must work on a novel.' So I promised her that I would. When we were leaving Prague on 31 January 1969, on what I was sure would be only an excursion or tour, I took my diary and notes, thinking that while we lived in the United States I would be able to work on it. Josef would be away all day at work at Berkeley, and since I didn't speak any English and didn't know anyone, I would be able to spend all my time writing.

We lived in Berkeley, he worked at the university, and I wrote. It was an ideal situation, though I was full of homesickness, longing for Prague, for Czechoslovakia, and depressed over the invasion. I finished the novel in three months. I rewrote it after we settled in Toronto. Josef then sent it to Harper and Row, and it was published in 1973.

SOLECKI As you were writing it, did you know that you wouldn't be returning to Prague?

SALIVAROVÁ No, no. In fact, I was so naïve that I even sent a first draft of the novel to Marie Vodičková, and she replied to me, giving me advice which passage should be shortened or which character should be developed. While this was going on I was also translating Sylvester's *Fantomas* from the French, for which I had a contract from Prague. That book was published in 1969 in Czechoslovakia.

You know, if Marie had worked with me on the novel I would have revised more than I did. Without her, I left it pretty much as it was when I finished rewriting it in Toronto.

SOLECKI Did Josef see *Summer in Prague* while you were working on it, or are you a secretive, private writer?

SALIVAROVÁ Oh no. This was our daily subject of conversation. When he would come home at five or six o'clock for supper, I would read him the day's work. He always told me that it's fine, it's good. He never told me to do this or that – he always said finish it first and then we will talk some more.

When we drove across the United States from California to Canada in a huge five-hundred-dollar V-8, whenever we stopped anywhere, the first thing Josef carried in to the motel was the suitcase with the manuscript of my novel. I had written it in longhand in a dozen or so scribblers, and so there was Josef protecting it from motel to motel across the length of the United States. It was very touching, because I probably would have left it in the car and not worried about vandals or car thieves or anything.

SOLECKI He's a Hemingway fan and probably remembered that Hemingway lost an early draft of *The Sun Also Rises* on a train.

SALIVAROVÁ Josef was right, of course, because if I had lost the manuscript I wouldn't have been able to write the same novel again. Maybe I would have written it again, but it would have been a different book.

SOLECKI How long was it after you finished the novel that you founded Sixty-Eight Publishers?

SALIVAROVÁ Oh, about a year. The novel was finished in 1970.

SOLECKI Whose idea was it to start the house?

SALIVAROVÁ It was mine.

SOLECKI Your father had been a small publisher in the 1930s and 1940s, hadn't he?

SALIVAROVÁ Oh that, that was just a coincidence, though people always think that it must be in my blood or in my genes. My father was a very small publisher, not at all successful. In fact, his story is very sad. He started his first bookshop in 1928, almost at the worst possible time for a book business. He lost a lot of money and we were very poor. It's ironic that the only time he had any success was during the war, because people had money but there was nothing to buy except books – no food, no clothing, nothing – and he published books for children and ran a bookshop. Then after the war he was nationalized – that's what it was called – and lost everything.

We were moved out of our apartment in Prague's Old Town into a worse one, and he was locked up.

Of the four children, my oldest sister and my only brother were supposed to go into the family business, and I was supposed to develop my musical talents and become a Paganini. Anyway, I didn't become a Paganini but, by coincidence, I became a Czech publisher, though not in Prague.

I got the idea to start Sixty-Eight Publishers in 1971, when the Society for Arts and Sciences, based in Washington I think, sent Josef a letter asking him for the manuscript of *Tankový prapor* (*The Republic of Whores*), because they wanted to publish it. I had the feeling that any group made up of people who had emigrated in the thirties or forties wouldn't really understand or be sympathetic to a very realistic novel about army life in the 1950s. I thought that they might find the language obscene, objectionable. So I told Josef that we should publish it ourselves. Josef didn't want to but he went along. We had about five thousand dollars in savings and he gave me the money to print the book. I found a Polish printer, Uncle Gutenberg, who set it up for us. It was a paperback, and we sent out announcements about it to everybody in our address book, and asked them to let their friends know about it. We began with about three hundred addresses and ended up with about two thousand. That's how our mailing list began. Today, it's at twelve thousand or so.

Josef was very insecure, anxious, nervous. He said, 'What if we get bankrupt? Everybody in Prague will be so happy.' I remember he used to talk in his sleep, sigh, toss and turn, worried that something terrible, a catastrophe, was going to happen. So I kept reassuring him, 'Don't worry. It won't lose money. We must do it this way.' And, in fact, we made enough money to publish another book, and then another and then another. And two decades later we're still here.

Early on, we established a Reader's Club based on advance subscriptions, which allowed us to have a bit of working capital. And that's how it works today. We announce a group of books and wait for the subscriptions. So our editorial year is like a roller coaster. When we send out our catalogue and get our subscriptions, we have a full bank account; by the end of the year when the books have been sent out, we're back where we were at the start. There just aren't enough booksellers to allow us to run the house the way that most North American publishers run theirs. We have people in Australia, South Africa, Germany, and Switzerland selling our books by mail order to the Czech community.

You know, when this all started I didn't plan to be a publisher forever. It was a solution to an immediate problem – what was I going to do in Canada, and how were we to publish Josef's novel, a novel, by the way, which had been written in 1954 and never published, although it was supposed to appear in 1968, but the invasion took care of that edition.

SOLECKI What's Josef's role in Sixty-Eight?

SALIVAROVÁ Perhaps the easiest way to indicate what he does would be to say that the whole business couldn't work without him. He is in touch with all our writers; he reads and comments on and edits all the manuscripts we work on. He prepares the catalogue every year, and that includes deciding what prices to charge for the books! We really are fifty-fifty. Neither one could do it alone. We've done 220 books, and Josef has been involved with each one.

SOLECKI Are there any that are particular favourites?

SALIVAROVÁ Oh yes. Some, I'm particularly proud of, especially the ones that Josef managed to provoke out of two or three talented young men and women. Jan Novák, for example, was nominated for the Pulitzer Prize; Eva Pekárková has a novel that Farrar Straus is going to publish. These are books that you could say have been inspired or encouraged into being by Josef. He really has that talent to provoke people into writing.

If you look at this from another angle, Sixty-Eight provides the writers with an audience, a Czech audience, they might not have had. I thought of this when we first published Josef. There were many other writers like him who had left in 1968 or 1969, Arnošt Lustig, for example, and who wouldn't have an outlet for their work in Czech.

SOLECKI Do you have any obvious best sellers?

SALIVAROVÁ Josef's *The Republic of Whores* and *The Miracle Game*. In fact, all of Josef's books sell really well.

SOLECKI Why do you think *The Republic of Whores* is so popular? It's a novel I like very much, but I would have thought others like *Miss Silver's Past* or *The Engineer of Human Souls* would have had a larger readership.

SALIVAROVÁ I think it's popular because everybody was in the army. I mean that most of our male readers are of Josef's generation, and so when they read that novel they are really reading about themselves and their youth and the reality that they all lived through in the fifties. All the men love the book; most of the women don't understand it, don't really see the humour. It's a bit like *The Good Soldier Švejk*, Hašek's book. You rarely meet a woman who really likes, sincerely likes Hašek. I don't. I never finished reading it even though I tried. I told myself it belongs to my education, but I just couldn't get through it. But men are crazy about it.

Another of our books that has sold well is my own novel *Summer in Prague*, which has gone through four editions.

SOLECKI In Czech it's *Honzlová*, which has a very different sound and general effect than the English title, which I find much more romantic, much more like a title by Françoise Sagan.

SALIVAROVÁ You're right and I didn't want it to sound romantic, because the novel isn't like that at all. You know Honzlová has certain definite implications or connotations. It's the surname of a woman, but if in Czech you call a woman just by her last name, leaving off the Miss or Mrs, it can be very insulting. There's a world of difference between Jana Honzlová, or Slečna (Miss) Honzlová, and Honzlová. If somebody calls you Solecki in Czechoslovakia, it's almost always unfriendly, cold. So in the title I wanted to indicate that Jana Honzlová was seen as Honzlová by the people she worked with, the world she lived in, a zero.

SOLECKI Since *Honzlová* is an autobiographical novel, let's turn to some biographical questions. Do you remember the first time that you met Josef?

SALIVAROVÁ Oh, of course. Of course, I remember when I met him. My oldest sister had a boyfriend who was deeply involved in American litera-ture, especially in detective novels, which he used to translate. He was quite a well-known translator. He came to our place one day and asked me to go with them to visit Mikuláš Medek, a surrealist painter, at whose place there was to be a gathering of writers and intellectuals. And I was so pleased, a singer and dancer, to be going to visit *intellectuals*. So I put on my best dress, went to the gathering, and sat quietly and listened to what was being said.

And Josef was there. He was very skinny, his ears stuck out, and his nose was red because he had a cold. It must have been in the spring. Yes, yes, in the spring of 1957. And so this was the first time we met. Josef later told me that František, my sister's boyfriend, had told him to come that evening because 'Vlasta's sister will be there and she's a dancer.' So that's how we met. And in the fall of that year my sister married František, and when Jan Zábrana refused to be best man, Josef filled in. And since the wedding took place at our apartment, Josef and I met again, talked, and he asked me to go to a movie with him. And so we started dating in October 1957 and were married in March 1958. We dated for about half a year, and then Josef said, 'That's enough, I'm a Catholic, let's get married.' And that's what happened. It's funny, but I knew when I first saw him that he would become my husband.

SOLECKI Did he work as hard then as he does now?

SALIVAROVÁ Oh yes. Once when we were on a date in the old days – the fifties are now the old days – he told me that he couldn't walk me home because he had to get back to his work. Now in Prague in the fifties, a boy always took his date back to her house. It was a question of custom, manners, politeness. But Josef was too busy, had too much work to do.

And then when we married, I moved to his one-room apartment, which was crowded with the landlady's furniture, including two large beds and a table at which Josef did all his work. Every day he would come home after five from the Odeon or *Světová literatura* offices and he would start translating and finish around ten o'clock at night. If he was really busy, I would dictate to him and he would type. So, as you can see, he was very busy all the time. Even when we took holidays in the Krkonoše mountains for a week or two, he brought his translation work and notebooks with him. And when he found out that I could write, he forced me to bring my work with me on our holidays as well. So there would be the two of us spending our vacation writing in the hotel room. I wrote my first three novellas on holidays.

Josef cannot sit doing nothing. Never. He's that kind of temperament. If he's not writing fiction he's writing letters or reading. If he comes to bed he brings a detective story so that he can read at least a few pages before sleep. He's up at six in the morning and often shaved and dressed and working even before I get up.

SOLECKI You said earlier that you always discussed your writing with him. Does he discuss his writing with you or do you read the work in progress?

SALIVAROVÁ It's almost impossible for me to read it because he writes the first draft in longhand and I just can't make it out. You've seen it, it's impossible. I still have a pile of his love letters at home, and I still don't know what's in them. That's a bit of an exaggeration. I understand a sentence here and there, but most of the letter might as well be in a foreign language. So with his fiction I wait until he types the second draft, and then I talk to him about it because he's usually quite eager to hear what I think of it. My problem with Josef's work is that I never find anything wrong. I always like it so I'm not much use to him as a critic or reader.

I remember when he was writing *Miss Silver's Past* in 1965. I would come home and he would be depressed. He would say, 'This novel isn't going to be any good, I can't get it any better.' And all I could do was keep on encouraging him. Maybe that's enough. I think he was really feeling the burden of having to produce something even better than his previous work. You know how readers and critics always expect an author to do something better or different than what he has done before? This kills writers, I'm sure of it. Or at least it stops them from writing.

SOLECKI Do you feel that way about your own work?

SALIVAROVÁ Oh no, I guess I don't care enough about critics. I'm working on a new novel now and it's going slowly, but not because of these kinds of worries. It's slow work because I can't find the time for it. The manuscript is half done and it's under my bed waiting for me.

SOLECKI This is your Canadian novel, the immigrant novel *Hnůj země* (Dung of the Earth).

SALIVAROVÁ Yes. It's a novel in letters, starting in 1860 and ending with our generation, all written by immigrants from Bohemia to Canada and America. The letters go back and forth between Bohemia or Czechoslovakia and North America, some are by the immigrants writing to each other and so on. The sections dealing with the invasion and after are about the confrontation between the generations.

I started it in Amherst in 1985, when I would visit Josef for a couple of weeks at a time when he was visiting writer there. But I really need a stretch of time for writing. A week here, a week there just isn't any good to me. I need to sit down and write until I'm finished. Every time I think I'm going to have some time for writing, something happens to the business, and I have to spend all my time on it.

SOLECKI Have you and Josef given any thought to what will happen to Sixty-Eight after you?

SALIVAROVÁ We have thought about it because we both realize that we can't go on forever at the pace at which we've been working. I doubt, you know, whether I could find anyone to take over because I can't believe anyone would be devoted enough to work the number of hours it takes to keep the business going, to make it a success. Maybe I am underestimating other people. I hope I am, because we would gladly give the business to someone else if we knew they would keep it alive. It's not for sale.

Anyway, that's our long-range plan, to publish fewer and fewer titles each year until I can once again move the operation back to our house and do each book from start to finish by myself.

SOLECKI Let me turn back for a moment to Josef's work. Do you have a favourite among his novels?

SALIVAROVÁ Oh no, that's impossible to answer. Maybe I can answer it with a question: Do you have a favourite child?

SOLECKI No.

SALIVAROVÁ Well, that's how I feel about the novels. But I do have favourite characters. Nadia, for example, in *The Engineer of Human Souls* is one of his best characters. I also like Emöke in the novella he wrote in the early sixties. Then there are some minor figures that are personal favourites even though they are so minor that they never get mentioned in book reviews. Sometimes I like them because I know the real-life person who was the model for the character.

SOLECKI I'm particularly fond of the committed Leninist, Laura, in *The Miracle Game*, especially in those late scenes between her and Danny Smiřický when we know she is dying.

SALIVAROVÁ I have a very different reaction to her, because I know that she is still very much alive and still very, very beautiful. It's a case in which life gets in the way of the fiction. Nadia, by contrast, is like something out of a dream, something created, imagined from small images and details that Josef picked up in the mountains somewhere.

Then there is Irena, or rather all the Irenas from *The Cowards* to the present day. I should be jealous because I know who they are based on and we even have a portrait, as you know, of the first one. I'm not jealous, but I would be if he had another Irena today. It's all in the past.

SOLECKI Speaking of the past, what did you miss most about Czechoslovakia, Prague during the two decades when you couldn't return?

SALIVAROVÁ Well, I am not that nostalgic, maybe not nostalgic at all for my country. I'm nostalgic for the past. I miss people, friends that I was young with. The other day I saw a very unusual photograph of an old Prague street that I know very well. A corner with old Gothic houses, that kind of thing. And for a second I felt myself falling into nostalgia and so I forced myself to stop looking.

So, what do I miss most? People, people. But even though many of them are still alive, they're different today, I'm different today. There's a gap of twenty years and we've all changed. When we meet after twenty years, after half an hour we don't know what to talk about because we've had completely different lives. Our lives have been completely separate, our interests have been completely different. Even when you still like each other very much and find things to talk about, it still feels very strange.

SOLECKI You've returned to Czechoslovakia several times since the 'velvet revolution' of 1989, but you've indicated that you plan to continue to live in Canada. What made the two of you decide to stay?

SALIVAROVÁ I can only answer for myself. And if I may, I'll do it, slightly indirectly, by quoting from my acceptance speech on the occasion of being awarded an honorary doctorate by the University of Toronto. I don't think I can formulate my answer any better than I did there:

I am often asked: Do you consider Canada as your home: Or is it still Czechoslovakia where, after all, you were born?

Like every exile, I have often pondered this question, and I have come to the following conclusion: my feelings can be compared to those of a child with both a mother and a stepmother. But in the case of this particular child, the traditional expectations associated with motherhood and stepmotherhood have been reversed. Czechoslovakia is my natural mother, and I'll never forget that; but, in the past, she has been a rather nasty mother, often quite cruel to me. Canada, my stepmother, on the other hand, has shown me only affection; so, as often happens with good stepmothers, I love her.

In my native country, my life had been marked by catastrophes: my father, a bookseller and publisher, lost his business in the Great Depression just at the moment I was born in 1933. Throughout the thirties we lived the life of a family whose breadwinner was unemployed, and there was neither unemployment insur ance nor welfare in those days.

My father had two great hopes for his children: he wanted to bequeath the family business to his only son, and he hoped that I would graduate from the Prague conservatory of music and pursue the career of a violinist. He did not live to see his dreams come true. On the contrary, he saw them cruelly destroyed, this time not by the Depression but by a terrorist regime. Shortly after he had re-established himself in business after the war, he earned the sad distinction of being the first Czech publisher to have his business confiscated by the Communists. He was arrested and sentenced to two years in jail. While serving his sentence, he learned that his only son had also been apprehended on trumped-up charges – there were almost no other in those days – and also sent to prison where he eventually served ten years. By 'prison' I mean the uranium mines of the Czechoslovak *gulag*.

I did not make it to the conservatory, either. I was not even permitted to take the entrance exam because, at the time, my father and my brother were already political prisoners, and my violin teacher, Professor Feld, had been fired from the conservatory staff as politically incorrect. After his release from jail, my father defected to the United States. He died there in poverty and doesn't even have his own grave.

In 1969 my husband and I followed his example and came to North America. The rest of my story is simple: my stepmother gave me everything my natural mother had denied me. I became a publisher and even a writer, for my stepmother doesn't ban books, no matter who writes them or what his political persuasion. She also gave me social security, which I had so badly lacked as a child and a teenager. But, above all, my stepmother gave me the most precious possession one can have: she gave me freedom.

NOTE

The title of the interview is taken from the dedication to Josef Škvorecký's first novel, *The Cowards*: 'To Zdena, the girl I met in Prague.'

Chronology

1924   Josef Škvorecký is born on 27 September 1924 in the northern provincial town of Náchod, Bohemia, Czechoslovakia, near what is now the Polish border to Anna Kurážová (1896–1947) and Josef Škvorecký (1897–1967). Škvorecký's father is a bank clerk and the chairman of the local Sokol Gymnastic Association, a patriotic organization.

1930–5   Škvorecký attends primary school (Obecná škola chlapecká v Náchodě). He begins to study German in 1932.

1935   Between 1935 and 1943, Škvorecký attends gymnasium (Státní reálné gymnasium v Náchodě).

1938   29–30 September, the Munich Pact is signed.

    1 October, the German occupation of western Czechoslovakia begins.

    Škvorecký begins to study English, and over the next decade reads American writers like Ambrose Bierce, Bret Harte, Jack London, Theodore Dreiser, Upton Sinclair, and Sinclair Lewis in Czech translations. Mark Twain was an early favourite since his father owned a set of his works in translation.

1939   15 March, German troops enter Prague.

1943   Škvorecký graduates from the gymnasium in 1943 and works until 1945 in the Messerschmidt factories in Náchod and neighbouring Nové Město. The period, characters, and events form the substance of the novels *The Cowards* and *The Engineer of Human Souls*, the novella *The Bass Saxophone*, the short-story collection *The Swell Season*, as well as of several other short stories.

1945   Škvorecký enters the Faculty of Medicine at Charles University in Prague but after a year transfers to the Faculty of Philosophy; he graduates in 1949, and receives a PhD in 1951 for a thesis on Thomas Paine, 'Thomas Paine and His Significance Today.'

1948   Škvorecký is awarded first prize for fiction in a Charles University literary contest for the short-story collection *Nové canterburské povídky* (The New Canterbury Tales). Soon after, he becomes a member of the Prague underground circle of writers and artists that includes, among others, artist Jiří Kolář, composer Jan Rychlík, and writers Bohumil Hrabal and Věra Linhartová. Between October 1948 and September 1949 Škvorecký writes *The Cowards* (*Zbabělci*), which remains unpublished for ten years. Also writes short stories and the novel *Nylonový věk* (The Nylon Age), set in 1945–6, about a Charles University student who has a love affair with an actress and then with a shop girl named Maggie. (The novel was never published, and the manuscript was left behind in Prague when Škvorecký emigrated. A fragment, *Věk nylonu*, appeared in 1992.) Škvorecký teaches for a month in Broumov, near Náchod.

1950   Škvorecký teaches for a year, until 1951, at a girls' school in Hořice v Podkrkonoší, an experience that provides much of the background for his novel *The Miracle Game*.

He writes *Konec nylonového věku* (The End of the Nylon Age), a novel about a dance given by the American Institute of Prague in February 1949. The story is told from the points of view of various individuals at the dance: Škvorecký describes it as 'a portrait of the "golden youth" of Prague, the bourgeois society at the beginning of their tragedy.' The original title was 'Sadness in Socialism.'

1951   Škvorecký is drafted into the army and serves two years with the Tank Division stationed at the Mladá military post near Prague. By 1954 he completes *Tankový prapor* (*The Republic of Whores*), the novel based on the army years. (It remained unpublished until 1969 when a French edition appeared in Paris.)

1954 Škvorecký begins to establish his reputation as an essayist, critic, and translator.

1956 He becomes the deputy editor-in-chief of the magazine *Světová literatura* (World Literature). He now begins to write extensively on modern American literature – Hemingway, Steinbeck, Sinclair Lewis, and Faulkner. He writes 'Really the Blues.'

He offers his novel *Konec nylonového věku* (The End of the Nylon Age) for publication; the censors turn it down.

1957 Škvorecký marries the singer and actress Zdena Salivarová, who was born in Prague in 1933.

1958 Ten years after being written, *Zbabělci* (*The Cowards*) is published, widely praised, then almost immediately banned. In the ensuing very public controversy Škvorecký loses his editorial post with *Světová literatura* and witnesses the firing of the editors and directors responsible for publishing the book.

During 1958 Škvorecký also publishes translations of Ernest Hemingway's *A Farewell to Arms* and, with Lubomír Dorůžka, Henry James's *The Aspern Papers*. He writes but does not publish the novella 'Emöke.'

1958–68 Between 1958 and 1962 the repercussions of 'The Cowards affair' leave Škvorecký with little official work. He survives by working on translations and by working in collaboration and publishing his work under his partner's name. In 1962, for example, he publishes *Vražda pro štěstí* (Murder for Luck), but the only author's name on the cover is that of his collaborator, Jan Zábrana. Over the next five years the two produce two more mystery novels and one children's adventure novel: *Vražda se zárukou* (Guaranteed Murder, 1964), *Vražda v zastoupení* (Murder by Proxy, 1967) and *Tána a dva pistolníci* (Tanya and the Two Gunmen, 1966). (The last was made into a film in 1967 by R. Cvrček, and won international prizes at the 1968 Moscow Film Festival of Children's Film and at festivals in Rimini and Cannes.)

During this difficult period Škvorecký collaborates on a number of translations with Dorůžka: F. Scott Fitzgerald's *The Great Gatsby* and *Tender Is the Night*, William Faulkner's *A Fable* (1961), Sinclair Lewis's *Babbitt* (1962), and Dashiell Hammett's *The Glass Key* (1963). The translation of Faulkner wins the annual award for the best translation from the Czechoslovak Writers Union. Some of the translations appear under Škvorecký's name, some under Dorůžka's.

(One of the more interesting never-to-be-completed projects of this period involved the Czech new wave director Miloš Forman, who wanted to make a film based on Škvorecký's story, 'Eine kleine Jazzmusik,' about a student swing band that outwits the Nazis. Unfortunately, despite several rewrites, the script never outwitted the censor. A second collaboration in the summer of 1968 on a script for *The Cowards* ended when 'the Russians came, Miloš left for Hollywood, and I for Canada.'

1961   Ernest Hemingway dies on 2 July. Škvorecký writes the obituary notices in *Kultura* and *Plamen*.
       A change in the political climate makes it possible for Škvorecký to publish 'Emöke.' His wife, in the meantime, is working as an actress.

1962   William Faulkner dies on 6 June. The notices in *Kultura* and *Plamen* are by Škvorecký.

1964   Škvorecký publishes the short-story collection *Sedmiramenný svícen* (The Menorah) as well as, with Lubomír Dorůžka, *Tvář jazzu* (The Face of Jazz), an anthology of biographies and autobiographies of famous jazzmen and essays on the history and aesthetics of jazz.

1965   Škvorecký publishes the short-story collection *Ze života lepší společnosti* (From the Life of High Society); translations of Raymond Chandler's *The Lady in the Lake*, Alan Sillitoe's *The Loneliness of the Long Distance Runner*, and William Styron's *The Long March*; and the book of criticism, *Nápady čtenáře detektivek* (Reading Detective Stories).

1966   Škvorecký publishes the first of his Borůvka collections, *Smutek poručíka Borůvky* (*The Mournful Demeanour of Lieutenant*

Boruvka). Škvorecký also works during the year with Jiří Menzel on the film *Zločin v dívčí škole* (Crime in a Girls' School), based on three of his short stories.

1967   Škvorecký's *Konec nylonového věku* (The End of the Nylon Age) receives the Writers Union annual award for the year's best fiction. In the same year he publishes *Babylónský příběh* (A Babylonian Story), a collection of short stories. With Lubomír Dorůžka he edits *Jazzová inspirace*, an anthology of American and Czech poems inspired by jazz.
   Zdena Salivarová publishes *Pánská jízda* (Gentleman's Ride).

1967   Škvorecký's father dies.
   La Légende d'Emöke is published by Gallimard; Kundera publishes *Žert* (*The Joke*); Jiří Menzel's film *Closely Watched Trains* wins an Academy Award for Best Foreign Film.

1969   On 31 January Škvorecký and his wife leave Prague on Air India and arrive on the same day in Toronto. They spend parts of the year at Cornell University and at Berkeley before returning to Toronto on 1 September. Škvorecký is Writer in Residence at the University of Toronto before joining the Department of English as a full-time member. Over the next two decades, he teaches film, creative writing, and American literature.
   Lvíče (*Miss Silver's Past*) and *Tankový prapor* (*The Republic of Whores*) are published in Prague. The first printing of *Lvíče* sells out; the second, together with the plates of *Tankový prapor*, is destroyed by government authorities in 1970.
   Farářův konec (The End of a Priest), a novella, and *Hořkej svět* (The Bitter World), a short-story collection, are published in Prague; *L'Escadron blindé* (*The Republic of Whores*) is published by Gallimard.

1970   *Zbabělci* is translated into English (*The Cowards*) and Polish (*Tchórze*).

1971   *All the Bright Young Men and Women: A Personal History of the Czech Cinema* is published in English in Canada.

1972   Zdena Salivarová and Škvorecký found Sixty-Eight Publishers, which over the next two decades becomes the most important Czech publishing house in the world. Škvorecký is involved as reader, editor, and best-selling author.

Mirákl (*The Miracle Game*), Škvorecký's novel about the Stalinist fifties and the Prague Spring, is published by Sixty-Eight Publishers. *Le Lionceau* (*Miss Silver's Past*) is published by Gallimard.

1973   *Hříchy pro pátera Knoxe* (*Sins for Father Knox*), a collection of detective stories, is published by Sixty-Eight Publishers.

Zdena Salivarová publishes the novel *Honzlová* (*Summer in Prague*).

Škvorecký begins monthly broadcasts for Voice of America; on occasion these deal with Czech literary matters, but for the most part they are reviews of recently published books such as Graham Greene's novels, Leszek Kolakowski's *Main Currents of Marxism*, Lewis Feuer's *Marx and the Intellectuals*, Saul Bellow's *To Jerusalem and Back*, and Norman Mailer's *Ancient Evenings*.

1975   *Prima sezóna* (*The Swell Season*), a collection of interrelated stories about the war years, and *Konec poručíka Borůvky* (*The End of Lieutenant Boruvka*), a detective novel; are published.

1976   Salivarová publishes her novella *Nebe, peklo, ráj* (translated in 1987 as *Ashes, Ashes, All Fall Down*).

1977   *Příběh inženýra lidských duší* (*The Engineer of Human Souls*) appears, a Danny Smiřický novel counterpointing the war years in Náchod and the years of exile in Canada.

The Bass Saxophone, the first book of Škvorecký's fiction to be published in translation in Canada, is brought out by Anson-Cartwright.

1978   *Les Lâches* (*The Cowards*) and *Miracle en Bohême* (*The Miracle Game*) are published by Gallimard.

1980   Škvorecký is awarded the prestigious Neustadt Prize by the University of Oklahoma. The occasion is marked by a special Škvorecký issue of *World Literature Today*, featuring articles by European and North American critics.

Škvorecký's play *Bůh do domu* (God Help Us!) is premiered in Czech in Toronto.

1981   *Návrat poručíka Borůvky* (*The Return of Lieutenant Boruvka*), a detective novel, is published.

1982   *Jiří Menzel and the History of Closely Watched Trains* is published.

1983   *Scherzo capriccioso* (*Dvorak in Love*) is published.

1984   *The Engineer of Human Souls* (English translation of *Příběh inženýra lidských duší*) is published.

Jaroslav Seifert (1901–86) is awarded the Nobel Prize for Literature; Škvorecký writes the article 'Czech Mate: Meet Jaroslav Seifert, the Nobel Laureate' for *New Republic*; he also reviews in the same journal Vassily Aksyonov's *The Burn*, the first of Aksyonov's novels to be published abroad after his departure from the Soviet Union.

1985   *The Engineer of Human Souls* is awarded the Governor General's Award for Fiction in English. It is the first translation ever to win the award for best novel of the year.

1985–6   Škvorecký is Visiting Writer at Amherst College.

1986   *Dvorak in Love* (English translation of *Scherzo cappricioso*) is published.

1987   Škvorecký publishes *O americké literatuře* (On American Literature).

Helena Kosková publishes *Hledání ztracené generace* (Searching for the Lost Generation), a study of modern Czech fiction with a substantial chapter on Škvorecký's fiction.

1988   *Talkin' Moscow Blues: Essays about Literature, Politics, Movies, and Jazz* and *Sins for Father Knox* are published. Škvorecký exchanges letters with George F. Kennan in *The New York Review of Books* over Kennan's positive view of Mikhail Gorbachev's glasnost and perestroika.

Škvorecký is the subject of an hour-long BBC documentary, the first in a six part series with the title 'Exiles.'

1989   *The End of Lieutenant Boruvka* is published.

1990   Škvorecký publishes *Hlas z Ameriky* (A Voice from America), *The Return of Lieutenant Boruvka*, and *The Miracle Game.*

Škvorecký and Salivarová return to Prague where President Václav Havel awards them the order of the White Lion, Czechoslovakia's highest award for foreigners (the Škvoreckýs are Canadian citizens).

1992   Škvorecký publishes *Nevěsta z Texasu* (The Bride from Texas). In June, he and his wife receive honorary degrees from the University of Toronto.

1993   Škvorecký publishes *The Republic of Whores* (English translation of *Tankový prapor*).

1994   The *Review of Contemporary Fiction* devotes an issue to discussion of Škvorecký's work.

Bibliography

This is a selective bibliography. It is based on the two following bibliographies of Škvorecký's work and criticism of it: Jana Kalish's annotated *Josef Škvorecký: A Checklist* (Toronto: University of Toronto Library, 1986), and Ilja Matouš' three-volume *Bibliografie Josefa Škvoreckého* (Praha: Společnost Josefa Škvoreckého, 1990, 1992, 1993). Information for subsequent years will probably be available in *Danny*, the Czech journal issued quarterly by the Společnost Josefa Škvoreckého and dedicated to discussion of Škvorecký's life and work.

1 FICTION, POETRY, DRAMATIC WORK, AND SCREENPLAYS

Babylónský příběh a jiné povídky. Praha: Svobodné slovo, 1967
The Bass Saxophone. Trans. Káča Poláčková-Henley. Toronto: Anson-Cartwright, 1977
Blues libeňského plynojemu. Plzeň: Bauer, 1992
Bůh do domu ('God Help Us!'). A Play. Trans. Josef Škvorecký. Toronto: Sixty-Eight Publishers, 1980
The Cowards. Trans. Jeanne Nemcova. Harmondsworth: Penguin, 1972
'The Death of a Priest.' Screenplay. Trans. Josef Škvorecký. Author's ms
Divák v únorové noci. Prague: Společnost Josefa Škvoreckého, 1991
Dívka z Chicaga: Básně z let 1940–45. Munich: PmD, 1980
Dvě legendy. Toronto: Sixty-Eight Publishers, 1982
Dvorak in Love. Trans. Paul Wilson. Toronto: Lester & Orpen Dennys, 1986
The End of Lieutenant Boruvka. Trans. Paul Wilson. Toronto: Lester & Orpen Dennys, 1989
The Engineer of Human Souls. Trans. Paul Wilson. Toronto: Lester & Orpen Dennys, 1984

L'Escadron blindé. Trans. F. Kérel. Paris: Gallimard, 1969
Farářův konec. Hradec Králové: Kruh, 1969
Hořkej svět: povídky z let 1946–67. Toronto: Sixty-Eight Publishers, 1978
Hříchy pro pátera Knoxe. Toronto: Sixty-Eight Publishers, 1973
Konec nylonového věku. Praha: Československý spisovatel, 1967
Konec poručíka Borůvky. Toronto: Sixty-Eight Publishers, 1975
Le Lionceau. Trans. F. Kérel. Paris: Gallimard, 1969
Lvíče. Praha: Československý spisovatel, 1969
Miracle en Bohême. Trans. Claudia Ancelot. Paris: Gallimard, 1978
The Miracle Game. Trans. Paul Wilson. Toronto: Lester & Orpen Dennys, 1990
Mirákl. 2 vols. Toronto: Sixty-Eight Publishers, 1972
'Miracles.' *Granta* 13, 22–48
Miss Silver's Past. Trans. Peter Kussi. London: Picador, 1980
The Mournful Demeanour of Lieutenant Boruvka. Trans. Rosemary Kavan, Káča
　　Poláčková, and George Theiner. Toronto: Lester & Orpen Dennys, 1987.
'The New Men and Women.' Radio Play. Trans. John Reeves. Author's ms
'Můj táta haur a já.' *Plamen*, January 1961, 146–52
Nevěsta z Texasu. Toronto: Sixty-Eight Publishers, 1992
Návrat poručíka Borůvky. Toronto: Sixty-Eight Publishers, 1981
'Oh, My Papa.' Ed. Itaru Iijima. Tokyo: Asahi Press, 1972
'Povídky tenorsaxofonisty: Malá pražská Matahara.' *Host do domu* 4 (1967), 20
Příběh inženýra lidských duší. Toronto: Sixty-Eight Publishers, 1977
Prima sezóna. Toronto: Sixty-Eight Publishers, 1975
Prima sezóna, Zbabělci, Konec nylonového věku. Prague: Odeon, 1991
The Republic of Whores. Trans. Paul Wilson. Toronto: Knopf Canada, 1993
The Return of Lieutenant Boruvka. Trans. Paul Wilson. Toronto: Lester & Orpen
　　Dennys, 1990
Scherzo capriccioso. Toronto: Sixty-Eight Publishers, 1983
Sedmiramenný svícen. Zürich: Konfrontace, 1974
Sins for Father Knox. Trans. Káča Poláčková-Henley. Toronto: Lester & Orpen
　　Dennys, 1988
Smutek poručíka Borůvky. Toronto: Sixty-Eight Publishers, 1966
'The Song of the Forgotten Years.' *New Writing in Czechoslovakia*. Ed. George
　　Theiner. Harmondsworth: Penguin, 1969, 69–80
The Swell Season. Trans. Paul Wilson. Toronto: Lester & Orpen Dennys, 1982
Tankový prapor. Toronto: Sixty-Eight Publishers, 1980
Tchórze. Trans. Emilia Witwicka. Katowice: RSW 'Prasa,' 1970
Věci. Praha: Společnost Josefa Škvoreckého, 1992
Věk nylonu. Praha: Společnost Josefa Škvoreckého, 1992
Zbabělci. Praha: Československý spisovatel, 1958

Ze života české společnosti. Toronto: Sixty-Eight Publishers, 1985
Ze života lepší společnosti. Praha: Mladá fronta, 1965

2 NON-FICTION

'Afterword' to Arnošt Lustig's *Indecent Dreams.* Evanston, IL: Northwestern
   University Press, 1988, 157–9
'A Judgment of Political Judgments,' *Canadian Literature,* 110 (1986), 171–6
All the Bright Young Men and Women: A Personal View of the Czech Cinema.
   Trans. Michal Schonberg. Toronto: Peter Martin Associates, 1971
'Are Canadians Politically Naive?' *Canadian Literature,* 100 (Spring 1984), 287–97
'At Home in Exile: Czech Writers in the West.' *Books Abroad,* 50, no. 2 (Spring
   1976), 308–13
'Bohemia of the Soul.' *Daedalus,* 119 (Winter 1990), 111–39
'Cesta (s překážkami) za Egonem.' In *Egon Hostovský.* Ed. Rudolf Sturm. Toronto:
   Sixty-Eight Publishers, 1974
'Drops of Jazz in My Fiction.' *Black American Literature Forum,* 25 (Fall 1991),
   621–32
'The Fear of Literature,' (a review of André Brink's *Mapmakers: Writing in a
   State of Siege*). *New Republic,* (20 April 1984), 29–33
Franz Kafka, jazz a jiné marginálie. Toronto: Sixty-Eight Publishers, 1988
'The Gorbachev Prospect: An Exchange between Josef Škvorecký and George F.
   Kennan.' *New York Review of Books* (17 March 1988), 44
Hlas z Ameriky. Toronto: Sixty-Eight Publishers, 1990
'Hipness at Dusk.' *Cross Currents 6.* Ed. Ladislav Matějka. Ann Arbor, MI:
   Department of Slavic Languages and Literatures, 1987
'Hovoří Josef Škvorecký.' *Listy,* 3 (16) (1986): 193–8
'How I Learned German, and Later English.' *Antaeus,* 63 (Autumn 1985) 217–26
'In Memoriam Vratislav Blažek.' *Listy,* 3, no. 4 (1973), 39–40
'Ještě o kritice vraždící.' *Host do domu,* 7 (1967), 73
Jiří Menzel and the History of Closely Watched Trains. Boulder, CO: East Euro-
   pean Monographs, 1982
Leading a Literary Double-Life in Prague. Toronto: Ontario Institute for Studies
   in Education, 1991
'Like Two Peas in a Pod.' *Západ* (March 1982), 28–34
'The Mess of Mother Russia,' (review of Vassily Aksyonov's *The Burn*). *New
   Republic* (31 December 1984), 28–34
Nápady čtenáře detektivek. Praha: Československý spisovatel, 1965
O americké literatuře. Praha: s.n., 1987
O nich – o nás. Hradec Králové: Kruh, 1968

'The Onset of my Literary Career.' *Antaeus*, 63 (Spring–Autumn 1990) 275–9
'Pokus o chápání modernosti v literatuře.' *Literární noviny*, 6: 17 (24 April 1957), 6–7
'A Psychopathology of Contemporary Czech Fiction.' *Canadian Forum* (November 1979), 13–17
Rozhovory s Josefem Škvoreckým. Praha: V. Krištof, 1990
Samožerbuch. Toronto: Sixty-Eight Publishers, 1977
'Some Contemporary Czech Prose Writers.' *Novel*, 4, no. 1 (1970), 5–13
Talkin' Moscow Blues: Essays about Literature, Politics, Movies, and Jazz. Ed. Sam Solecki. Toronto: Lester & Orpen Dennys, 1988
'The Troublemaker,' (a review of Ludvík Vaculík's *A Cup of Coffee with My Interrogator*). *New Republic* (7 March 1988), 38–9
Velká povídka o Americe. Toronto: Sixty-Eight Publishers, 1980
Všichni ti bystří mladí muži a ženy: osobní historie českého filme. Praha: Horizont, 1991
'What was Saved from the Wreckage,' (a review of Peter Hames's *The Czechoslovak New Wave*). *Sight and Sound*, 55 (Autumn 1986) 278–81

3 CRITICISM OF ŠKVORECKÝ AND CZECH LITERATURE

Anonymous. 'Kulturu a umění prodchnout stranickým duchem.' *Život strany* (February 1959), 209–12
– 'Záběry z některých sekcí.' *Literární noviny*, 8: 5 (1959)
Banerjee, Maria Nemcova. 'Nezval's "Prague with Fingers of Rain": A Surrealistic Image.' *Slavic and East European Journal*, 23, no. 4 (1979)
Běhounek, Václav. 'Políček živým i mrtvým.' *Práce* (11 January 1959), 4
Blumenfeld, Yorick. *Seesaw: Cultural Life in Eastern Europe*. New York: Harcourt Brace and World, 1968
Bradáč, Karel. 'V kavárně.' *Dikobraz* (29 January 1959), n.p.
Brich, Hans and Ivan Volgyes, eds. *Czechoslovakia: The Heritage of Ages Past*. Boulder, CO: East European Quarterly, 1979
Brink, André. 'The Girl and the Legend: Josef Škvorecký's "Emöke." ' *World Literature Today*, 44 (Autumn 1980), 552–5
Burgess, Anthony. 'Laughing It Off.' *Observer* (3 March 1985), 18
Carlisle, Olga. 'Letter from Prague – Voices of a Captive City.' *New York Times Book Review* (23 November 1986), 3, 43
Corbeil, Carol. 'Playing the Critic's Game by a Different Set of Rules.' *Globe and Mail* (19 July 1984), E3
Czarnecki, Mark. 'The Engineer of Human Souls.' *Quill and Quire*, 50 (May 1984), 30

Doležel, Lubomír. *Narrative Modes in Czech Literature*. Toronto: University of Toronto Press, 1973

French, Alfred. *Czech Writers and Politics 1945–1969*. Boulder, CO: East European Monographs, 1982

– *The Poets of Prague*. London: Oxford University Press, 1969

Gellner, Ernest. 'An Exile and His Leftovers.' *Times Literary Supplement* (8 March 1985), 256

Gibian, George, 'Škvorecký's *The Cowards* Twenty Years Later.' *World Literature Today*, 44 (Autumn 1980), 540–4

– 'Jiří Orten's Elegies.' *Cross Currents* (1982). Ed. Ladislav Matějka. Ann Arbor, MI: Department of Slavic Languages and Literatures, 1982, 243–59

Goetz-Stankiewicz, Marketa. 'Literary Mirrors.' *Canadian Literature*, 110 (1986), 165–71

– *The Silenced Theatre: Czech Playwrights without a Stage*. Toronto: University of Toronto Press, 1979

Goldie, Terry. 'Political Judgments: A Review of *The Engineer of Human Souls*.' *Canadian Literature*, 104 (Spring 1985), 163–7

Hájek, Jiří. 'Novoroční úvahy o nové české próze.' *Literární noviny*, 8: 3 (17 January 1959), 1–3

– 'Zatím jen svědectví.' *Literární noviny*, 7: 51–2 (23 December 1958), 4

– 'Novoroční anketa.' *Literární noviny*, 8: 1 (January 1959)

Hancock, Geoff. 'Interview with Josef Škvorecký.' *Canadian Fiction Magazine*, no. 45–6, (1983), 63–96

Havel, Václav. 'On Dialectical Metaphysics.' Trans. Michal Schonberg. *Modern Drama*, 23: 1 (1980), 6–12

Heim, Michael Henry. 'Dangerously Wonderful.' *Nation* (4–11 August 1984), 87

Henighan, Stephen. 'Josef Škvorecký and Canadian Cultural Cringe.' *Canadian Literature*, 116 (Summer 1988), 253–9

Jungman, Milan. *O Josefu Škvoreckém*. Praha: Společnost Josefa Škvoreckého, 1993

Kalish, Jana. *Josef Škvorecký: A Checklist*. Toronto: University of Toronto Library, 1986

Kejík, František. 'Bludný kámen.' *Obrana lidu* (18 January 1959), 7

Kloboučník, Jan. 'Proč jsou tu Zbabělci?' *Mladý svět*, (2 February 1959)

Kosek, Helena. 'The Demolisher of False Myths.' *World Literature Today*, 44 (Autumn 1980), 565–71

Kosková, Helena. *Hledání ztracené generace*. Toronto: Sixty-Eight Publishers, 1987

Kott, Jan. 'The Emigrant as Hero.' *New Republic* (27 August 1984), 34–7

Kucera, Henry. 'The Language Dilemma of a Czech Writer.' *World Literature Today*, 44 (Autumn 1980), 577–81

Kussi, Peter. 'The Engineer of Human Souls.' World Literature Today, 59 (Summer 1978), 655

Leckie, Barbara. 'Interview with Josef Škvorecký.' In So to Speak: Interviews with Contemporary Canadian Writers. Ed. Peter O'Brien. Montreal: Véhicule Press, 1987, 12–34

Lederer, Jiří. 'Zbabělci Josefa Škvoreckého.' Večerní Praha (20 December 1958), 3

Liehm, Antonín. 'Hovoří Josef Škvorecký.' Listy, 3 (16) (1986), 193–8

– ed. The Politics of Culture. Trans. Peter Kussi. New York: Grove Press, 1968

Magnuszewski, Józef. Historja literatury czeskiej: zarys. Wrocław: Zakład narodowy, 1973

Měšťan, Antonín. Česká literatura 1785–1985. Toronto: Sixty-Eight Publishers, 1987

Mináč, Vladimír. 'Proud proti proudu.' Květen, 3: 12 (1958), 666

Nawrocki, Witold. 'Josef Škvorecký: epik przeżyć pokoleniowych.' Introduction to Tchórze. Katowice: RSW 'Prasa,' 1970, 5–38

Novák, Arne, ed., with supplement by William Harkness. Czech Literature. Trans. Peter Kussi. Ann Arbor, MI: Michigan Slavic Publications, 1976

Nový, Jan. 'Živočichopis pásků.' Tvorba, 24: 3 (1959), 62–3

Otčenášek, Jan. 'K otázkám ideové činnosti Svazu čs. spisovatelů.' Literární noviny, 8: 11 (10 March 1959), 3

Rothstein, Edward. 'New World Symphonietta.' New Republic (1 June 1987), 27–30

Rybák, Josef. 'Červivé ovoce.' Rudé právo (14 January 1959), 4

Schonberg, Michal. 'The Case of the Mangy Pussycat (An Account of the Literary Scandal Surrounding the Publication of Josef Škvorecký's The Cowards).' World Literature Today, 44 (Autumn 1980), 532–9

Schubert, Peter. 'Příběh inženýra lidských duší.' World Literature Today, 52 (Spring 1978), 655

Solecki, Sam. 'The Laughter and Pain of Remembering.' Canadian Forum, 64 (August–September 1984), 39–41, 51

– Prague Blues: The Fiction of Josef Škvorecký. Toronto: ECW Press, 1990

Souckova, Milada. A Literary Satellite: Czechoslovak-Russian Literary Relations. Chicago: University of Chicago Press, 1970

Společnost Josefa Škvoreckého. Zbabělci ... a co bylo potom. Prague: Společnost Josefa Škvoreckého, 1991

Štoll, Ladislav. 'Literatura a kulturní revoluce.' Umění a ideologický boj, vol. 1. Prague: Svoboda, 1972, 202–58

– 'Úkoly literatury v kulturní revoluci.' Literární noviny, 8: 10 (7 March 1959), 7

Štuka, Ivo. 'Nesouhlasím se Zbabělci.' Československy voják, 8: 3 (1959), 24

Svoboda, Svatoslav. 'Cesta za hrdinou šoucasné prózy.' *Mladá fronta* (12 December 1958), 5

Trensky, Paul I. *The Fiction of Josef Škvorecký.* London: Macmillan, 1991

Vohryzek, Josef. 'Próza dnes.' *Květen*, 3: 14–15 (1958), 780–5, 842–6

Voskovec, George. 'Danny: Škvorecký's Shadow, Persona, Alter Ego, Man Friday, etc.' *World Literature Today*, 44 (Autumn 1980), 544–7

Vrabec, Vladimír. 'Trojí slibný úspěch naší románové tvorby.' *Svobodné slovo* (30 December 1958), 3

Žekulin, Gleb. '*Miss Silver's Past*: The Tragedy of an Intellectual.' *World Literature Today*, 44 (Autumn 1980), 547–51

4 MISCELLANEOUS

Brousek, Antonín. *Na Brigádě.* Toronto: Sixty-Eight Publishers, 1979

Deschodt, Eric. *Le Royaume d'Arles.* Paris: Lattes, 1988

Elgrably, Jordan. 'Conversations with Milan Kundera.' *Salmagundi*, 73, (Winter 1987), 3–24

Hašek, Jaroslav. *The Good Soldier Švejk.* Trans. Cecil Parrott. London: Heinemann, 1973

Kaufmann, Thomas DaCosta. *The School of Prague: Painting at the Court of Rudolf II.* Chicago: University of Chicago Press, 1988

Koestler, Arthur. *Darkness at Noon.* Harmondsworth: Penguin, 1988

Kundera, Milan. *The Art of the Novel.* Trans. Linda Asher. New York: Grove Press, 1988

Liehm, Antonín. *The Politics of Culture.* New York: Grove Press, 1968

Mann, Thomas. *Doctor Faustus.* Harmondsworth: Penguin, 1980

Miłosz, Czesław. *The Captive Mind.* Trans. Jane Zielenko. New York: Octagon, 1981

– *Nobel Lecture.* New York: Farrar, Straus & Giroux, 1981

Miner, Earl, et al. *The Princeton Companion to Classical Japanese Literature.* Princeton: Princeton University Press, 1985

Murdoch, Iris. 'Against Dryness.' In *The Novel Today.* Ed. Malcolm Bradbury. London: Fontana/Collins, 1977, 23–31

Pešina, Jaroslav, ed. *České umění gotické, 1350–1420.* Prague: 1970

Petro, Peter. *Modern Satire: Four Studies.* Amsterdam: Mouton, 1982

Salivarová, Zdena. *Ashes, Ashes, All Fall Down.* Trans. Jan Drabek. Toronto: Larkwood, 1987

– *Summer in Prague.* Trans. Marie Winn. New York: Harper, 1973

Solzhenitsyn, Aleksandr. *One Word of Truth: The Nobel Prize Speech on Literature 1970.* Trans. Thomas P. Whitney. London: Bodley Head, 1972

– *Nobelevskaia lektsia po literature 1970 goda*. Paris: YMCA Press, 1972

Součková, Milada. *The Baroque in Bohemia*. Ann Arbor, MI: Ardis, 1980

Theiner, George, ed. *The New Writing of Czechoslovakia*. Harmondsworth: Penguin, 1969

Wagenbach, Klaus. *Franz Kafka: Pictures of a Life*. New York: Pantheon, 1984

Contributors

STANISŁAW BARAŃCZAK holds the Alfred Jurzykowski Chair of Polish Language and Literature at Harvard University. He is the author of numerous collections of poetry and critical studies, including *Breathing under Water and Other East European Essays* (1990). He writes a regular column for *Salmagundi*.

ANDRÉ BRINK has written several novels – *A Chain of Voices* (1982); *An Act of Terror* (1991) – and a collection of essays, *Mapmakers: Writing in a State of Siege* (1983).

LUBOMÍR DORŮŽKA is a Czech jazz critic living in Prague, who has collaborated with Josef Škvorecký on several books about jazz as well as translations of Henry James's *The Aspern Papers* (1958) and William Faulkner's *A Fable* (1961).

GEORGE GIBIAN is Goldwin Smith Professor of Russian and Comparative Literature at Cornell University and has written extensively on Russian and Czech literature. Together with Ewald Osers he edited and translated *The Selected Poetry of Jaroslav Seifert* (1986). He has also edited the Norton Critical Editions of Dostoevsky's *Crime and Punishment* (1989) and Gogol's *Dead Souls* (1985).

MARKETA GOETZ-STANKIEWICZ is the author of *The Silenced Theatre* (1979), and is a professor in the Department of Germanic Studies and the Program in Comparative Literature at the University of British Columbia.

IGOR HÁJEK, a senior lecturer in Czech studies at the University of Glasgow, is the author of many articles on modern Czech literature and the co-author of *Slovník českých spisovatelů: pokus o rekonstrukci dějin české literatury, 1948–1979* (1982).

PETER HRUBÝ is an honorary fellow (social sciences) at the Curtin University of Technology, Western Australia. His books include *Fools and Heroes: The Changing Role of Communist Intellectuals in Czechoslovakia* (1980) and *Daydreams and Nightmares: Czech Communist and Ex-Communist Literature 1917–1987* (1990).

HELENA KOSKOVÁ is the author of *Hledání ztracené generace* (Searching for the Lost Generation), a 1987 study of postwar Czech fiction. She lives in Sweden.

JAN KOTT's works include *Shakespeare Our Contemporary* (1967), *Kamienny Potok: Eseje* (1986), *The Bottom Translation: Marlowe and Shakespeare and the Carnival Tradition* (1987), *The Memory of the Body: Essays on Theatre and Death* (1990), and *Still Alive: Autobiographical Essays* (1993).

MILAN KUNDERA's novels include *The Book of Laughter and Forgetting* (1981), *The Unbearable Lightness of Being* (1984), and *Immortality* (1991). He lives in Paris.

PETER PETRO is a professor in the Department of Slavonic Studies at the University of British Columbia. He is the author of *Modern Satire: Four Studies* (1982).

JOSEPH N. ROSTINSKY is a professor of Russian and East European studies at Tokai University, Tokyo. He has published numerous articles in books (*Sinn und Symbol*) and journals both in Europe and Japan.

EDWARD ROTHSTEIN lives in New York and is the music critic of the *New York Times*.

ZDENA SALIVAROVÁ's fiction includes the novel *Summer in Prague* (1973) and the novella *Ashes, Ashes, All Fall Down* (1987).

MICHAL SCHONBERG, a professor in the University of Toronto's Drama Centre, is the author of *The Liberated Theatre of Voskovec and Werich* (1992).

SAM SOLECKI is a professor of English at the University of Toronto. He is the author of *Prague Blues: The Fiction of Josef Škvorecký* (1990), and has edited *Spider Blues: Essays on Michael Ondaatje* (1985) and Josef Škvorecký's *Talkin' Moscow Blues: Essays about Literature, Politics, Movies, and Jazz* (1988).

GEORGE WOODCOCK has written many books on a wide range of political and literary subjects – *Anarchism* (1962), *The Crystal Spirit: A Study of George Orwell* (1967), *Canada and the Canadians* (1970). He is also the founder of the quarterly *Canadian Literature*. He lives in Vancouver.

GLEB ŽEKULIN is professor emeritus in the Department of Slavic Studies and former director of the Centre for Russian and East European Studies at the University of Toronto and has written extensively on Russian and Czech literatures.

Index